Theory and Practice in Action Research

University of
Chester

Theory and Practice in Action Research

EDITED BY

Christopher Day, John Elliott
Bridget Somekh & Richard Winter

SYMPOSIUM
BOOKS

Symposium Books
PO Box 65 Wallingford, Oxford OX10 0YG, United Kingdom
www.symposium-books.co.uk

Published in the United Kingdom, 2002

ISBN 1 873927 44 4

Typeset in Melior by Symposium Books
Printed and bound in the United Kingdom by Cambridge University Press

Contents

Preface

The work of public service professionals all over the world has become more complex in recent years as they have had to manage new realities of the intensification of work, persistent demands for regular responsibilities for raising standards without the power to influence the nature, direction or pace of these, and associated increases in bureaucracy. There are increasing case loads for social workers, output targets for health workers and massive assessment demands upon teachers in schools and universities. Alongside these their 'clients' are from societies which are increasingly fragmented in terms of values and social ligatures. As a result they are either alienated or less easily satisfied by what they are offered. It is hardly surprising therefore that public services are suffering recruitment and retention problems in many countries.

Yet this rather pessimistic picture is not universal. Many professionals, despite the inevitable pressures, have managed to survive and even thrive and this applies also to organisations. They have found 'room to manoeuvre' and have been able to rediscover, articulate and communicate a set of core values which promote the care and concern for welfare and the public good which are essential components of work in the public service sector.

Many have achieved this by regularly and systematically reflecting upon their thinking and practice, the personal professional values and the social, economic and political contexts which inform and influence these. Alone and working in collaboration with others they continue to fulfil the primary responsibility of all professionals – to interrogate the nature, purposes, processes and outcomes of their practice with a view to improving it. Many use action research, for reflection itself is a necessary but insufficient condition for change.

This book contains 16 articles from across the professions and from different countries which explore and examine the nature, purposes, processes and outcomes of action research – its importance to professional growth and the challenges of collaboration and change. Written by practitioners from schools and universities, health and social services, it provides a comprehensive yet focussed critical appraisal which we believe is essential reading by all for whom lifelong learning is an essential part of being and remaining a professional.

Christopher Day
University of Nottingham
John Elliott
University of East Anglia
Bridget Somekh
Manchester Metropolitan University
Richard Winter
Anglia Polytechnic University

PART 1

Conceptualisations of Action Research

These four articles have been selected for their inspirational analysis of the key issues that have concerned those engaged in action research during the last decade. The first, by Susan Noffke, looks forward, at the beginning of the 1990s, to ways in which action research needs to engage with critical issues emerging in the post-Soviet world. It sets the scene for this book as a whole with its scholarly analysis of the history of action research, touching on its origins in the work of Collier and Lewin in the USA; followed by a focus upon two different strands of development, in the progressive education movement embedded in the imperative for social change of the disciples of Dewey, and the new conceptions of the teachers' role in curriculum reform in the work of Stenhouse and Elliott. Noffke sets the scene for the articles that follow by opening up the tensions that quickly developed between those who adopted a political stance in their action research and those who did not. In particular, she locates this within the explicitly political focus upon social action led by J.L. Moreno in Austria and participatory action researchers such as Fals-Border in Latin America and feminist researchers in the USA, as opposed to the focus of some in the USA, especially in the post-sputnik era, upon improving the practice of teaching.

One of Noffke's 'emergent' critical issues concerns the nature of knowledge and the role of action research in knowledge production. This is the main focus of the article by Winter which starts with the question, 'Where does theory come from in action research?' It opens with a tentative definition of 'theory' as 'speculative play with possible general explanations of what we experience and observe', and probes and reflects upon this through a reflexive conversation in response to a number of critical questions. The author engages with questions that span not only the nature of knowledge – in practice and the university – but also the inter-relationship between theory and practice, the role of the university in supporting work-based research and the moral responsibility of citizens to engage in research that 'makes a difference'. Employing a playful, dialogic voice, and incorporating narrative journal extracts that locate the seeds of the ideas in the author's personal history, the article models the process of developing theory as more fully defined during the course of the article: '"Theory" means: conceptions of general significance, initially located outside the immediate events we wish to interpret, but with a potential bearing on how we may eventually decide to explain them'.

One of the 'contemporary challenges' identified by Noffke is the need to understand that action research is 'about relationships', as well as the operation of power in society and organisations and 'the social relations of knowledge production'. This leads into Winter's concern with citizenship and engagement, which university academics must 'embrace and sponsor' as a pre-requisite for retaining the independence of the university in the current political climate that 'threatens the humanity of (all) workplaces'. This theme of the individual's moral responsibility and commitment is taken up in the article by Biott, which is located in the work of the European project, Management for Organisational and Human Development. The article begins with a quotation from a poem by Seamus Heaney about the revelatory nature of intense experience, the process whereby 'what has been gone through' is the origin of revelatory insights that were already 'foreknown' within one's understanding. Personal growth through engagement in the process of enquiry, portrayed through the metaphor of the latent photographic image emerging, is the main theme of the article. Biott goes beyond traditional notions of practitioner 'voice' and presents a conception of action research as the process whereby professionals develop a sense of 'the emerging force of their newly established identities as researchers'. The practice of action research is presented as an individual's engagement with change, involving challenges to his/her overlapping identities (personal, occupational, professional, researcher) through which latent understanding and personal growth are forged.

All three of these articles incorporate critical questions and self-challenges. The final article by MacLure, on postmodernism, sharpens this critique in a coda of deliciously provocative 'play' with ideas. After an opening tour de force which manages to summarise the key ideas of the leading postmodern theorists without over-simplification, MacLure presents two key metaphors for postmodernism – Deleuze and Guattari's 'rhizome' standing for non-hierarchical, formlessness, and Derrida's 'bricolage' of knowledge consisting of bits and pieces through which the best we can do (and indeed 'the best' we can do) is rummage. The challenges for action research are forcefully presented in the penultimate section, Education Matters. According to MacLure, a 'postmodern or deconstructive reading' of action research would identify spurious claims for unsustainable givens (the right ways of going about action research) in the constant recourse to a narrative of 'opposition between practice and theory'; and the 'continuing appeal to/of the *self* (of 'the practitioner') as a singular, knowable, knowing, perfectible entity' (her emphasis). We hope that the reader will take these challenges back to a re-reading of the opening three articles in the section and ponder 'how the writers have done?' All three are concerned with these very issues, but not, we the editors think, in the expected ways. Postmodernism and deconstruction have savaged the academic world in the last decade in a way that has left it never the same again. Thank goodness. Ultimately, conceptions of actions research need to allow for a continuing belief that 'our actions can make a difference' (as Winter says we must keep telling ourselves this, no matter how many times we forget it), but we need to abandon our anxiety about the need to demonstrate some old-style validity using the 'metaphorical tool box' of modernism (Derrida cited by MacLure). Our three opening articles in this book present the musical theme and variations of a fascinating, if incomplete, response to the challenge in MacLure's coda.

Action Research:
towards the next generation

SUSAN E. NOFFKE

For those interested in action research or its close relative, teacher research, the current context is certainly a good one. The terms are recognized internationally in increasingly wider educational research circles, in teacher certification programs, and in programs for masters or even doctoral degrees as a legitimate form of inquiry. It is also growing in its presence in inservice programs and in funded projects. While the exceptional growth in the extent of action research practices may seem to be a cause for celebration among those who have long advocated greater attention to the generation of knowledge at a grassroots level, it should also be recognized that there has been a proliferation of meanings and uses of the term action research. Some of the efforts heralded under the label of action research have differences which seem to be minor responses to particular contexts and are overall quite complementary. Between others, however, there are frequently contradictory aims and outcomes (Hult & Lennung, 1980; Peters & Robinson, 1984; Noffke, 1990). The rapid growth of acceptance of the term, especially within Western university settings, may signal a need for some cautionary notes. A central core of action research is once again quite visible in the academy, but it may also be that an important sustaining force lies in its practice in less domesticated arenas.

   In this article, I lay out some areas in which historical and conceptual work in action research has been done. As a concept and as sets of projects, action research encompasses and embodies a whole range of practices across various fields, not only in arenas apart from the academy, but also in fields far removed from education. After more than fifty years, action research is reaching a crossroads, one at which particular turns may greatly influence its potentials. The examination of historical and current 'generations' (McTaggart & Garbutcheon-Singh, 1988) of action research will emphasize the importance of a clarity of vision over what 'potentials' might mean for the 'next generation' of action research. The first section highlights recent attempts to understand the history of action research. After a brief overview of recent developments, issues and contemporary challenges arising both from within its practice in education and from the larger context are addressed. The task has been to outline areas in which much work has been done and to explore those areas which have emerged as problematic. Clearly, those involved in action research over its many decades have made substantial contributions. Yet identifying some tensions and dilemmas in action research highlights the ways in which action research might continue to grow into the next century.

Many Ancestors, Many Descendants

Studies of the history of action research, as with retrospectives of some other educational innovations, have revealed a host of predecessors, many of which serve to help us understand the diversity of meanings the term has acquired. Several of these (Kemmis, 1982; Wallace, 1987; McKernan, 1988; Noffke, 1989; McTaggart, 1991a) have emphasized some common roots, especially in the works USA Commissioner of Indian Affairs, John Collier, during the 1930's and in those of the social psychologist, Kurt Lewin. A Jewish refugee from Germany, Lewin's work in the USA during the years surrounding World War II is most frequently cited (see, for example, Adelman, 1993). He and his associates focused on understanding and changing human actions, often around issues of reducing prejudice and increasing democratic behaviors. This work had effects not only in the USA, but through the Tavistock Institute and the *Journal of Social Issues* (see Bargal et al, 1992), it reached into the United Kingdom as well, often affecting social programs, especially at the community level. While Lewin's work has been cited, there has been little note in the educational literature of the continuance of that legacy in other fields of social inquiry. His efforts, and those of many other social psychologists of his time, emphasized the role that social science could play in initiating a host of changes in social practices, reaching beyond education to industry and the military, for example.

Works which address the history of action research in education frequently locate it also within broad, but differing, traditions in educational innovation, often varying in response to context. For example, while Schubert & Lopez-Schubert (1997) and Noffke (1989) highlight the roots of USA action research in the progressive education movement, particularly in the work of John Dewey, Elliott (1990) discusses efforts in the United Kingdom towards curriculum reform and greater professionalization of teaching as factors. Kemmis (1982) and McTaggart (1991b) locate Australian efforts within a broad-ranging movement toward collaborative curriculum planning. Each of these directs attention toward action research as an effort toward the development of more participatory education, yet there are differences which in turn highlight divisions over the scope and nature of action research practices.

One of the recent debates within the action research movement has emerged around issues which could loosely be described as discussions over the boundaries of educational practices, including their articulation to efforts towards social change (Weiner, 1989). In the USA, for example, while action research efforts have been associated with 'progressive education', that term has sheltered a whole range of educational innovations, with technical, scientific management orientations often lumped together with more developmental, 'child-centered', or even 'social meliorist' change efforts (Kliebard, 1986). Recent efforts in action research and teacher research in the USA do, indeed, seem to foster one over the other of these orientations to progressivism, albeit under different labels. These differences can be clearly seen in the early Interactive Research & Development projects (Jacullo-Noto, 1984), in some of the teacher researcher efforts (Cochran-Smith & Lytle, 1990), and in some of the action research in teacher education work at the University of Wisconsin (Liston & Zeichner, 1990).

In the United Kingdom, work in action research developed during an era in which considerable innovation in curriculum theorizing was evident in response to a change in the overall configuration of educational policy at the secondary school level (Elliott, 1990). Perhaps best exemplified in the works of Lawrence Stenhouse (1975), the pattern for action research manifested itself in a struggle for a changing view of curriculum and pedagogy, one which sought to move conceptions of curriculum away from notions which predetermine that which is to be learned by students, toward those which emphasize the student's own search for meaning. In tandem with this came efforts to highlight a conception of teachers not as the implementors of educational theory, but rather as professionals who theorize in practice, and whose deliberations are often moral in nature (Elliott, 1990; Noffke, 1992).

Early works of action research in education during the post-World War II era in the USA present a progression towards a starkly contrasting set of assumptions. Some of these projects took place through the efforts of the staff of the Horace Mann-Lincoln Institute at Teachers' College of Columbia University, New York City, among them, Stephen Corey (1953) and A. W. Foshay (Foshay et al, 1954). This work was later expanded and modified through the work of Hilda Taba at San Francisco State College, an influential figure in curriculum planning (Taba & Noel, 1957), and Abraham Shumsky (1958), a student at Teachers' College and later on the faculty at Brooklyn College. Whether a function of growing McCarthyism in the USA, of a shortage of fully qualified teachers for the 'baby boom' generation, or of the growth of federally funded educational research in part in response to the then growing Soviet–USA competition in space, there was a gradually developing silence over issues relating to a political agenda for education and for action research. Instead, issues related more to professional and personal development, as well as establishing action research as a legitimate form of educational research, supplanted concerns with children's social values and with creating curriculum which fostered democratic thinking (Noffke, 1990).

Concerns with both moral and political issues have thus played an ambiguous role in the development of action research in education, especially when considered alongside assumptions about the nature of teacher development. Recent work by Altrichter & Gstettner (1997) has highlighted that ambiguity by foregrounding the indirect influence of social philosopher, J. L. Moreno, in developing a social activist form of action research in German-speaking countries during the early years of the twentieth century. Although there may be no direct historical links, this same form of action research can be seen in research based efforts to deal with social problems, for example, in the monumental efforts of women in the Love Canal region of New York to address problems of toxic waste disposal (Bogden & Biklin, 1992), in the work of Maria Mies (1983) who highlights efforts to create shelters for women who have been battered, and in the various projects in participatory action research (Brown & Tandon, 1983; Gaventa, 1988; Fals-Borda & Rahman, 1991).

Efforts to explore the history of action research still have many avenues left to explore. We have but touched the surface in understanding its multiple origins and their implications for current manifestations. 'Reading' the history of action research, for example, in the documents of people mostly based in universities adds little to our understanding of what teachers hoped to gain from their involvement in action research. We do not know how widespread the influence of the movement was in its earlier manifestations. Nor do we have any way to consider the implications of voices which are primarily Northern European or Northern European–American or Australian males representing the practices of teacher and student populations which include many other voices. What is clear from readings of its history, is that it has taken root in a multitude of contexts, ones in which the education of children was an issue much in transition and in which the role of the teacher in the education of those children and in social transformation was greatly contested. Such a context clearly resonates with many contemporary situations.

While the action research movement in education clearly has its roots in the efforts of many people, it shares those roots with a host of other fields. Not surprisingly, the process of action research – its methods, and also the basic assumptions and purposes – varies greatly. This is well evident in comparing works already mentioned with presentations at the recent Second World Congress on Action Learning (Bruce & Russell, 1992), with a second kind of participatory action research which makes no attempt to connect with other, more grassroots orientations (Whyte, 1991), with efforts to promote 'action science' (Argyris et al, 1985; Argyris & Schön, 1989), and even with current explorations of 'quality circles' and the management studies of W. Edwards Deming (Holt, 1993). Given the increasing interconnections between industry and education in many areas of the world, a look at the linkages as well as the dissonances between the many 'cousins' in the action research family, might prove useful in identifying future directions.

Emergent Issues in the Practices of Action Research

If one had looked fifteen years ago for material on action research in education, one would have found very little in the mainstream of educational research. The few references in the USA literature are to be found in journals related to fields such as industrial arts or home economics, for example, far removed from the center stream of massive curriculum reform efforts in the natural and social sciences. A search of the literature now reveals hundreds of articles, books and book chapters on the subject spanning several continents, resembling one another, yet differing in assumptions about the purposes and goals of research or the actual procedures involved in the research process. Action research seems to be gaining credibility on a number of fronts and in many countries, yet also to be developing multiple meanings.

In the United States, for example, the increasing visibility of action research begins with several projects funded by the National Institute of Education (Tikunoff et al, 1979; Oja & Smulyan, 1989). Since that time, there has not only been a growth in action research activities both at the level of federally or foundation funded projects and at universities, but also an emergence of a distinct 'teacher research' movement. Its kinship with action research is clear, yet its antecedents lie more in the traditions of progressive pedagogy than in the search for an alternative to traditional social science through the work of teachers. Recently, much work has been done in identifying the distinctive characteristics and assumptions of teacher research, arguing strongly for the contributions that teacher knowledge can make to the educational community of both practitioners and academic researchers (Cochran-Smith & Lytle, 1990 & 1993; Noffke, 1991).

An examination of action research efforts in the USA reveals obvious differences. In some of the projects, one of the goals of the research is to facilitate the development of 'reflective' teachers – ones who are capable of making both ends and means of education problematic, and who can act on the basis of such deliberations (Gore & Zeichner, 1991). For others, the function of action research is to acquaint teachers with the techniques of university researchers, making them

Susan E. Noffke

better 'consumers' of research or more willing data collectors, thereby helping to 'close the gap' between research and practice (Connelly & Ben-Peretz, 1980). Such efforts help to raise the question of whose knowledge is being 'reflected' on or 'applied'. The development of 'teachers' practical theories', a phrase often heard in conjunction with action research, can be seen as a form of knowledge production by teachers, but it can also be seen as the 'better' use of theories generated in university settings or through foundation sponsored research.

Research topics under the broad label of action research have also varied greatly. Unlike the action research of the earlier era in the USA, some recent projects have shown a tendency to emphasize changes in specific teaching practices within given parameters, rather than to situate action research as part of broad efforts towards reconceptualizing curriculum or schooling. While this trend is not, in and of itself negative (and there are many exceptions), when taken within a context in which the parameters of teaching practice are increasingly subject to external controls, it is certainly an area for concern (Apple, 1986; Noffke, 1992). Importantly, the teacher research movement, with its increasing focus on issues of power and organizational reform, along with the growing awareness of the international literature on action research efforts (Kyle & Hovda, 1987/1989; Oberg & McCutcheon, 1990), may provide an impetus for clarifying the scope of action research in the USA.

In England, writings on action research are extensive and varied. From the early works of Stenhouse and of John Elliott and others involved in the Ford Teaching Project and in the Teacher–Pupil Interaction and the Quality of Learning Project, action research efforts have grown to a both broadly based and theoretically complex literature. Books, both analyzing and developing the concepts and methods for action research, have become widely available (e.g. Winter, 1987 & 1989; McNiff, 1988; Elliott, 1991; McKernan, 1991; Altrichter et al, 1993), but perhaps more significantly, the efforts of the Collaborative Action Research Network, founded in the mid-1970s, have brought not only the works of academics involved in writing about action research, but also the works of practitioners, to a wider audience through both publications and the sponsoring of conferences (see, for example, Holly & Whitehead, 1986; Edwards & Rideout, 1991). In much of these works, there is a clear emphasis on the role of action research in the development of a profession which is concerned with ethical issues as well as technical ones.

Alongside these efforts, several action research projects have also been carried out within the United Kingdom which are distinct, in terms both of their assumptions and purposes. Two of these are representative not only of a continuance of action research in the Lewin–Tavistock model, with 'outside' researchers providing technical assistance with traditional research methods, but also retain the concern with an explicit

18

social agenda (Chisholm & Holland, 1986; Whyte, 1986). Similar, too, in terms of its orientations toward both social research and social agendas is the work of Grudgeon & Woods (1990) in researching efforts towards practices which further 'education for all'. While not specifically labelled as action research, the efforts are clearly part of the same stream of thought.

Developments in action research in Australia, while slow in arriving in the USA, share common roots with both the USA and United Kingdom contexts. Building as in the United Kingdom from a strong tradition of school-based curriculum development, action research efforts emerged both around implementation of curriculum reform efforts, sometimes originating in the USA, and notions of 'negotiating the curriculum' (Boomer, 1982). The influence of Stenhouse is clear, but also salient is an effort to locate action research efforts within a framework influenced by critical social thought, in particular that of Habermas (Carr & Kemmis, 1986). Much has been accomplished in developing historical and theoretical works (Kemmis & McTaggart, 1988a & 1988b) as well as locating action research, cross culturally, within the struggles of indigenous peoples (McTaggart, 1991c). In addition, social organizations with interests beyond education have developed efforts to use action research in areas of social services (Wadsworth, 1984).

It should be noted, too, that action research efforts are not limited to English language countries. Germany, Switzerland, and Austria, for example, have experienced resurgences of action research works, first in the 1970s and more recently in connection with CARN (Klafki, 1973; Moser, 1975; Altrichter et al, 1993). Work is also being done in several developing nations (McTaggart, 1997) and in South Africa (Walker, 1993). An analysis of these works is unfortunately beyond the scope of this short review.

In all of these contexts, issues in action research have emerged both from its practices within the domain of academic research and in the world of educational work in schools. Issues of purpose as well as methodology will become more salient as both groups begin to address directly the role of action research in personal and professional development, in the political economy of knowledge production, as well as in social movements. Rather than locating debates solely within either site, it may be wise to look at practices in both sites and at attempts to work collaboratively between them. Identifying points of divergence, forming categorizations, whether by geography or by types, while important ways of discussing action research, often lead us away from essential questions of epistemology, ethics, workplace, and politics. In this respect, works which cut across both sites are sorely lacking.

Contemporary Challenges

One of the things which emerges quite clearly from the study of previous and current 'generations' of action research is that its practices in various contexts differ greatly. How then ought we to see the 'potentials' of action research across a number of dimensions? The growth and proliferation of action research means that whole hosts of questions need to be addressed not only by academics writing about action research but also by those working within it. These questions can be arranged into several broad areas.

One important dimension is that of purpose or expected outcomes of the research process. To some working in action research, its goal has been represented as lying primarily within the areas of personal and/or professional development. Action research, in this way, is valued less for its role in the production of knowledge about curriculum, pedagogy, and the social contexts of schools, and more for its ability to help teachers 'grow' in their self-awareness or in terms of their professional skills and dispositions. This is clearly an important 'potential'. Yet as I've argued elsewhere (Noffke, 1989), a sole emphasis in this area not only misses important aspects to the work of education, it can provide an avenue for the 'social engineering' of particular attitudes and dispositions among teachers to the exclusion of others, primarily the focus on technical questions of 'delivery' to the exclusion of questions of curriculum and social justice.

A growing concern with action research is highlighted by seeing its outcomes in terms of knowledge production. This raises some interesting questions. Is action research simply, as many portray it to be, 'real research' writ small enough for practitioners, or is it a new form of research, a new paradigm, whose methods, methodology, and epistemology are only now being clarified? The works of Winter (1987), Elliott (1987), and Carr & Kemmis (1986) have of course been very helpful in this area. Yet for much of action research practices, questions about the standards of quality as raised, for example, by Adelman (1989), Noffke (1991), & Reid (1992), are largely unaddressed. Is action research merely the following of standard measures of validity in qualitative and quantitative research, just in cyclical fashion? If not, how are knowledge claims to be addressed? What kinds of data are used and in what ways? In whose interests is research to be evaluated and by whom? While we do have some theoretic resources, the voices of practitioners themselves need to be heard. If action research is a form of knowledge production, then we enter into a sphere where we can ask such questions as: In whose interests is knowledge produced? Who 'owns' and benefits from knowledge? and an interesting question, given this post-Soviet era, to what extent can we begin to talk about collectivities instead of assuming proprietary notions of knowledge production? Placing action research into existing frames for epistemology may also lead to new ways of maintaining privilege systems as they are. Here the works of feminist and post-colonial scholars (hooks, 1990; Collins, 1990; Spivak, 1990; Harding, 1993) may be particularly helpful.

The question of collectivity leads into another area of 'potentials' for action research. Work with teachers is more than a debate over political economies, although this attention to the social relations of knowledge production is clearly needed, especially when the academic community is involved. It is also about relationships. In much of the literature, this area is discussed in terms of breaking down the barriers of isolation within teaching and across schools and universities. These, too, are clearly important areas. Yet much of what is written sidesteps issues of the nature of relationships in action research. Are they 'new', in the sense of alternative configurations of existing forms of power (and oppression) in society? Or are they ways of maintaining existing patterns of privilege? Relationships are formed out of things which encompass more than issues of 'rights' and 'ownership'. Yet what language will we need to discuss mutual sustenance and the transformation of the dynamics of power in education?

The 'potentials' of action research are often claimed in another area – one that highlights its role in social transformation – in concerted efforts towards systemic change. The literature in this area is larger than a simple search of the educational documents might reveal, and resonates with some of the early 'generations' of action research. The literature on Participatory Action Research, the records of the ongoing efforts of the Highlander Center in the USA (Morris, 1991), point toward a legacy of social action within the action research traditions. Yet here, too, are many questions, especially important to those of us connected with universities. Given that academics exist within structures which actually aid in maintaining their positions of authority and privilege within society, whose very systems of validating knowledge have historically and continuously excluded other epistemic communities (in the USA that is women, African-American men and women, working class people and a host of what are often called 'others'; see Harding, 1993), how can links be formed to social movements which inherently challenge academic privilege?

This article's title includes 'the next generation', not only because of a fondness for *Star Trek*. It highlights the long history of action research through a succession of 'generations' as well as expresses hope for future ones. While much has been done in identifying the historical roots of action research in education in various contexts, little has been done to try to understand the relation of the action research movement to other areas with clearly similar orientations, some of which share the same roots. Action research does not 'belong' to the educational world alone. There is a need to look carefully at recent trends in areas such as women's studies and in community development, but also at areas such as management. The term is used in areas which have seemingly disparate, when not also antagonistic, assumptions and purposes: Quality circles, action learning, soft systems, innovation research, evaluation research, community action studies, case study research, etc. We need to think of these things in terms of what they mean for educational work, to think more broadly about trends in the production sector. While I'm not certain what these will tell us in terms of linkages for social change, we do need to address them in more ways than just thinking that our way is better, has clearer linkages, either to the holy sphere of education or to oppressed peoples, or just that we are on the 'side of the angels' (Reid). The New Right, at least in the USA, seems often to be able to create an umbrella bringing in many to support their causes. Our deliberations with educational practitioners have to include strategies toward more ethically defensible, politically strategic action, to be sure. But they must also cut through our own tendency to create new orthodoxies, ways in which our efforts, as well as those of the Right, create umbrellas, which protect us and make sure there is no real challenge to the pattern of the rain.

We are living in an era of rapid social, economic and political change. The legitimation crisis experienced by many of the old forms, while certainly a source of worry for many, also affords an opportunity to create new linkages – new forms in society, ones which could be guided by an understanding that our attempts will always be partial, our outcomes contradictory. Yet one of the basic ideas of action research has to do with creating a constant interplay between our principles – hearing a wider range of voices, social justice, greater humanity, greater reverences for our precarious earth, along with desires for more technical efficiency, etc. – and our practices. The 'next generation' has much to do.

References

Adelman, Clem (1989) The Practical Ethic Takes Priority over Methodology, in Wilfred Carr (Ed.) *Quality in Teaching: arguments for a reflective profession*, pp. 173-182. London: Falmer Press.

Adelman, Clem (1993) Kurt Lewin and the Origins of Action Research, *Educational Action Research*, 1, pp. 7-24.

Altrichter, Herbert & Gstettner, Peter (1997) Action Research: a closed chapter in the history of German social science?, in Robin McTaggart (Ed.) *Participatory Action Research: international contexts and consequences*, pp. 45-78. Albany: State University of New York Press.

Altrichter, Herbert, Posch, Peter & Somekh, Bridget (1993) *Teachers Investigate their Work: an introduction to the methods of action research*. London: Routledge.

Apple, Michael W. (1986) *Teachers and Texts: a political economy of class and gender relations in education*. New York: Routledge.

Argyris, Chris, Putnam, Robert & Smith, Siana McLain (1985) *Action Science.* San Francisco: Jossey-Bass.

Argyris, Chris & Schön, Donald (1989) Participatory Action Research and Action Science Compared, *American Behavioral Scientist*, 32, pp. 612-623.

Bargal, David, Gold, Martin & Lewin, Miriam (1992) Introduction: the heritage of Kurt Lewin, *Journal of Social Issues*, 48(2), pp. 3-13.

Bogden, Robert C. & Biklin, Sari K. (1992) *Qualitative Research for Education: an introduction to theory and methods*, 2nd edn. Boston: Allyn & Bacon.

Boomer, Garth (1982) *Negotiating the Curriculum.* Sydney: Ashton Scholastic.

Brown, L. David & Tandon, Rajesh (1983) Ideology and Political Economy in Inquiry: action research and participatory research, *Journal of Applied Behavioral Science*, 19, pp. 277-294.

Bruce, Christine & Russell, Anne L. (Eds) (1992) *Proceedings of the Second World Congress on Action Learning.* Nathan, Queensland: Action Learning, Action Research and Process Management Association.

Carr, Wilfred & Kemmis, Stephen (1986) *Becoming Critical: education, knowledge and action research.* London: Falmer Press.

Chisholm, Lynne & Holland, Janet (1986) Girls and Occupational Choice: anti-sexism in action in a curriculum development project, *British Journal of Sociology of Education*, 7, pp. 353-365.

Cochran-Smith, Marilyn & Lytle, Susan L. (1990) Research on Teaching and Teacher Research: the issues that divide, *Educational Researcher*, 19(3), pp. 2-11.

Cochran-Smith, Marilyn & Lytle, Susan L. (1993) *Inside/Outside: teacher research and knowledge.* New York: Teachers' College Press.

Collins, Patricia Hill (1990) *Black Feminist Thought: knowledge, consciousness, and the politics of empowerment.* Boston: Unwin Hyman.

Connelly, F. Michael & Ben-Peretz, Miriam (1980) Teachers' Roles in the Using and Doing of Research and Curriculum Development, *Journal of Curriculum Studies*, 12, pp. 95-107.

Corey, Stephen M. (1953) *Action Research to Improve School Practices.* New York: Teachers' College.

Edwards, Gwyn & Rideout, Paul (1991) *Extending the Horizons of Action Research.* Norwich: CARN Publications, University of East Anglia

Elliott, John (1987) Educational Theory, Practical Philosophy, and Action Research, *British Journal of Educational Studies*, 35, pp. 49-169.

Elliott, John (1990) Teachers as Researchers: implications for supervision and for teacher education, *Teaching and Teacher Education*, 6, pp. 1-26.

Elliott, John (1991) *Action Research for Educational Change.* Buckingham: Open University Press.

Elliott, John & Adelman, Clem (1973) Reflecting Where the Action Is: the design of the Ford Teaching Project, *Education for Teaching*, 92, pp. 8-20.

Fals-Borda, Orlando & Rahman, Mohammad Anisur (Eds) (1991) *Action and Knowledge: breaking the monopoly with participatory action-research.* New York: Apex Press.

Susan E. Noffke

Foshay, Arthur W., Wann, Kenneth D. & associates (1954) *Children's Social Values: an action research study.* New York: Teachers' College.

Gaventa, John (1988) Participatory Research in North America, *Convergence*, 21(2 & 3), 19-28.

Gore, Jennifer M. & Zeichner, Kenneth M (1991) Action Research and Reflective Teaching in Preservice Teacher Education: a case study from the United States, *Teaching and Teacher Education*, 7, pp. 119-136.

Grudgeon, Elizabeth & Woods, Peter (1990) *Educating All: multicultural perspectives in the primary school.* London: Routledge.

Harding, Sandra (Ed.) (1993) *The 'Racial' Economy of Science: toward a democratic future.* Bloomington: Indiana University Press.

Holly, Peter & Whitehead, Dido (1986) *Collaborative Action Research.* Cambridge: CARN, Cambridge Institute of Education.

Holt, Maurice (1993) The Educational Consequences of W. Edwards Deming, *Phi Delta Kappan*, 74, pp. 382-388.

hooks, bell (1990) *Yearning: race, gender, and cultural politics.* Boston: South End Press.

Hult, Margareta & Lennung, Sven-Ake (1980) Toward a Definition of Action Research: a note and bibliography, *Journal of Management Studies*, 17, pp. 241-250.

Jacullo-Noto, Joann (1984) Interactive Research and Development – partners in craft, *Teachers' College Record*, 86, pp. 208-222.

Kemmis, Stephen (1982) Action Research in Retrospect and Prospect, in Stephen Kemmis, et al (Eds) *The Action Research Reader*, 2nd edn, pp. 11-31. Geelong: Deakin University Press.

Kemmis, Stephen & McTaggart, Robin (1988a) *The Action Research Planner*, 3rd edn. Geelong: Deakin University Press.

Kemmis, Stephen & McTaggart, Robin (Eds) (1988b) *The Action Research Reader*, 3rd edn. Geelong: Deakin University Press.

Klafki, Wolfgang (1973) Handlungsforschung im Schulfeld, *Zeitschrift fuer Paedagogic*, 19, pp. 487-516.

Kliebard, Herbert M. (1986) *The Struggle for the American Curriculum*, 1893-1958. Boston: Routledge.

Kyle, Dian W. & Hovda, Ric A. (1987, Winter, Spring/1989) The Potential and Practice of Action Research, Parts I & II, *Peabody Journal of Education*, 64(2 & 3).

Liston, Daniel P. & Zeichner, Kenneth M. (1990) *Teacher Education and the Social Conditions of Schooling.* New York: Routledge.

McKernan, Jim (1988) The Countenance of Curriculum Action Research: traditional, collaborative, and emancipatory–critical conceptions, *Journal of Curriculum and Supervision*, 3, pp. 173-200.

McKernan, James (1991) *Curriculum Action Research: a handbook of methods and resources for the reflective practitioner.* London: Kogan Page.

McNiff, Jean (1988) *Action Research: principles and practices.* London: Routledge.

McTaggart, Robin (1991a) *Action Research: a short modern history.* Geelong: Deakin University Press.

McTaggart, Robin (1991b) Action Research is a Broad Movement, *Curriculum Perspectives*, 11(4), pp. 44-47.

McTaggart, Robin (1991c) Action Research for Aboriginal Pedagogy: beyond 'both-ways' education?, in Ortrun Zuber-Skerrit (Ed.) *Action Research for Change and Development*, pp. 157-178. Aldershot: Avebury.

McTaggart, Robin (1997) *Participatory Action Research: international contexts and consequences.* Albany: State University of New York Press.

McTaggart, Robin & Garbutcheon-Singh, Michael (1988) A Fourth Generation of Action Research: notes on the Deakin seminar, in Stephen Kemmis & Robin McTaggart (Eds) *The Action Research Reader*, 3rd edn, pp. 409-428. Geelong, Australia: Deakin University Press.

Mies, Maria (1983) Towards a Methodology for Feminist Research, in Gloria Bowles & Renate Duelli Klein (Eds) *Theories of Women's Studies*, pp. 117-139. London: Routledge & Kegan Paul.

Morris, Aldon (1991) Education for Liberation. Introduction to Issues on Myles Horton and the Highlander Folk School, *Social Policy*, 21(3), pp. 2-6.

Moser, Heinz (1975) *Aktionsforschung als kritische Theorie der Sozialwissenschaften.* Munich: Koesel.

Noffke, Susan E. (1989) The Social Context of Action Research: a comparative and historical analysis. Paper presented at the Annual Meeting of the American Educational Research Association, San Francisco, March.

Noffke, Susan E. (1990) Action Research: a multidimensional analysis. Unpublished PhD thesis, University of Wisconsin.

Noffke, Susan E. (1991) Hearing the Teacher's Voice: now what? *Curriculum Perspectives*, 11(4), pp. 55-59.

Noffke, Susan E. (1992) The Work and Workplace of Teachers in Action Research, *Teaching and Teacher Education*, 8, pp. 15-29.

Oberg, Antoinette A. & McCutcheon, Gail (Guest Eds) (1990) Teacher as Researcher, *Theory into Practice*, 29(3), pp. 142-221.

Oja, Sharon N. & Smulyan, Lisa (1989) *Collaborative Action Research: a developmental approach.* London: Falmer.

Peters, Michael & Robinson, Viviane (1984) The Origins and Status of Action Research, *Journal of Applied Behavioral Science*, 20, pp. 113-124.

Reid, William A. (1992) The State of Curriculum Inquiry, *Journal of Curriculum Studies*, 24, pp. 165-177.

Schubert, William & Lopez-Schubert, Ann (1997) Sources of a Theory of Action Research in the United States of America, in Robin McTaggart (Ed.) *Participatory Action Research: international contexts and consequences*, pp. 203-222. Albany: State University of New York Press.

Shumsky, Abraham (1958) *The Action Research Way of Learning: an approach to in-service education.* New York: Teachers' College.

Spivak, Gayatri C. (1990) *The Post-colonial Critic: interviews, strategies, dialogues.* New York: Routledge.

Stenhouse, Lawrence (1975) *An Introduction to Curriculum Research and Development.* London: Heinemann.

Taba, Hilda & Noel, Elizabeth (1957) *Action Research: a case study.* Washington: Association for Curriculum & Supervision.

Tikunoff, William J., Ward, Beatrice A. & Griffin, Gary A. (1979) *Interactive Research & Development on Teaching: final report.* San Francisco: Far West Laboratory for education research and development (ERIC ED 186385).

Wadsworth, Yoland (1984) *Do It Yourself Social Research.* North Sydney: Allen & Unwin.

Wallace, Mike (1987) A Historical Review of Action Research: some implications for the education of teachers in their managerial role, *Journal of Education for Teaching*, 13, pp. 97-115.

Walker, Melanie (1993) Developing the Theory and Practice of Action Research: a South African case, *Educational Action Research*, 1, pp. 95-109.

Weiner, Gaby (1989) Professional Self-knowledge Versus Social Justice: a critical analysis of the teacher–researcher movement, *British Educational Research Journal*, 15, pp. 41-51.

Whyte, Judith (1986) *Girls into Science and Technology.* London: Routledge & Kegan Paul.

Whyte, William F. (Ed.) (1991) *Participatory Action Research.* Newbury Park: Sage.

Winter, Richard (1987) *Action Research and the Nature of Social Inquiry.* Aldershot: Avebury.

Winter, Richard (1989) *Learning from Experience: principles and practice in action-research.* London: Falmer Press.

First published in *Educational Action Research*, Volume 2, Number 1, 1994

Managers, Spectators and Citizens: where does 'theory' come from in action research?

RICHARD WINTER

An obvious first response to the question posed in the title is: 'Why pose it? Why is it important?' In order to begin to answer that question, however, I need to start with a couple of preliminary definitions.

To begin with 'theory'. First, I intend to take 'theory' to be a mode of understanding which has some degree of *generality*. According to my dictionary, one meaning of 'theory' is 'a set of *abstract* principles which *explains* a given phenomenon'. However, this is not a sufficient definition: 4-year-old infants have their general explanatory schemas, and racists have general justifications for their bigotry; indeed 'generalisation' may well be a *spontaneous process* – simply the way our minds tend to work and the way language itself operates. Secondly, 'theory' is derived from a Greek word meaning 'spectator', and so another meaning of theory is to do with 'speculative' explanations, conjectures or hypotheses which do not (or not yet) have a tightly established connection with observable facts. So 'theory' therefore refers to a recognition that the observable facts of a situation are not self-explanatory and that understanding may be helped by being slightly removed from involvement. Putting these two points together, I'd like to begin by defining 'theory' as 'speculative play with possible general explanations of what we experience and observe'.

So much for 'theory'. What about 'action research'. What is specific to 'action research' as a form of inquiry is that it uses the experience of being committed to trying to improve some practical aspect of a practical situation as a means for developing our understanding of it. It is research conceived and carried out mainly by 'insiders', by those engaged in and committed to the situation, not by outsiders, not by 'spectators' (although outside 'facilitators' may also, indeed, have rather an important role to play). One important point follows from this definition: if we are inquiring into a practice or a situation that we are engaged with and committed to, it follows that action research will always have a 'reflexive' dimension. In some way, to some extent, at some stage, we will be inquiring into (amongst other things) our *own* practice, i.e. the impact of our engagement, the nature of our commitment. Action research thus undermines the simple distinction between the researcher and the researched which seems to be presupposed by defining the theorist as a spectator. So a preliminary review of the two terms has already begun to show the tensions which give rise to the question and, thus, give an impetus to the argument.

However, I can also already imagine an objection to this way of proceeding. What *authority* do I have for these definitons? What about John Elliott's definition of action research? Or Jack Whitehead's? Or Carr & Kemmis's? Or Pam Lomax's? Not to mention Peter Reason on participative inquiry, Reg Revans on action learning, or the work of Carol Gilligan & Mary Field Belenky re-defining inquiry from a feminist perspective? As regards 'theory', what about, for example, Aristotle, Kant and Popper. Isn't that the way to start an argument?

This takes us right to the heart of the matter. Because one widespread interpretation of the proper relationship between 'theory' and knowledge derived from involvement in practice is that speculative play with possible general explanations (my introductory definition of 'theory') requires an initial mastery of a corpus of learning located in academic institutions – libraries and university course reading lists – and thus, institutionally, separated from professional workplaces. So one crucial dimension of my question is 'What is the relationship between book-based learning and action research inquiry?' I want to keep that question open, rather than accidentally lending support to one answer by starting off my own argument with a conventional review of what previous writers have already said.

This aspect of the question was, indeed, the origin of my argument. My interest in the relationship between theory and action research initially arose several years ago when I was discussing the concept of action research with a highly respected colleague, an academic yet highly critical of conventional definitions of academic curricula, and very interested in the relationship between academic knowledge and the world of workplace practice. 'That's all very well', he said (or something like it), 'but where's the theory? Your understanding of action research' he said to me, 'is clearly based on theory derived from your academic learning. But nothing in the action research process seems to be making this form of learning available to the practitioners taking your action research courses.' So I want to answer this (for me) long-standing question both by considering the relationship between academic knowledge and action research, and also (and this is the other central issue) by considering what 'theory' might mean other than the content of an academic curriculum. In the end, I will try to argue that action research itself points towards a specific conception of theory which should command intellectual respect even in circles where academic definitions of knowledge are taken as the norm.

And now I really am going to explain why this seems a worthwhile question. I'll start by explaining why it is important for me as a practitioner, in my professional role as a member of staff in a university trying to teach action research courses. From time to time, I will draw on comments based on the reflective diary I have been keeping over several years, and one thing will become clear: in order to explain the origin of the question in my *practice* I shall find myself in an argument which itself is *theoretical* in most of the senses outlined so far – which, in itself, seems quite significant. So from time to time I will pause to consider where the theory informing this argument 'came from'.

Most of my work, at present, involves either running courses to support social workers, nurses and university teachers in their own action research projects, or working as a consultant to social work staff wishing to use the methods of action research to develop aspects of their role. The form of my practical problem is that I am caught between a number of conflicting demands.

One of the most important of these conflicts is inherent in the workplace, and concerns how far workplaces can provide resources and support for developmental inquiry. Practitioners wishing to undertake action research find it extremely difficult to find time to consult with colleagues and clients, to arrange and attend meetings, to gather and interpret data. They come along to course meetings and say they haven't had time to do anything since the last meeting because a colleague is off sick and they are all under pressure – or they just don't come.

> *An early entry in my research diary is a plaintive little note*
> *about low levels of attendance and about how I might arrange*
> *to 'increase the students' motivation'. That already implies an*
> *explanatory theory, Where did it come from? From my reading*
> *of texts on educational psychology during my teacher training*
> *about thirty years ago and also the current 'staffroom culture'*
> *of the university. As theory, I think we can agree that it is*
> *highly inadequate, because it ignores alternative possibilities;*
> *in particular, the contribution of the organisational and*
> *political context . It may be 'explanatory' but it lacks any form*
> *of 'speculative play'. So let me try to present the problem more*
> *broadly.*

The globalisation of international capital has undermined the ability of nation states to operate a welfare-orientated approach to the provision of professional services. Instead, market forces are allowed to drive down public expenditure and workplaces are increasingly dominated by short-term budgetary considerations. This means that staff time is seen as a *cost* which is continually being reduced to demonstrate increasing 'efficiencies'. Managers (of schools, universities, hospitals and social services agencies) thus find themselves accountable for staying within budgets that seem to render impossible the provision of effective services (for which they are also held accountable). This, in turn, tends to reduce the scope for professional satisfaction and creativity, and thus makes engaging in action research particularly hard, even though the managers who enforce this state of affairs lament it almost as much as anyone else.

> *Now that theory feels more convincing. Where did it come from? Mainly from listening to the radio, reading newspapers, and – most importantly – listening to comments made by my students, by their managers, and also by colleagues and managers in my own and other universities ... It is certainly a general explanation and it has broadened its scope, from the psychological to the socio-political dimension. But it still seems more dogmatic than speculative. So what makes an explanation 'speculative'?*

My argument is that if action research is to be feasible in the workplace, budget-driven organisations need help from outside to resolve their own inherent contradictions. Because there really are contradictions at work here. It's not simply that senior managers find themselves forced to prioritise profitability over service quality at the expense of staff and their clients. What is also true is that the auditing of outputs and the reduction of costs is seriously intended to improve the quality of the service to consumers. Organisations increasingly wish to describe themselves as 'Learning Organisations' – committed to continuous development of their processes and services as a condition of their survival in the marketplace – and as 'Investors in People' – committed to supporting the development of staff as the organisation's main 'resource' in the struggle to remain successful in the competitive struggle with its rivals. The contradiction is there in the concept of a market for services: on the one hand, the market is seriously intended to enfranchise clients – reducing their dependency on paternalist definitions of their needs and increasing their power to influence the services they receive; on the other hand, the market process reinforces all the inequalities and injustices represented by the current distribution of wealth and social power, so that attempts to allocate resources on the basis of need are ruled out as 'interfering with' effective market forces.

> *As a theory this, at last, seems better. The focus on a central contradiction gives it a speculative feel and opens up various possible continuations, conclusions, and practical strategies.*

Returning to my practical context (as the origin of the question in the title) let me sum up the argument so far. On the one hand, the contemporary workplace provides *scope* for action research, and many staff at all levels appreciate its potential contribution; on the other hand, the contemporary workplace finds it difficult to resource action research, and staff who try to undertake it find themselves under enormous physical and moral pressures which undermine their motivation to do so.

My next point is that this general state of affairs creates a need and an opportunity for the university to *support* practitioner action research in the workplace. Now this, obviously, goes to the heart of my professional role, as a university teacher, and it returns us explicitly to the role of theory, because universities have, as it were, a vested interest in theory. Universities are like warehouses, where knowledge is kept separated from particular practical situations and, thus, potentially available to be used in any situation. This knowledge is made available through libraries, embodied in academic traditions, organised into subject disciplines and taught in award-bearing courses. Admittedly, new models of university curricula are breaking down some of the boundaries between disciplines and beginning to accommodate practice-based knowledge, but this is a slow process. Essentially, the university still draws its cultural authority from its institutional *separation* from the immediate motives of practical life. It sees itself as specifically standing for the value of knowledge pursued for purposes other than practical effectiveness (Kant, 1979 [1795]; Newman, 1960 [1873]), as representing, therefore, a *critical* rationality (Barnett, 1997) or, as Edward Said put it, 'a Utopian space' (1994a, p. xxix) – a refuge of political safety where, committed purely to ideas and values, we may freely 'speak truth to power' (Said, 1994b, p. xiv).

The university, then, is drawn to embracing a 'spectator' model of theory, and so the other conflict I find myself in, in my professional role as a teacher of action research courses under the aegis of a university, is the conflict between the university model of theory and the practice-based definition of knowledge espoused by action research. This conflict structures my negotiations concerning the acceptabilty of my course documents with university validating committees, and the acceptability of my students' work with colleagues on assessment boards and with external examiners. It also structures interactions with my students, since they are not only professional practitioners committed to the principles of action research, but also see themselves as students undertaking a university-based course, of which they have familiar expectations.

F writes in her final report, 'I sent the questionnaire to my tutor' (Research Diary entry.) [What worries me here is that she invokes her student role in an activity which is supposed to be part of her professional role.]

P said he felt strange presenting himself to agencies in the role of a 'student' asking for help with a course project, instead of in his usual professional role. (Research Diary entry.) [But why did he choose to do so? Again this seems like 'taking refuge' in the student role.]

K asked the course group for feed-back on her interpretation of what had happened before asking the workers she was collaborating with. I was disappointed by this misunderstanding. (Research Diary entry.) [What had happened to the principle of work-based collaboration?]

As these comments based on my research diary indicate, I am worried that the involvement of the university can have a distorting effect on action research, fostering an unhelpful dependency on the course and on the tutor, and moving the action researcher's attention away from the workplace process.

However, it's not just the students I worry about. Here is another example:

W. said that all her notes on the session were based on comments that H [a fellow student] had made. At this I felt disappointed that none of her points were based on what I had said, because I felt I had made some extremely useful and pertinent suggestions concerning her work! But now I have the worry that my attempts to elaborate on students' themes may be experienced by them somehow as a process of 'theft'. It makes me feel clever, but perhaps they try (rightly) to resist my interventions. So do I trust myself in this role? (Research Diary entry, expanded)

I hope I have shown, now, why I think the issue of theory in action research is an important one. It not only refers to key conflicts in my own role, but also raises the question of the relationship between the university and the workplace as potential partners in fostering both a learning society and an educated society. I am nearly ready to approach my main theme, which is the link between action research, theory and citizenship. However, before I address that, I want to acknowledge that, so far, I have presented too simplistic a contrast between the workplace and the university, by making two points by way of reservation.

1. The first point is quite simple: universities are workplaces like any other. My colleagues and I experience the same budget-driven reductions in time and resources, and the same difficulties when we try to find time

to reflect upon our practice as any school teacher, nurse or social worker. University staff undertaking my action research courses are just as likely as anyone else to say that they just haven't been able to find the time. Universities are no more convincing than other workplaces in their claims to embody the ideals of 'learning organisations' or 'investors in people'. Universities may hark back to a tradition of knowledge for its own sake and may aspire to be safe havens for critical reason, but nowadays they are also engaged in the competitive business of marketing, and delivering products (degree courses) and services (teaching and funded research) in a struggle with rival universities. So the conflict between spectator theory and work-based inquiry is a dilemma-ridden relationship within the university, as well as a relationship between the university and the organisations it claims to serve.

2. The second point is more complex and also serves to take my general argument forward. It is this: workplaces have their own direct involvement with the sort of theory espoused and produced by universities. Hospitals, schools and social services agencies have their own libraries of professional theory, and books on the theory of organisations by Peters, Handy and Senge can be seen above the desk of every self-respecting manager. Analytically, it is clear that professional work is actually defined as being based on a body of general theory acquired during initial training (Parsons, 1954, pp. 27-28; Friedson, 1994, pp. 18-19). The question at issue is how far the subsequent process of professional development can be equated with the ideal of systematically applying theory to experience. The work of Benner (1984), based on Dreyfus (1981), emphasises that as one becomes more experienced, more 'expert', this process rapidly ceases to be 'systematic' and becomes instead intuitive, creative, elliptical. However, this stress on the interpretive discretion of individual staff comes into conflict with the current organisational culture of managerial accountability and also with the rights of clients/students, etc. Organisational managers, therefore, with strong political backing, are currently encouraging a different model of the relationship between theory and professional work, summed up in the phrase 'evidence-based practice'. This notion of 'evidence-based practice' throws further light on my main question, so I want to examine briefly some details of the UK 'Research In Practice' initiative which attempts to introduce evidence-based practice in the social work profession.

    To begin with, although it is a partnership between university social work researchers, the government and social services departments, it was initiated by the Association of Directors of Social Services. Its aims are described in the first 'Newsposter':

> ... to provide a link between social work professionals and the best research knowledge available ... to assemble and assess findings about good practice ... and make them available in a variety of forms to practitioners, senior managers, elected members and consumers ... to assist all those working in social services departments who want to build an evidence base for their practice. [Research In Practice, Dartington Social Research Unit, 1997 [my emphasis]]

So here we have a managerial initiative assembling research findings provided by universities as a 'base' for practice. This fits with my earlier argument that the new organisational culture of accountability reduces staff members' sense of professional autonomy, as follows. Research findings can be treated as general explanations (i.e. in one sense at least, 'theory') with which to justify subsequent decisions in particular contexts and thus provide managers with a basis for controlling the professional decisions of staff. Assembling a body of general theory in this sense can be seen as a pre-emptive move to defend the service against possible legal actions for malpractice – always a real danger in social work and medicine, and now beginning to arise also in educational contexts. Theory invoked in this way thus threatens to become the basis for *codifying* professional work, with the university co-opted by organisational management into providing a prescriptive authority for the codification.. Which is why 'managers' feature in my title. 'Theory' for managers risks being theory-as-authoritative-prescription.

However, although this is a very real danger, it can be exaggerated. I have already referred to another model of the link between theory and practice, one which emphasises the interpretive discretion of the professional worker, and it has a strong philosophical pedigree, stretching back through Wittgenstein (1967) to Kant:

> An aggregation of rules, even of practical rules, is called a theory ... [But] between theory and practice, no matter how complete the theory may be, a middle term that provides a connection and transition is necessary. For to the concept of the understanding that contains the rule must be added an act of judgement by means of which the practitioner decides whether or not something is an instance of the rule. (Kant, 1983 [1793], 'On the proverb: that may be true in theory but is of no practical use, p. 61)

It is precisely this 'liberal' spirit which informs the actual volume of theory provided by the Research In Practice initiative (*Child Protection – Messages From Research*, Department of Health, 1995). The volume presents summaries and findings from 20 research studies carried out in universities on behalf of the government, but in the Foreword, by the

Parliamentary Under-secretary of State (no less), we read, 'This document is not intended as a practice text-book ... Professionals must be experienced, knowledgeable and skilled and no amount of central or local guidance can substitute for this.' The introduction repeats the message: 'This publication ... is not a text book or practice guide which tells professionals what to do with individual cases' (p. 8). The rest of the document demonstrates why such a non-prescriptive emphasis is inevitable. Most of the text consists of discussion and argument, rather than rules-to-be-followed, and the summaries of the research findings are of such generality that they verge on the banal:

> *Five features of best practice have been identified; sensitive*
> *and informed professional/client relationships; an appropriate*
> *balance of power between the key parties; a wide perspective*
> *on child abuse; effective supervision and training of social*
> *workers; and a determination to enhance the quality of*
> *children's lives.*

> *Clients suffered whenever professionals became preoccupied*
> *with a specific event, ignored the wider context, chose the*
> *wrong 'career avenue' for the child, or excluded the family*
> *from the enquiry.*

> *Protection is best achieved by building on the existing*
> *strengths of the child's living situation. (p. 52)*

Now, I am not saying all this is unhelpful. What I am saying, though, is that in the context of social interaction (which is the context for any action research inquiry) theory as *generalisation* does not even begin to build up to a prescriptive basis for professional action, even though some senior managers and government ministers might wish that it did. So the attempt to place managerial authority behind spectator theory produced by university researchers creates, at best, a very incomplete model of the relationship between theory and the professional workplace. What is needed, rather, is an account of how professional workers *use* the knowledge they either already possess or can readily acquire, and how engaging in an action research inquiry creates a process which is genuinely 'theoretical' in accordance with the definitions we have been using. This is what I will now try to describe, and in the end I will call it 'theory for citizens'. My argument is in four stages.

Let me begin my first point by restating (in a slightly amended form) some aspects of my original definition. 'Theory' means: conceptions of general significance, initially located outside the immediate events we wish to interpret, but with a potential bearing on how we may eventually decide to explain them. Guidelines for the presentation of conventional 'academic' inquiry prescribe this in a specific form: the initial 'literature review'. In some ways, this convention can be seen as the non-controversial recognition that we always conduct an inquiry in the light of previous work by others. Inquiry is always historically and culturally located; implicitly or explicitly, it will inevitably draw on prior knowledge. We never 'start from scratch'. Insofar as we wish an inquiry to gain the support or the interest of others (i.e. potential participants, sponsors or readers) we will need to demonstrate that we are aware of key issues, that our work is worth taking seriously, that we are neither ignorant nor naive. (Some very popular nineteenth century novelists placed a 'learned' quotation at the head of each chapter!)

However, the basis for referencing prior work in academic research is significantly different from its function within an action research project. In academic research, the review of prior work is supposed to define the starting point for the inquiry *as a whole*, to pre-define its analytical parameters and, indeed, the very topic itself. For this, the initial review of prior work (both in a research proposal and in a research report) needs, above all, to be *comprehensive*. In action research the argument is different. The essence of action research is that, although an inquiry may have an individual initiator with a specific *provisional* focus, this focus can change as soon as the inquiry is under way, as other participants contribute crucial insights. Also, action research follows a developing situation as it changes over time. For both these reasons the later phases of an action research inquiry will need to take into account theory which was not envisaged at the outset. So, whereas academic research is set up as a carefully designed response to a body of theory as it exists at a given moment, action research, having initially established the scope and significance of its provisional topic by reference to general intellectual and professional debates, then becomes a relatively free-flowing dialogue with various bodies of theory as the progress of the work brings new aspects into significance. Action research, therefore, does not aim to make an initial 'comprehensive' review of all previous relevant knowledge; rather it aims instead at being *flexible and creative* as it *improvises* the relevance of different types of theory at different stages in the work. (This improvisatory process probably also describes the actual *practice* of 'academic' inquiry, but for an action research project it describes the underyling *principle* as well.)

So, my first direct answer to the question 'Where does 'Theory' come from in action research?' is: *not* mainly from a computer search of 'The Literature', but from a process of improvisation as we draw on different aspects of our prior professional and general knowledge in the course of the inquiry. This theoretical dimension of an action research inquiry may be thought of as a sort of journey of self-discovery. Every time a colleague or a student or a client presents us with something new and surprising (in the data), or a new possible interpretation pops into our head concerning some event or part of the data, we find new relevance in theories which we were 'aware of' beforehand, but which until this moment had not seemed significant. Theory, in the sense I defined it (prior knowledge of possible general relevance) does not, then, always require a trip to the university library: quite apart from our initial general and professional education, we have spent a life-time in a culture with rich and varied resources of information and interpretive commentary. We can thus improvise links between perspectives which previously had been lying dormant in different areas of our brains, so to speak. We find ourselves remembering things we had forgotten we knew, suddenly realising we need to think hard about a set of ideas that had previously been in the background, not yet apparently 'anything to do with' the inquiry. Often, the process is so familiar that we hardly notice it occurring, but its existence and significance is persuasively described in Susan Hart's analysis of five 'interpretive modes' which constitute professional thinking and decision-making, ending with the 'hypothetical mode', in which one recognises the need to suspend judgement for the time being 'in order to learn more' (Hart, 1995, p. 224).

Some examples of this: Alice Otto *ends* her account of her work teaching student anaesthetists with what she calls a '*re*-examination' of relevance of the work of John Dewey (Otto, 1993, pp. 38-40). Val Childs observes that the unanticipated problems she encountered in her work with a children's support group led her to recognise, quite late in her inquiry, the relevance of systems theory (Childs, 1997, p. 17). Finally, an extract from my own research diary:

> *Today the students said that it takes so long to get participants 'on board' for the first phase of the inquiry that there isn't time for a second 'cycle' within the twelve-month duration of the course. So [a 'sudden' thought] I suggested that perhaps we emphasise too much the 'repeated cycles' model of action research and that we might use Morgan's 'holographic' model (Morgan, 1986, chapter 4) in which the structure of the whole is embodied in each particle. The students took up the general idea but, perhaps because they are nurses, preferred the biological image of the gene which, again, carries the structure of the whole organism. Another link: the ideas in Capra's 'The Web of Life' (1996) on biological and mental evolution might be helpful in developing this.[I read it a year or more ago out of an interest in Buddhist philsophy.]*

My first point, then, is that theory in action research is a form of improvisatory self-realisation, where theoretical resources are not predefined in advance, but are drawn in by the process of the inquiry.

My second point is that theory in action research is inherently both reflexive and multidisciplinary, because action research is necessarily just as much to do with the process of the inquiry as with the substantive topic. The negotiations through which we involve participants, resolve ethical and political issues, establish and develop the focus of the work, and construct strategies for agreeing interpretations of events; all contribute to what we learn from an action research inquiry. This learning could be placed generally under the heading of action research 'methodology', but, more specifically, it draws on a whole variety of different types of *theory*: social interaction theory (language, learning, group dynamics, motivation), ethical theory (professional values and role conflict), organisational theory (management cultures, patterns of influence, change processes) and political/economic theory (macro-contextual influences). In view of this, it is not surprising that the articles in *Educational Action Research* focus so much on the processes and methods of the inquiry, and their general implications. I don't think this is because action research is still at a preliminary stage of refining its methods before going on to the 'real business' of reporting concrete developments in specific contexts. I think it is because action research raises key questions about the actual experience of taking responsibility for attempting to initiate change. It is about the possibilities and limits for responsibility and creativity within the lived experience of highly problematic organisational and political conditions. Theory thus also enters action research through its reflexive attention to its own methods, i.e. to the general considerations which make such methods both possible and necessary. (A fine example here is Hazel Hampton's article 'Behind The Looking Glass' [Hampton, 1993] on her experience of working with issues of power and cultural diversity in primary school classrooms.)

Thirdly, action research requires theory in the sense of speculation on the hypothetical meanings of the immediately observable. Theory in this sense is absolutely central to action research: it involves questioning the meaning of data so that participants can go beyond the already 'expert' understandings which defined their starting points. It is essential to the *reflective* process, the search for the contradictions and discrepancies which bring alternatives into view; it is part of the *dialogue* between participants engaged in the work in differing roles and, thus, with differing standpoints and practical interests; it is part of the *pluralism* of action research, the collaborative, negotiating process and, thus, also part of the search for change – both in practice and in understanding. Action research is inherently theoretical in this sense because of its aim to *challenge* existing interpretations, to make distinctions within what had been seen as a single phenomenon and to make links between what had been seen as separate. (As an example, see Rebecca Luce-Kapler's exploration of feminist education in 'Becoming a research community' [Luce-Kapler, 1997]) This, then, is theory as a dialectical exploration – the negotiation of alternative conceptions, based in metaphor, multidisciplinarity and critique. It is this aspect of theory in particular which I had in mind when I referred earlier to theory as speculative *play*. It refers directly back to the university's definition of its cultural role, and my suggestion of its inherent significance within the action research process completes my argument that, in principle, a university *ought* to be able to play a part in supporting action research in the workplace.

This brings me to the fourth and final stage of my argument. At the outset I suggested that to talk of theory and practice is not merely to talk of epistemology – of different types of knowledge – but also of institutional relationships and thus (in a general sense) of politics. The argument I now wish to make concerns, once more, the relationship between the university and the workplace, and the significance of this link for conceptions of citizenship in a democracy.

I have argued that engaging in action research necessarily brings us up against a *varied* set of theoretical perspectives. However, action research is, above all, about deciding on courses of action. In order to act, we need to make choices and this means that we have to establish an *effective relationship* between these different theoretical perspectives. So action research entails the *integration* of theory – in and for action. Because the action research process itself involves *deciding how best to intervene here and now*, in this situation, with these various individuals, in the light of these social and professional values, amidst the complex pressures of this organisational and political context.

> *A final 'aside': where did this concept of action research as a process of theoretical integration come from? (I present the following references to other people's thinking on this matter as another example of theory as autobiographical exploration, as the re-collection of personal resources.)*

> *I think, to begin with, it was prompted by the opening sentence of a book I happened to be reading (out of a current interest in religion): 'The idea of a self-contained unity or limited whole is a fundamental instinctive concept' (Murdoch, 1993, p. 1). Over the summer, I have been reading George Eliot's novel 'Daniel Deronda', in which the theme is the search for a life that is justifiable in terms of one's widest moral, political and spiritual self-understanding, situated in a historical society. However, that then took me back to Sartre's 'Search for a Method' (1968) and the term 'totalisation' (p. 165) i.e. understanding the details of a complex situation as 'a unique totality' (p. 25). Now Sartre gives his method a familiar name – 'praxis' – which is also a central term for Gramsci, so this reminded me of Gramsci's presentation of the relationship between our spontaneous 'common sense' and 'philosophy':*

> common sense gives all of us a rudimentary but 'disjointed'
> basis for making sense of our world (1971, p. 323), and by
> 'philosophy' Gramsci means 'intellectual order' (p. 325) and
> 'critical awareness' (p. 323). And, amongst other things,
> Gramsci says: 'To criticise one's conception of the world
> means ... to make it a coherent whole' (p. 324). Finally there
> was Stella Clark's delicate yet inspiring article 'Finding Theory
> in Practice', (Clark, 1996) which I first read about two years
> ago: 'To conceive of other worlds and other intentions is
> actually theoretical' (p. 13). I interpret this as: it is when we
> see a set of alternatives as integrated into a conception of an
> alternative possible world *that we have grasped their*
> *theoretical significance.*

However, we must beware of simplifying this unity, this integretation, this coherence. As concepts, they also need to be treated critically. Yes, the process of action research does require us to find what Aristotle called a 'prudent' political path (Aristotle, 1976, p. 209) amidst the variety and complexity of different perspectives, but our 'totalisations' are never compete or final, and what seems careful political 'prudence' to one person may be shameful political compromise to another. Action research, then, cannot be free of contradictions and ambiguities – indeed, one of its central terms, 'collaboration', is notoriously ambiguous: 'collaborators' may be friends or traitors – it all depends on who they are collaborating *with*! (I was reminded of this point by a group of action research students recently when they responded very critically to what they took to be the prescriptive tone of moral and intellectual superiority in some action research writing, including my own!). To claim 'integration' and 'coherence' is to risk losing dialectical pluralism and openness, and descending into prescriptive authority (as my students were suggesting).

Nevertheless, I would like to insist on the argument that what distinguishes action research from 'spectator research' is that its action focus necessarily means that it must seek to integrate the various theories it draws upon. Furthermore, the action focus means that the theoretical work of action research has, in some sense a political purpose, even if it is only concerned with negotiating a shift in organisational policy or resource allocation. This is an important point, because the concept of 'praxis' not only implies 'informed and committed action' (Carr & Kemmis, 1986, p. 190), but an understanding of the ways in which, although human action is massively constrained by political, economic and cultural forces beyond our direct control, there always remains a specific scope for creative innovation (see Sartre, 1968, p. 87, p. 171ff.; Carr & Kemmis, 1986, pp. 33-34; Winter, 1989, p. 51). This conception of action research is particularly significant, I think, because it reminds us of the intellectual, emotional and, indeed, the spiritual demands involved in trying making sense of a powerless life, i.e. a life in which our sense of moral responsibility for events contrasts sharply with a sense that the power to affect those events is largely located 'elsewhere'.

However, to say 'powerless' is to go too far. It is all too easy to conceive of power simply as existing like a hierarchical chain of command in a bureaucracy. It does, of course, but – as I mentioned earlier – we also know that every general rule is only implemented through specific acts of interpretive judgement, and the work of Michel Foucault has reminded us that power also exists as a *network* of relationships, in which power is created 'everywhere', on the basis of particularised local knowledge (see, for example, Foucault, 1977, pp. 27-28). So, although power is always 'elsewhere' (and, thus, a constraint), it is also always 'here' as well. This provides an argument for a degree of residual political courage and a certain spiritual hope also: that we can make intellectual and moral sense of a life which is always constrained, but never entirely powerless. Our actions do 'make a difference'. (I keep telling myself this – and then forgetting it and getting depressed, and telling myself again, and wondering why I keep forgetting and what strategies I might adopt to try to keep this perfectly familiar understanding 'in mind'!)

So this, finally, returns us to the notion of theory for citizens. In a democracy, citizenship implies not only possessing rights, but exercising real responsibilities Both concepts entail a degree of personal autonomy (see Roche, 1992, chapter 9). Part of my argument has been that the processes of action research provide a strategy for embodying a sense of professional autonomy and responsibility in employment contexts, where both autonomy and the exercise of real professional responsibility are otherwise continuously threatened. A second aspect of my argument has been that the university can be a source of support in resisting such threats, although – as my references to my own experience have illustrated – this will entail responding sensitively to deeply ambiguous power relationships. The final component of my argument has been that this 'support' need not mean accepting the poisoned chalice of conventional academic courses, which entail their own threat of reinforcing, yet again, the gap between theory and practice. Rather, I have argued, the process of action research generates its own form of theory. This is a form of theory which is integrative, critical and political; it is both personal and collective, a synthesis of values and understandings, and a response to the many methodological dimensions of practical action in complex organisations profoundly influenced by external political forces. It is a form of theory which is required for the full exercise of a citizen's responsibilities in the workplace, and it is also a form of theory that the university must embrace and sponsor if it is to retain its aspiration to be a place of critical reason in a social and political order which threatens the independence of the university through the very same political and economic forces which threaten the humanity of other workplaces.

Acknowledgements

An earier version of sections of this article was originally presented at the annual CARN Conference in October 1997. The author wishes to thank Susan Hart, Pam Lomax, Stephen Rowland and Michael Young for helpful suggestions on earlier drafts.

References

Aristotle (1976) *Ethics*. Harmondsworth: Penguin Books.

Barnett, R. (1997) *Higher Education: a critical business*. Buckingham: Open University Press.

Benner, P. (1984) *From Novice to Expert*. Menlo Park: Addison-Wesley.

Capra, F. (1996) *The Web of Life – a new synthesis of mind and matter*. London: Harper Collins.

Carr, W. & Kemmis, S. (1986) *Becoming Critical: education, knowledge and action research*. Lewes: Falmer Press.

Childs, V. (1997) What Does an Elephant Look Like? a Social Worker's Journey of Innovation, in R. Winter (Ed.) *Action Research in Social and Health Care Settings*, Vol. 1. Cambridge: CARN/Anglia Polytechnic University.

Clark, S. (1996) Finding Theory in Practice, *Educational Action Research*, 4, p. 1.

Dartington Social Research Unit (1997) *Research in Practice: newsposter 1*. Dartington: Social Research Unit.

Department of Health (1995) *Child Protection – messages from research*. London: HMSO.

Dreyfus, S. (1981) *Formal Models vs. Human Situational Understanding*. Schloss Laxenburg: International Institute for Applied Systems Analysis.

Foucault, M. (1977) *Discipline and Punish*. Harmondsworth: Penguin Books.

Friedson, E. (1994) *Professionalism Reborn*. Cambridge: Polity Press.

Gramsci, A. (1971) *Selections From The Prison Notebooks*. London: Lawrence & Wishart.

Hampton, H. (1993) Behind the Looking Glass: practitioner research: who speaks the problem? *Educational Action Research*, 1, p. 2.

Hart, S. (1995) Action-in-reflection, *Educational Action Research*, 3, p. 1.

Kant, I. (1983) [1793] On the Proverb: that may be true in theory but it is of no practical use, in I. Kant, *Perpetual Peace and Other Essays*. Indianapolis: Hackett.

Kant, I. (1979) [1795] *The Conflict of the Faculties*. New York: Abaris Books.

Luce-Kapler, R. (1997) Becoming a Community of Researchers, *Educational Action Research*, 5, p. 2.

Morgan, G. (1986) *Images of Organisation*. London: Sage Publications.

Murdoch, I. (1993) *Metaphysics as a Guide to Morals.* London: Penguin Books.

Newman, J. H. (1960) [1873] *The Idea of a University.* Notre Dame: University of Notre Dame Press.

Otto, A. (1993) Graduate Medical Education: action research's outer limits, in T. Ghaye & P. Wakefield (Eds) *The Role of Self in Action Research.* Bournemouth: Hyde Publications.

Parsons, T. (1954) The Professions and Social Structure, in T. Parsons, *Essays in Sociological Theory.* New York: Collier Macmillan.

Roche, M. (1992) *Rethinking Citizenship.* Cambridge: Polity Press.

Said, E. (1994a) *Culture and Imperialism.* London: Vintage Books.

Said, E. (1994b) *Representations of the Intellectual.* London: Vintage Books.

Sartre, J-P. (1968) *Search for a Method.* New York: Vintage Books.

Winter, R. (1989) *Learning From Experience: principles and practice in action research.* Lewes: Falmer Press.

Wittgenstein, L. (1967) [1953] *Philosophical Investigations.* Oxford: Blackwell.

First published in *Educational Action Research*, Volume 6, Number 3, 1998

43

Latency in Action Research: changing perspectives on occupational and researcher identities

COLIN BIOTT

Strange how things in the offing, once they're sensed,
Convert to things foreknown;
And how what's come upon is manifest

Only in light of what has been gone through.
Seventh heaven may be
The whole truth of a sixth sense come to pass.

At any rate, when light breaks over me
The way it did on the road beyond Coleraine
Where wind got saltier, the sky more hurried

And silver lame shivered on the Bann
Out in mid-channel between the painted poles,
That day I'll be in step with what escaped me

(Seamus Heaney, 'Squarings', Seeing Things, 1991, p. 108)

I have prefaced this article with a Seamus Heaney poem because of the way he catches the everyday 'grain of things' and because, at the same time, he is so ready for surprise; so able to re-remember experiences, and to merge the commonplace and the transformed. As a researcher in familiar settings of daily professional life, I find his work both inspiring and humbling. Perhaps, the poem above will resonate with others like me who try, in more prosaic ways, to sense what is 'in the offing' and to get in touch with what escapes us.

In a recent interview Heaney talked of writing a poem being 'a line crossed in the self in secret'. This set me thinking more about what it might mean to cross frontiers between a researcher self, an occupational self and a social self in doing action research.

The ideas and illustrative cases in the article arise mainly from my work over about 15 years with experienced professionals from all phases of education, and more recently from health care, and also from my current involvement in a European Union funded project on Management for Organisational and Human Development. This project is essentially about the reflective transformation of practice, grounded in action research methodologies (Elliott, 1991; Altrichter et al, 1993). Action research is being carried out by practitioners in their own organisations, in collaboration with colleagues and university-based researchers at seven centres in five countries. The project poses a number of questions about relationships between self agency, personal learning, individual practice development and impact upon whole organisational development.

As part of the project at the University of Northumbria, we are working with a group of practitioners who are at various hierarchical positions in different kinds of organisations in education and health services. They have varying lengths of experience of action research, which all of them began as part of higher degree programmes. Whilst their own purposes and circumstances vary, they are working together to explore a number of shared concerns, one of which is is to explore their emerging sense of identity as practitioner researchers with reference to their sense of self as experienced professionals in their daily work.

Daily Life and Latency in Action Research

This brings us to a paradox of practitioner research; that of dailiness and latency. When the adjective 'daily' is used as in daily-life or daily-care it denotes common place concerns, or, as in the term 'daily-round', it suggests 'sameness'; the regular recurrence of routines. In contrast, latency implies expectancy and revival, and it highlights potential for change in daily life at work. The prospects and promise of learning through practitioner research hinge around the familiar, the 'looked for', the unexpected and the newly constucted. Perhaps we should focus less on how we uncover tacit knowledge or activate dormant selves, and spend more time exploring how practitioners constuct new preferred identities through being action researchers.

As daily work and enquiry become intertwined, practitioner researchers often begin to feel a sense of professional and personal risk. Their research becomes self-referential, inclusive and often highly charged emotionally. Dadds (1993), for example, has traced, two teachers' projects on their own teaching, and shown how they both became uncomfortably self-judgemental and deeply vulnerable. She makes the point that such risk cannot be divorced from the biography of the researchers and contexts in which the research is carried out, and in line with the central argument of this article, she notes how we should be 'tentative in our predictions of where processes started by self-study may lead' (p. 301).

For these reasons, projects cannot be pre-planned very far ahead and, as facilitators or supervisors of action research projects usually learn, it is inappropriate to expect projects to be confined to predetermined goals. As projects unfold, questions are often reformulated and new ones emerge. Interests are re-shaped, foci shift, and observations or findings are frequently combined with self-revelation including practitioners' sense of the emerging force of their own newly established identities as researchers.

Latency in Practitioner Research

There are three broad ways in which the concept of 'latency' helps us think about expectancy, revival and change when practitioner researchers study their daily work:

emergence of a new researcher identity;
expectancy of what has not yet been made visible by the processes of research, as in the photographers' term 'latent image';
awakening or revival of what is dormant or in abeyance.

First, latency suggests promise of what is in the 'offing'. For me, this catches the notion of emergence of a researcher identity which does not simply follow a familiar or linear course or appear like a new suit of clothes. Its form cannot be forecast or pre-planned in designated phases of an action research cycle, even by experienced supervisors, co-researchers or supporters who may have learned that its emergence is always a possibility.

A second and related form of latency refers to expectancy of what has not yet been made visible by the processes of development, as in the photographers use of the term 'latent image'. Whilst the processes of practitioner research are not quite as procedural or technical as those in the photographer's darkroom, they often do reveal surprising insights just as when photographs are developed and printed we sometimes find things in the pictures which we were not aware of when we pointed the lens. Like photographers, practitioner researchers learn to be prepared and willing to be surprised in the apparently familiar circumstances of their daily lives and so see more than they looked for. This is one of the ways in which practitioner research is potentially transforming.

I am not suggesting that it is unusual to discover emergent themes or patterns through ordinary, painstaking procedures of data collection and analysis in research, nor am I implying that practitioner research offers short cuts to avoid sustained effort. However, when we come to study ourselves in our daily working lives our most striking discoveries frequently involve more than steady labour over data handling. Indeed, to realise the potential of new ways of seeing and understanding, we may need to experiment with alternative approaches to perceiving and representing what we experience. Sanger (1994), for example, has suggested practical strategies for creative and anarchic data analysis as an antidote to mechanistic ordering. He suggests that the shape of research can resemble the structure of good jokes, essentially that it is about 'putting knowns together and coming up with a striking unknown which makes sense of what precedes it' (p. 185). Sanger is not writing specifically about insider action research, but he does offer two key ideas relevant to the discussion of latency in this article; first, that research which makes a difference is more likely to come from the imagination of researchers than from the coding and ordering of data, and secondly, that 'visionary experience in all cases was prefaced by intense periods of concentrated work' in the research undertaking.

A third use of the concept of latency refers to revival of what is in abeyance, implying suspension of activity or, perhaps more strikingly in contemporary professional practice in the United Kingdom, restoring to view what is temporarily off the prevailing, managerialist agenda. In a political sense we may ask whether action research might help to maintain continuity of fundamental beliefs at a time of self-doubt arising from enforced change, imported vocabularies and new inspection and accountability arrangements.

Practitioner enquiry has been seen as one possible source of sustenance for professional ideals and as a way of restoring the status of teachers' commitments to self-managed improvement at a time of unprecedented external meddling. Elliott (1994), for example, suggests that action research 'may not offer teachers with battered souls much therapy but it does offer even battered souls the prospects of enhancing the quality of their students' learning experiences' (p. 137), and Beattie (1995) argues that 'narrative ways of knowing', an established intellectual resource in the arts, can help teachers to both construct and reconstruct their personal practical knowledge. At a time of populist suspicion of professionals' motives of self-interest, it is heartening that Beattie values teachers' ways of knowing and holds that narrative:

> *allows us to acknowledge that educators know their situations*
> *in general, social and shared ways, thus validating the*
> *interconnectedness of the past, the present, the future, the*
> *personal, and the professional in an educator's life. (p. 54)*

Placing emphasis on teachers' personal and shared ways of knowing and on connecting the past, present and future are consistent with a key theme of this article; that change is experienced mainly with reference to the self. This is in sharp contrast to research which aims to check school effectiveness or imposed arrangements, but discounts the need to understand the continuities in which they are placed.

Making Meanings with Reference to Self and Social Identities

Holly (1993) has shown how teachers who wrote daily journals 'found themselves describing other teachers' (or pupils') motives and then slowly turned to themselves to find the same motives' (p. 176). In a similar vein, two practitioner researchers in our project have demonstrated the inclusive nature of action research in unanticipated ways. Both have made sense of new revelations in ways which have validated their social identities and emphasised their preferred images.

One cited Daly's (1978) use of the term an 'a-mazing process' to describe what happened when she had foregrounded the concepts of 'ceremony and ritual' in her analysis of data from newly-qualified teachers, and then realised, after responding to a friend's questions, how this was related to their importance in her own life. Daly, a feminist writer, refers to 'a-mazing processes', in the politics of patriarchy. In these processes, dormant senses become alive to break through 'a maze of deception' and spring into free space:

> *Each time we succeed in overcoming their numbing effect,*
> *more dormant senses become alive. Our inner eyes open, our*
> *inner ears become unblocked. We are strengthened to move*
> *through the next gateway and the next. This movement*
> *inward/outward is be-ing. (Daly, 1978, p. 3)*

A similar kind of sudden breakthrough was conceptualised in a different way by another researcher. A chance remark during a discussion had jolted her to a sudden and vivid insight into the meaning of her whole project. She had already identified tensions between parents' views and her staff team's views of their work with pre-school children with severe communication disorders. At the time, she was seeking a starting point from within her overall picture and beginning to draw out some of its key elements. To explain the process of how she did this, she subsequently used Barthes's (1981) notion of an element in a photograph that punctuates and disturbs our first, vague, inconsequential encounter with a photographer's intentions. The point that disturbs, Barthes calls the 'punctum'. It is this punctum point that becomes a focus for the whole picture. It pricks sensitivities and 'whilst remaining a detail fills the whole picture' (p. 45).

It is a focal point that draws you in, holds you and then fires you out. Barthes also suggests that:

> *sometimes, despite its clarity, the punctum ... (is) revealed*
> *only when the photograph is no longer in front of me. (p. 53)*

She described how she found a way to begin to write about them with clarity and how this gave her an impetus to make changes in practice. Recalling a discussion, she wrote:

> *One night when describing the 'disasters' of week four, ... a*
> *remark suddenly brought me to what I considered to be the*
> *'punctum' point of this project. It took me from a despondent*
> *retelling of the unhappy situation to beginning to develop my*
> *thinking towards improving the work we did with parents.*
> *(Cook, 1995)*

Notably, both had derived and shared some of their ideas about their studies from and with friends, as well as with project participants. The former is guided by feminist principles and Daly's notion of 'a-mazing moments' is used amongst her friends. The other conveyed her leanings towards arts and art criticism. For example, near the end of a recent project she likened her own sense of self as a practitioner-researcher with Pierre Bonnard's note about himself 'acquiring the soul of a landscape painter':

> *I have become a painter of landscapes, not because I paint*
> *landscapes – I have done very few – but because I have*
> *acquired the soul of a landscape painter in as much as I have*
> *been able to free myself from the picturesque, the aesthetic*
> *and other conventions which have been poisoning me.*
> *(Pierre Bonnard, Notebook, letter to Vuillard 2 January 1935)*

Like him she did not mean that she had become a good at it, but she was beginning to see, feel and think like an action researcher. Now that she had done some research with people she knew well, in real circumstances of her daily work, she was starting to free herself from some supposed research conventions which had inhibited her at the outset.

In both cases, these practitioner researchers had re-interpreted and recast new ideas in familiar forms which helped to maintain the momentum of their work. A key challenge to the practitioner research community is to extend such re-interpretation beyond familiar frameworks, and to represent ideas to themselves and others, in ways which are not fixed.

Sumara & Luce-Kapler (1993) use this notion to advocate action research as 'writerly text', referring to another idea of Barthes (1974) of 'a text that forces us explicitly and deliberately to write while reading' (p. 389), rather than a 'readerly text' which tries to predetermine and control a reader's experience. Action research as writerly text:

> *expects research to be like our reading of (a writerly literary*
> *text); unpredictable, often uncomfortable, challenging, yet*
> *always infused with the possibility of what the next page*
> *might bring. (p. 394)*

They refer to education in postmodern terms as a tangle or mosaic of texts:

which are constantly being written, re-written, read and re-read. Working as an educational researcher, then, entails critically reflective re-writings and re-readings of the day-to-day phenomena which present themselves to us. (p. 388)

This broadens processes of meaning-making so that all participants are given opportunities to interpret, influence and shape its movement. The discomfort associated with this kind of participation is referred to by Sumara & Luce-Kapler (1993) as co-labouring and 'toiling together' rather than as collaboration, which, they suggest, implies a much too comfortable and comforting enterprise.

'Research as text' seeks to evoke the professional imagination. Not only does it invite us to re-remember our own experiences, it also offers possibilities for new meanings to be constructed at any time between the reader, the author and the text. This is a helpful idea for the way in which it alerts us to keep open possibilities of seeing anew until the point of writing, re-drafting and beyond.

Changing Perspectives on
Researcher Identities: two illustrative examples

The Growth of a Practitioner-Researcher Identity

Extracts from the writing of two project members, with whom I have worked, are offered here to illustrate ways in which latency, as growth of researcher identity, became evident as their enquiries progressed. The first example is of a lecturer in a college of further education who published two pieces which together traced part of his research biography over a period of about 7 years. The second example is from the notes of a new researcher who has reached a point, after about a year of research, when he has become interested in comparing and relating his thought processes as an experienced educational psychologist with his thinking as a novice researcher, especially in his decision making in his research and in his daily work. It will be apparent from the ways in which both descriptions try to convey a sense of change and movement, that these pictures will be out of date by the time this article is published.

In the first example, Andy Convery (1991), recalled his own modest start in action research as he tried to avoid risk and reduce his own vulnerability:

As a teacher I strongly resisted one form of change – that which implied that my existing classroom teaching behaviour was ineffective and therefore needed fundamental alteration. When I investigated my classroom experiences as part of an MA course, my insecurity as a teacher unconsciously drove me

> *to adopt a classroom research plan that avoided self-*
> *examination, and validated and affirmed my established style.*

He was also reluctant, at the beginning, to involve his colleagues in his enquiry:

> *through my research, I discovered that it was relatively easy to*
> *discuss externally administered changes with my colleagues in*
> *the staffroom, but it was extremely difficult to investigate my*
> *daily classroom practice and open it to the critical*
> *examination of my peers, as this would involve making myself*
> *personally and professionally vulnerable.*

When teachers, like Convery, undertake self-study in practitioner research for the first time their projects are often both deliberately and unwittingly circumscribed. This is not surprising given their insiders' knowledge of the political dimensions of their workplaces. This is also evident in a literary sphere, as when the eager Boswell began to keep his daily journal in 1762. He seemed to have a foreshadowed hunch that he would want to conceal some aspects of his daily life from his readers. He makes this appealingly explicit in the following passage:

> *I was observing to my friend Erskine that a plan of this kind*
> *was dangerous, as a man might in the openness of his heart*
> *say many things and discover many facts that might do him*
> *great harm if the journal should fall into the hands of my*
> *enemies. Against which there is no perfect security. 'Indeed',*
> *said he, 'I hope there is no danger at all; for I fancy you will*
> *not set down your robberies on the highway, or the murders*
> *you commit. As to other things, there can be no harm.' I*
> *laughed heartily at my friend's observation, which was so far*
> *true. I shall be on my guard to mention nothing that can do*
> *harm. Truth shall ever be observed, and these things (if there*
> *should be any such) that require the gloss of falsehood shall be*
> *passed by in silence. At the same time I may relate things*
> *under borrowed names with safety that would do much*
> *mischief if particularly known. (James Boswell,* The London
> Journal, 1762-63, *pp. 39-40)*

Boswell's anticipation of the possibilities of harming himself or others is similar to Convery's concern to avoid tactless disclosure. Judging by the number of metaphors in our language for keeping things 'under wraps' or 'under our hat', it seems that 'putting the lid on' and 'sealing our lips' are deeply embedded in our culture. At the same time, we often suspect that in other people's work there might be 'more than meets the eye', 'a hidden hand at work' or 'wheels within wheels'. While metaphors for uncovering or disclosing shadowy parts of daily professional life such as 'blowing the whistle', 'letting the cat out of the bag' or 'spilling the beans' are inappropriate for what action researchers try to do, the idea of gradually 'lifting the veil' or 'letting in the daylight' is nearer the mark for what Convery did over time.

Insider practitioner research, like many other aspects of social interaction in workplaces, is often shaped by caution, strategic common sense, compromise, reciprocity and unspoken truces. This is as much about establishing and maintaining favourable relationships, as it is about reducing risk and protecting self-interest. It is to be expected that many projects which aim to study daily professional life in political contexts will begin in modest ways. Convery's moves towards more risky and challenging investigation came through a process of gradual immersion, rather than through planning ahead and building discrete phases into a grand design.

One consequence of this was that his first ideas and early questions were subsequently reformulated, and this was influenced as much by his daily working activities and contacts outside work as by data collection and analysis within the project. Sticking solely to project tasks, fixing research questions too early and adhering to them relentlessly, sometimes hints at lack of responsiveness or authenticity in workplace projects. As Whitehead (1989) has argued, 'living educational theories' are created through a process of rethinking and re-focusing', and as with the photographer's 'latent image' some surprises may emerge.

During his project, Convery, gradually involved others, step-by-step, in a series of collaborative activities; first, with experienced researchers outside his own college of further education; secondly, with the students he taught; and thirdly, with a working colleague:

> *In the early part of my research I found that working with professional educational researchers provided challenging theoretical perspectives which both prompted me to examine my accepted teaching practices and indicated areas where progress was possible. My work with the students had revealed insights into their needs and had also encouraged me to continue with a student-centred approach. These collaborative relationships were further complemented by my work with a colleague, who provided the vital emotional support necessary if I was to continue taking risks in the classroom.*

At that time, Convery saw himself as operating in two worlds as a teacher-researcher: in his relationships with a research community across universities and with colleagues in his daily working life. He remembers how external researchers provoked reflection and gave guidance, but he still needed support in his institution to extend risk-taking in his classroom. At that time, he described his development as 'progressive focusing from the outside to the centre'. Concerns and foci shifted. He concentrated, at first, on questions about the use of a teaching aid (television) in his Communication Studies course. That led to a study of his teaching methods, which then provided evidence of his own role and his effects on students' learning. The pattern of his collaborative relationships also showed movement inwards from external beginnings (in reverse to Daly's idea of moving inward-outward, referred to earlier). Overall, however, he was discovering that he could only change the world around him by first learning how to change himself.

Convery has shown, and Rowland (1988) has argued, that learning from doing enquiry is a continuous process rather than a therapeutic interlude. 'Learning', Rowland says, 'is not only the result of what we do, but also how we give meaning to what we have done' (p. 63). Also, 'future events will alter the significance of what took place during the enquiry. All we can say about the educational value of an experience is: we'll have to wait and see' (p. 63).

In a similar vein, in a later article, Andy Convery (1993) describes how he had become committed to action research during his MA programme, but that when he had finished he felt 'disillusioned and slightly betrayed'. Whilst this may have been seen subsequently as a key phase in his research autobiography, at that time it had not offered promise of a clear route to continual improvement. After an interlude of about a year, and after discussion with me, he embarked upon a PhD at the University of East Anglia, as he says, 'to recapture a sense of identity, focus and direction' for his enquiring spirit. Growing from his previous research, his intention was to continue to improve his own planning and teaching by exploring the relationship between them. In another article, written after a total of about 7 years of action research experience, and after a period of trying to use a reflective journal, he traces his own journey of personal development even further. This time he focused on his experiments with 'form' as an aid to making meaning in his research. He explains how he came to find fictional writing to be an appropriate vehicle to get behind his own defence and to get deeper access to his own thinking:

> *Fictional writing seemed to act as a diversionary tactic which*
> *allows me access behind my own lines of defence. Perhaps*
> *what was critical to my research development was that*
> *fictional writing gave me the security to explore a real danger*
> *area in my teaching, whereas in writing a reflective journal I*
> *might have focussed on a safer, more controllable problem*
> *area. (p. 147)*

At that time, Convery found that fictional writing enabled him to uncover latent feelings and frustrations and also to understand feelings which were difficult to describe. Usher & Edwards' (1994) term 'resonance' seems best to catch the sense which Convery conveys; that something feels important, but its exact meaning is uncertain. In contrast to the release he now felt, he recalled how his former attempts at reflective journal writing had made him feel tense, 'restricted by the inflexibility of a single subjective reality' and vulnerable to the 'professional research community'.

His story of action research combines the latencies of self discovery and revival, partly because of the introspective nature of the topic of studying his own thinking, and partly because of his continuous struggle to make meaning and to find an appropriate form to help his quest. For example, he even tried two alternative ways to write about weekend preparation. The first, and less helpful version slipped into what he called "self description' – 'a mask or disguise' – 'self-disclosure' cloaked in a degree of objective anonymity' (p. 144):

> *I wondered whether the first version of Michael's Weekend –*
> *my disguised disclosures – may have poured onto the page as I*
> *needed to express and understand my frustrations, and that I*
> *wanted immediately and exactly to capture those tired feelings*
> *that weekend marking can produce. However, in returning to*
> *these disclosures, I found it unrewarding when I tried to*
> *explore the emptiness and could not get inspired to investigate*
> *my lack of inspiration. The second version, however, provided*
> *a sharp contrast to such lassitude. Sometimes, to understand*
> *experiences that of their nature are difficult to describe, it may*
> *be necessary to explore their opposites. The reality which one*
> *has lived with for a long period may be too familiar to provide*
> *a useful focus for reflection. So before I could focus on my own*
> *weekend weakness I had first to create a comparative 'ideal'*
> *against which which I could then evaluate and understand my*
> *own behaviour. With fiction, one is not restricted by the*
> *inflexibility of a single subjective reality. (p. 148)*

Time had given Andy Convery opportunities to find a form, through experimenting, reading and working with others, that has helped him to think imaginatively rather than to confirm what he already knew. Finding ways to learn through research may be seen by some researchers as little more than following a sequence of appropriate techniques to produce a set of findings. However, when doing practitioner research into our own daily professional lives, we need to do more than adopt ready-made techniques and resolutely follow established procedures. Nor should practitioner researchers be expected to conform to institutional house styles, however innovatory, or to judge themselves against the academic discourse of critical, social theorists. As Zeichner (1993) has put it 'an awful lot of time and energy is wasted arguing over who are the 'real' action researchers and who are the imposters' (p. 201).

Colin Biott

Becoming an Insider Practitioner–Researcher

For my second illustrative example, I have used some of the notes of Nigel Mellor, a new practitioner researcher, who has been making connections between his changing view of research and his existing ideas about how he thinks and solves problems in his work as an educational psychologist. His notes, up to this time, have been written in two sets: a collection of thoughts on individual casework, dictated along with conventional case notes; and a diary of 120 pages of rough jottings about his own thoughts (a kind of running commentary of the early part of his project as it unfolded).

These notes trace his understanding of processes of *becoming* a practitioner-researcher which he had noticed are not often represented in literature which is almost all about *being* a practitioner-researcher:

> *Several entries, particularly at the start of the diary, record my recollections of those factors which, it seemed to me, created the conditions for bringing about this research. It did not just appear one day ready planned. I hope to set out the dispositions, triggers and life events which made this inquiry possible.*

> *Although perhaps of only personal interest in studies carried out by full time researchers, for the practitioner researcher my feeling is that these issues form a key to understanding the research as a whole.*

As he developed his project, he read about grounded theory, ethnography, reflective practice and action research and then realised during his quest to locate and refine his methodology that what he had been doing was itself his methodology. He then set out to describe his own brand of what he called 'reflective practice research' and to clarify the predisposing and precipitating conditions that shaped it:

> *The diary records that my concept of 'my practice' has developed throughout the period. Thus, the questions I could possibly have posed at the outset are not necessarily the questions which exercise me now. For instance, some of my later diary notes record, as well as concerns over the progress of the case and other such matters, reflections on how and why I became involved with a particular client in the first place.*

> *Intimately connected with the above issue is that associated with my realisation 'the world won't go away'. From the earliest days of the project I was involved in decisions over casework, with my newly-acquired 'reflective practitioner*

'status, but with no clear idea what I was wanting to reflect on, or change my practice to. Thus, I identified problems and made changes without a plan or clear methodology. My contention is that it could not have been otherwise.

These two topics are closely tied to that of the methodology of the project. I hope to discover the history of these particular aspects, and how, if at all, they interacted with my changing view of methodology.

Initially, he had found the concept of 'setting conditions' useful in comparing and relating his ways of making decisions in his daily work and his research, but then he wanted to move on beyond what he had read:

Schön's (1983) professionals appear remarkably calm and unhurried. He seems not to take the side of matters into account. My slightly amended version, which more accurately describes my day-to-day work, takes into account the surrounding stresses and uncertainties of the job. As an example, I have considered the situation at the point of becoming involved with a problem, what I have termed 'setting conditions'. At this time, often in a review meeting at a school, information can be drawn out from participants in a way which allows me to consider becoming involved while delaying a commitment.

For Nigel Mellor, the 'setting conditions' in his daily work are the predisposing and precipitating events which lead up to a decision to intervene. These include things such as current stress level, judgement of the likely chance of success, aspects to do with feelings, consideration of alternatives and amount of pressure applied on him. In trying to compare himself as a novice researcher with himself as a experienced psychologist, he found it most useful to think about differences in the knowledge and expertise he is able to bring to bear when answering his own question, 'Do I like what I get?' As he compares how he thinks and solves problems in his daily practice with how he goes about these processes in his research, he is also coming to understand more about:

intertwined and yet separate identities as researcher and practitioner.

Congruence or Connections between Identities?

This article has focused on a key issue for further exploration in the Management for Human and Organisational Development Project at the University of Northumbria: to seek to understand frontiers between the professional identity of experienced practitioners and their emerging identities as practitioner researchers during a time when they investigate their own practices and try to contribute to organisational development. We are interested in learning about continuities and discontinuities, and also trying to understand differences in meaning and implications between trying to achieve congruity or merging, on the one hand, or, on the other, to maintain fruitful tensions as we cross lines between occupational, social and researcher selves. This work will be continued mainly through narrative accounts, interviews and focused discussions.

We are also interested in the potential of action research for learning about identity issues across professions. We are curious, for example, about whether there may be any patterns in and between, therapists', educationalists' and carers' ways of conceptualising practitioner research processes in relation to their occupational identities. In their daily work, all are likely to try to see things from the perspectives of 'patients', 'clients' or 'pupils', and it will be interesting to find out whether it makes any difference to also see them as research participants. For example, how do they take ethical considerations into account, and how do they review the practical utility of introducing an action research dimension into their daily work?

One challenge for us all is to listen, give space, question and encourage each other to strive for new ways of seeing and understanding, and then to communicate with each other about our own learning. This needs time and, because of the potentially inclusive nature of practitioner research, useful and timely support and learning seems to come, when least expected, from many sources in informal social, professional and academic settings. A key concern of mine is to avoid imposing my own limitations and placing boundaries around projects and, by so doing, cutting off wider sources of inspiration for seeing anew and thinking in fresh ways. A key challenge for the project as a whole is to express our collective and personal learning in a form that is not fixed, but which is publicly intelligible. As a final thought – perhaps one pitfall for us all may be to attach too much status to the ideas of those amongst us who are already trying to be opinion makers in the literature of practitioner enquiry.

Acknowledgement

I should like to thank Nigel Mellor for the use of his unpublished personal journal for the second illustrative case.

References

Altricher, H., Posch, P. & Somekh, B. (1993) *Teachers Investigate their Work.* London: Routledge.

Barthes, R. (1974) *S/Z*. New York: Hill & Wang.

Barthes, R. (1981) *Camera Lucida*. London: Vintage Press.

Beattie, M. (1995) New Prospects for Teacher Education: narrative ways of knowing teaching and teacher learning, *Educational Research*, 37, pp. 53-70.

Bonnard, P. (1935) *Notebook*. Laing Art Gallery, Newcastle upon Tyne.

Boswell, J., *London Journal, 1762-63*, (Ed. F.A. Pottle, 1952). London: The Reprint Society.

Convery, A. (1991) Insight, Direction and Support: a case study of collaborative enquiry in classroom research, in C. Biott & J. Nias (Eds) *Working and Learning Together for Change*. Buckingham: Open University Press.

Convery, A. (1993) Developing Fictional Writing as a Means of Stimulating Teacher Reflection: a case study, *Educational Action Research*, 1, pp. 135-152.

Cook, T. (1995) I Just Want Him to Talk, unpublished MEd dissertation, University of Northumbria, Newcastle upon Tyne, United Kngdom.

Dadds, M. (1993) The Feeling of Thinking in Professional Self-study, *Educational Action Research*, 1, pp. 287-304.

Daly, M. (1978) *Gyn/ecology: the meta-ethics of radical feminism*. London: Women's Press.

Elliott, J. (1991) *Action Research for Educational Change*. Buckingham: Open University Press.

Elliott, J. (1994) Research on Teachers' Knowledge and Action Research, *Educational Action Research*, 2, pp. 133-140.

Heaney, S. (1991) *Seeing Things*. London: Faber & Faber.

Holly, M.L. (1993) Educational Research and Professional Development: on minds that watch themselves, in R. Burgess (Ed.) *Educational Research and Evaluation for Policy and Practice*. London: Falmer Press.

Rowland, S. (1988) My Body of Knowledge, in J. Nias & S. Groundwater-Smith (Eds) *The Enquiring Teacher*. London: Falmer Press.

Sanger, J. (1994) Seven Types of Creativity: looking for insights in data analysis, *British Educational Research Journal*, 20, pp. 175-185.

Schön, D.A. (1983) *The Reflective Practitioner*. New York: Basic Books.

Sumara, D.J. & Luce-Kapler, R. (1993) Action Research as Writerly Text: co-labouring in collaboration, *Educational Action Research*, 1, pp. 387-398.

Usher, R. & Edwards, R. (1994) *Postmodernism and Education*. London: Routledge.

Whitehead, J. (1989) Creating a Living Educational Theory from Questions of the Kind, 'How Do I Improve My Practice?', *Cambridge Journal of Education*, 19, pp. 41-52.

Zeichner, K. (1993) Action Research: personal renewal and social reconstruction, *Educational Action Research*, 1, pp. 199-220.

First published as *Educational Action Research*, Volume 4, Number 2, 1996

Postmodernism: a postscript*

MAGGIE MacLURE

From In These Times, *the weekly newspaper.*

fashion accessory • boys' toy • zombie philosophy • bourgeois chique •
vanity ethnography • nihilist • relativist • dehumanising • facile •
elitist • reactionary • self-indulgent • excessive • faddish • old hat •
pestilent • intellectual consumerism • modish negativity • self
contradictory • superficial • bankrupt • proselytising • doctrinaire •
dilettante • apolitical • narcissistic • incoherent • obscurantist •
arrogant • frivolous

> *There is no reason for alarm: I have no influence on the*
> *profession to corrupt the young. (I. Hassan, American literary*
> *theorist of the postmodern)*

So – what is all the fuss about?[1] Postmodernism is hard to define, not least because definitions are about tying meanings down. And that is one of the things that postmodernism is 'against'. But as a starting point: think *fragmentation, ambiguity, loss of certainty.* Think of postmodernism as a kind of undoing of all the habits of mind of so-called Western thought that have prevailed over the last two centuries – the decidability of truth, the inevitability of progress, the triumph of reason, the possibility of a universal moral code, the objectivity of science, the forward march of history, the existence of the singular, autonomous self. These foundational principles are all to do with making the world knowable, accountable, unambiguous, generalisable, predictable, coherent, manageable, mutually comprehensible. They have all, at one time or another, been held to be characteristic of modernism.[2] And postmodernism says 'No' to them. You will begin to understand its widespread unpopularity.

Here are some of the ways in which that 'No' has been said, and some of the names in which it has been said.

In the name of *Lyotard* postmodernism says we're now living with/in the 'postmodern condition', where something funny is happening to the 'metanarratives' we live by – those big stories (of science, progress, Marxism, humanism...) that cultures tell themselves in order to understand and legitimate their practices. These narratives are fragmenting into a disorderly array of little, local stories and struggles, with their own, irreconcilable truths (Lyotard, 1984). An example would be the dissolution of the USSR and subsequent events in Eastern Europe.

In the name of *Jameson* postmodernism says this fractured condition is the outcome of late capitalism – of the global dispersion of production (bits and pieces of the object assembled in different countries); the indifference of multinational capital to boundaries, and loyalties, of nation, state or culture; and the rise of sectors whose trade is symbols, signs and simulacra – such as the finance, entertainment, information, and communications industries. All the old collectivities within which people worked, suffered, struggled and recognised one another – nationality, workforce, locality, family, race, gender, and even class itself – are breaking up, and so too are our cultural and intellectual traditions. Nobody 'belongs' anywhere in particular, so there is no ground on which to stand and fight. And the old enemy, though it is the same enemy, has made itself invisible. Capital and its oppressions are simultaneously everywhere and nowhere-in-particular. Our old theories, especially Marxism, can no longer cope with the infinitely expanded and complicated relations that now exist between the economic, the social, the personal and the cultural. So we need new 'cognitive maps' (Jameson, 1984).

Nissan United: an anecdote of the postmodern [3]

Sunderland, in the North of England, is heavily dependent on the Japanese Nissan car factory for its economic well-being. This has meant, amongst other things, accomodating new business practices – such as the 'Just in Time' policy, which commands suppliers to deliver Nissan's orders at very short notice, within tightly specified time targets. When Sunderland council proposed to build a new football ground near the car factory, Nissan objected, on the grounds that traffic congestion would slow down suppliers dashing to meet their Just in Time targets. However Nissan subsequently indicated that they would be willing to reopen discussions with the Council about the new football ground: but only on condition that the team's name be changed from Sunderland United to Nissan United. The Council refused.

In the name of *Foucault* postmodernism says: yes, but that's the way it's always been (in this century). In spite of our dominant theories with their boxy categories (power, class, social structure) and their top-down explanations, power has actually always worked in this insinuating, dispersed fashion. It is seeded through the everyday practices of our institutions – in the ways we inspect, name and blame one another in the routine procedures of our prisons, schools, hospitals or courts. Power lurks and works in *discourse*. It is tied to knowledge and to language. And so are 'we': in place of the centred self of modernism, the human subject has become the contested and shifting creature of different discourses (Foucault, 1977).

In the name of *Baudrillard* postmodernism says language has gone 'hyper'. Words and images (signs) no longer refer to anything except one another, as they hurtle round the electronic information/entertainment networks. Plugged into those hopeless little screens, we no longer have access to what is real, but have become passive spectators of events without consequence, as struggle, fear and pain take their place amongst the succession of images and lifestyle options that pass indifferently before our eyes. The Gulf War, said Baudrillard, notoriously, was an example of our fatal detachment from the real – a remote engagement via the screens of computerised weaponry and the media, which became (for 'us' in the West) an event without consequence (Baudrillard, 1988).[4]

In the name of *Derrida* postmodernism [5] says language is all. There's no point in looking outside language for the truth that lies behind it, or the thought that it expresses, or the reality that it reflects, or the objects to which it corresponds. There are no First, Last or Deepest things out there – no origins, eternal verities, first principles or final destinations to ground our theories, justify our politics, validate our beliefs, centre our selves. No way to track words (signs) back to their original meanings: scratch a sign and you'll find another sign underneath.[6] So what we must attend to is what happens between and amongst signs, because that's where meaning lives. Or as Derrida would say, where it plays. Much of our philosophy and science has been about stopping that play – about trying to subdue meaning so that it will point unambiguously to the conclusions we want, and exclude the disorderly voices that we don't. The logic of Western thinking is divisive and discriminating. It creates order by setting up 'violent hierarchies' between pairs of terms, which 'privilege' one of the pair as more important/basic/central/deep/stable than the other: thought-not-language, nature-not-culture, men-not-women, white-not-black, reason-not-emotion, theory-not-practice (or vice versa in each case). These binary oppositions work by setting one term against its excluded Other; yet they rely on that Other for their sense. It is the task of *deconstruction* to destabilise those oppositions and to challenge the closure of meaning and possibility that they inevitably bring about (Derrida, 1974).

Trying to look across all these accounts, you could say that postmodernism makes claims in two (indissolubly linked) domains.

(1) It says things are changing 'out there' [7] – in our forms of social organisation, economic activity and political economy, with profound implications for the way we live our lives. This is sometimes referred to as *postmodernity*, reserving the term 'postmodernism' for the intellectual and cultural dimensions referred to in (2) below. It says that class, race and gender have become (or perhaps always were, though we did not recognise it) fragmented and multiply-determined. We can no longer think, for instance, in terms of class interest in the old ways. Similarly, postmodernist, or poststructuralist versions of feminism say that, despite the enormous gains of the women's movement in organising its struggles around a specifically female subjectivity and experience, there is a need also now to understand the ways in which women's identity is far from unitary (see papers in Luke & Gore, 1992). As far as education is concerned, the most telling question is whether it still makes sense to think of education in essentially modernist terms: as (potentially, if not actually) a rational process for turning out citizens, or emancipated individuals, or a stratified workforce, or a democratic society. It would be possible to read UK educational policy in the first half of the 1990s, for instance, in postmodern terms. Think of the escalation of initiatives (TVEI, the various versions of a National Curriculum, local management, etc.) and the seeming lack of interest in measuring their success by

traditional methods; the endless parade of remedies and accusations (skills shortages, back to basics, enterprise skills...); the way educational policy seems to have disconnected itself from the work of educational theorists, or at any rate seems content to seize eclectically on any position or posture that fits the current bill. Policy seems to have become a simulacrum of itself – a spectacle of imaginary solutions (see Stronach & Morris, 1994).

(2) Postmodernism says that the nature of our *intellectual and cultural work* – our philosophy, science, social science, art, etc. – is changing. History, time, space, representation, causality, objectivity, authorial certainty, self-knowledge – all of these have lost their innocence. Old distinctions have become blurred – e.g. between 'high' and 'low' culture, amongst different literary genres, or artistic styles. Thinking of literature for example, postmodern texts tend to do several or all of the following: disrupt linear time, space and causality; mix genres and styles; 'refer' to other texts (e.g. through parody or pastiche), and play fast and loose with characters' identities. They also routinely expose the machinery of their own construction and undermine the author-ity of the author. Italo Calvino's *If on a Winter's Night a Traveller* would be one example.

These characteristics – self-reference, irony, pastiche, refusal of coherence and wholeness, mixing of styles and periods – can be found across art, architecture, TV and film, advertising and fashion. They have been noticed in the fast-forward, fragmentary structure of MTV; in the malls and DIY sheds of decentered urban life; in the 'heritage history' of theme parks and nostalgia films; in adverts that parody themselves, plunder film genres and 'quote' other ads in an endless intertextual loop. More to our point, they can now be found throughout the academic disciplines. Not only in literary theory and philosophy, but also in psychology, anthropology and various sociologies, you will find books and articles which try to renounce the authority of academic language by writing playfully in alien genres, which deliberately make meanings provisional, which challenge their own claims to knowledge. An example would be Mulkay's (1985) book about the social production of scientific knowledge, which is partly written in the form of a play script and imaginary conversations. Mulkay insists that scientific theories are just particular kinds of stories, and argues that 'discoveries' are not the product of heroic, unmediated encounters with the laws of nature, but the result of (far from heroic) arguments amongst (far from disinterested) groups of scientists. They are created, in other words, in *discourse*.

There is more than clever trickery at stake here, although playing with paradigms can often seem foolish and flippant. It may seem pointless to undermine your own arguments, to cherish ambiguity and openness over coherence and conclusiveness. It may even seem like an abrogation of your responsibilities to the 'subjects' of your research, if you fail to match the seriousness of their dilemmas with the solemnity of your writing. But those who do this kind of thing are motivated by a number of considerations.

(1) A loss of faith in the power of the old 'totalising' theories to account for social processes in the postmodern condition, and in the possibility of attaining what Jameson (1984) called the 'critical distance' that hitherto allowed theorists, whatever their particular allegiances, to make moral and critical judgements. The move towards theories built on ambiguity and openness seems better suited to the diffuse and shifting nature of postmodern experience.

(2) An acceptance of the argument that research is a set of *writing practices*. That disciplinary knowledge, like any other kind of knowledge, is produced in and through language. This means refusing to use any longer what Derrida called the 'metaphysical tool box' that allows us to pretend that our particular field – whether that is physics psychology, or qualitative research – can be grounded by appeals to stuff that lies outside language – to those foundational things mentioned above, such as truth, democracy, practice, experience.

(3) A conviction that there is a link between oppression and the very structure of 'Western' thought and language itself.[8] The certainty and intransigence of dominant cultures towards those who are (constituted as) marginal is matched by the certainty and intransigence of theoretical languages that set the researcher above and outside the dilemmas of the researched, and that work by dichotomous reasoning – true/false, either/or, us/them, right/wrong – that always leaves the 'other' on the wrong side of the equation. So, the argument goes, to write differently is to open up the rigid language of theory that keeps the dispossessed in their place.

Metaphors for Postmodernism

Various thinkers associated with the postmodern have come up with metaphors that try to describe the logic (or anti-logic) of postmodernism, to give a sense of what it might be like to abandon order, symmetry, wholeness, logic and causality. Deleuze & Guattari (1988) use the metaphor of the *rhizome*: an organism without roots or determinate shape, which grows by the dispersal of nodes across a flat surface, and links aspects of the social, cultural, political, and personal in complex and shifting ways that deny the reality of discrete levels, domains, disciplines etc. The rhizome 'ceaselessly establishes connections between semiotic chains, organisations of power, and circumstances relevant to the arts, science, and social struggles' (1988, p. 7). Deleuze &

Guattari were opposed to theories – whether of the individual, the social or the political – that are tree-like: that is, based on notions of roots, hierarchies, levels or cores. For Deuleuze & Guattari, the will to mastery (of self, of society) that animates this kind of thinking leads, ultimately, to fascism.

Derrida's older notion was that of the *bricoleur* – a kind of professional handyman who makes things by cobbling together bits of other objects, and often has no fixed idea at the start about how things are going to turn out. Derrida said our old ways of knowing – aesthetically and philosophically, as well as scientifically – were akin to those of the engineer, who isolates a well-defined problem within a well-mapped domain, and works step-by-step to a determinate solution (see Spivak, 1974, pp. xvii-xx). All sorts of different theories and frameworks are 'engineered': when we think of knowledge as the tracking down of the truth, or of ideology as a (repairable) distortion of the 'real' interests of people, or of human development as a process leading to the 'whole' person, we are thinking/acting as engineers. We are 'questioning the universe' as if it were a masterable, knowable thing. But, says Derrida, that's a myth: all knowledge is *bricolage* – a making do with the best that is at hand, in a world whose shape and boundaries are never finally knowable, because meaning is never finally decidable. It's just that we seldom recognise this, because we rummage in our metaphysical tool box, as noted above, for those (illusory yet indispensable) appliances that make the flux of the universe stand still.

Educational Matters

Now, ask yourselves what's in the metaphysical tool box of action research, or of naturalistic enquiry, or of case study. Let's start with action research. A postmodern or deconstructive reading might be interested in how the claims of action research often rest on an opposition between practice and theory, that privileges the former. (Older educational paradigms have, of course, tended to privilege the latter.) It would notice the special status given to *experience*, with its connotations of authenticity, directness, naturalness, immediacy, relevance, life-as-it-is-lived; and how this is counterposed to, *and thereby draws its power from*, the claimed remoteness and abstraction of research/theory/policy/positivism. A postmodernist reading would register the continuing appeal to/of the *self* (of the 'practitioner') as a singular, knowable, knowing, perfectible entity. A postmodern reading *of* action research would suggest, then, that it is a very modernist sort of enterprise. What might a postmodern *version* of action research look like? Well, it might start by trying to 'bother', as Britzman (1995) puts it, its own clear-cut distinctions and categories. It might ask what would happen to self-reflection and self-knowledge when the 'self' is no longer a comfortable category to put at the centre of your theoretical framework, but a contested and problematic thing – what the poststructuralists would call a 'site of struggle' between different discourses. It would ask similar questions about key notions such as 'experience' and 'practice' – refusing to treat these as somehow natural or in-need-of-no-further-explication, but as themselves criss-crossed by different régimes of truth, in Foucault's term. "The field of practice is a broken and uneven place', heavily inscribed with habit and sedimented understandings" (Lather, 1993, p. 674, quoting Spivak).

In so far as naturalistic inquiry has any clear consensual meaning amongst those who work under its label, a postmodern reading would start by looking closely at that weasel word, naturalistic. Natural as opposed to what? Is it trading off an implied opposition to artificiality, experimentation, intervention, the machinery of positivism? And thus claiming that its methods provide a window on what's 'really' going on in social and educational settings? A postmodern reading might also 'interrogate', to use one of the buzz-words, the theories of the political that underpin democratic evaluation, or responsive evaluation, with their shapely modernist conceptions of competing interests, or stakeholders, or constituencies, and their aspirations (or fantasies) of a more open and equitable flow of information. Are these modernist notions still applicable in the postmodern condition?

Lastly, let's think of the methods and techniques of qualitative research, such as observation, interview, data analysis. Derrida's metaphor of the engineer may have struck you as far-fetched in this world of 'soft', interpretive, empathetic stances. But don't we often construct research as a kind of *mining* operation? We still sometimes actually refer to our methods as tools. We 'interpret' interview transcripts by looking for the person/values/attitudes that lie behind or beneath the surface litter of their speech. We classify and categorize observational data to disclose its hidden patterns and meanings. We 'analyse' the data to make it yield its truths, trends or themes. We use 'triangulation' (a very 19th century metaphor) to get a bead on the accuracy of interviewees' accounts, and 'validity' to provide a secure foundation for our statements. Despite our rhetoric of keeping things complicated, of acknowledging the baffling complexity of human social action, we are usually, as researchers, engaged on a quest for the *singular reading* of the case. We have our own metanarratives, and they are always 'victory narratives', part of the 'discourse of deliverance', as Lather says, quoting other people (1994, p. 2). You could say that we even have our heroes and heroines – the evaluator as existential hero (arguably a masculine identity, even when assumed by women), the action researcher as knight, missionary or barefoot doctor. Except for politically correct asides, where we acknowledge our own complicity in the pictures we paint (reflexivity), we are pretty sanguine about the possibility of operating in a knowable and perfectible universe.

But What Else Are We To Do?

Still, I confess: I still have difficulty uncoupling myself from the persuasive promises of ethnography. I desire to construct good stories filled with the stuff of raising and falling action, plots, themes, and dénouement. (Britzman, 1995, p. 237)

This is hard to answer – partly because there are still relatively few examples of postmodernist educational research, as opposed to explorations (such as the present one) of what it *might* look like. But mainly it's hard because possible answers all seem to point to risk, renunciation, open-endedness, leaping in the dark, not having a clear end in mind. Patti Lather, one of the foremost educational theorists of the postmodern, puts it thus: 'What would it mean to reinscribe research outside of a victory narrative ..., to situate it, instead, as a ruin, to work its failures toward a less comfortable social science?' She is thinking, here, of her ongoing work with women living with HIV/AIDS, about what might count as praxis under postmodernism. She wants to work with some kind of rhizomatic notion of power and knowledge (see refs to Deleuze & Guattari above), and sees this as creating spaces where new understandings might emerge. 'Viewing power as capillary, nomadic, and circulating rather than as uni-directional creates the possibility of spaces in which no-one is as yet the master versus the 'giving' people power more typical of the 'emancipatory' projects' (1994, p. 5).

Some Unanswered FAQs about Postmodernism

[FAQs: Frequently Asked Questions]

Yes, but isn't postmodernism itself a grand narrative?
Isn't it nihilism/hysteria/political naiveté/any of the other words at the start of this piece?
How can you be so dismissive of the (real, living, breathing) 'subjects'?
You can't really believe there's 'nothing outside of the text'?
Isn't all this renunciation of the heroics of research itself a kind of covert heroism? (Postmodernists do it with their bare hands – look, no metaphysical tools.)

Derrida says we have no choice but to use metaphysical tools of some kind, even while we know they are impossible. This means that the arguments of postmodernism can always be turned back against postmodernism itself. Yes, it is, in a way, a grand narrative (and thereby ought to be witnessing its own demise). Yes, it's impossible not to sit on that branch that has already been sawn off – on some value position, or commitment, or principle. Yes, every attempt to characterize postmodernism (including of course this one) uses, while it abuses, the logics of causality and rationality that were the target of deconstruction in the first place. Critics often advance this sort of argument – about sawing off branches, shooting oneself in the foot, etc. – against postmodernism. It's part of a general objection to relativism. A postmodern rejoinder would be to refuse the dare to jump one way or the other, the invitation to solve an insoluble paradox. To accept would be to rejoin the modernist community of binary choosers. Derrida's argument (and Deleuze & Guattari's in a different way) is that we need to cherish the movement between the poles of these positions, and permanently resist the impulse to come to rest on one of them. Postmodernism refuses to choose between. Just as it refuses to choose between theory and practice, nature and culture, 'man' and machine, progressive and traditional education, school and work, etc., so it also refuses to say yes or no to the question of its own relativism. By saying yes *and* no.

Notes

* This is a slightly amended version of an article originally written for research degree students in the Centre for Applied Research in Education at the University of East Anglia, United Kingdom. The original version appears in *Coming to Terms with Research: an introduction to the language for degree students* (CARE, 1994). It is showing its age in this new millennium!

[1] I have borrowed this question from the title of a scathing review of postmodernism by Beverly Skeggs (1991). The terms of abuse listed at the beginning have all been applied to postmodernism. Amongst them is one from a reviewer of this article.

{2} It's confusing though, because literary 'high modernists' such as Joyce or Eliot also wrote of the breaking down of all these certainties. But the high modernists are/were deeply nostalgic for their loss, while postmodernists are often either feverishly exultant about this vertiginous state, or pessimistically resigned: see Jameson (1984).

[3] Thanks to Charles Sarland for this anecdote, which may or may not be 'true'. Note the postmodern blurring of domains – political, cultural, economic, national. Note also how the contestation takes place on the site of *identity* – i.e. the football team as emblem of local pride and sentiment. Perhaps the Council's refusal indicates a *resistance* to the claims of postmodernity?

[4] Baudrillard's account of the Gulf War was hugely controversial, and generally anathemised by leftist critics.

[5] Some people would characterise Derrida's position as poststructuralist rather than postmodernist. As usual, definitions in this area are contested.

[6] 'As even such empirical events as answering a child's question or consulting a dictionary proclaim, one sign leads to another and so on indefinitely' (Spivak, 1974, p. xvii).

[7] Although of course the distinction between inside and outside, and related boundaries, such as personal/political, economic/cultural, are no longer tenable in postmodernism. We need to keep these distinctions 'under erasure', in Derrida's words – to be permanently mindful of their impossibility, even as we acknowledge the continuing imperative to use them.

[8] Derrida called this *logocentrism*: the centrality of (logical) thought and reason in our intellectual systems. Poststructuralist feminists sometimes expand the term to *phallogocentrism*, to point to the privileging also of patriarchal values.

A Short Annotated Bibliography

On Postmodernism in General

Connor, S. (1989) *Postmodernist Culture*. Oxford: Blackwell. [Lucid exposition of cultural aspects of postmodernism, from an informed but critical position. Includes potted summaries of arguments of Lyotard, Baudrillard and Jameson.]

Geertz, C. (1988) *Works and Lives: the anthropologist as author*. Cambridge: Polity Press. [Not really postmodernist in its assumptions and values, but an entertaining critique of ethnography that contains postmodern themes: e.g. ethnography as a set of writing practices. Takes apart the styles, and thus the truths, of the Greats of anthropology: Levi Strauss, Malinowski et al.]

Jameson, F. (1984) Postmodernism, or the Cultural Logic of Late Capitalism, *New Left Review*, 146, July-August, pp. 53-92. [Seminal (or perhaps we should say rhizomatic) article that tries to maintain a link between postmodernism and Marxist analyses of capitalism and culture.]

On Postmodernism and Education

Aronowitz, S. & Giroux, H. (1991) *Postmodern Education*. Minneapolis: University of Minneapolis Press. [Critical pedagogy gets postmodern and becomes 'border pedagogy'. Uses the metaphors of decentering and working on the margins to open up a space where the dispossessed can 'speak'. Criticised by Luke & Gore (below) as old-fashioned modernist emancipation theory jumping on the bandwagon.]

Gough, N. (1994) Manifesting Cyborgs in Curriculum Inquiry. Paper presented to American Educational Research Association, New Orleans, April. [Uses the postmodern figure of the cyborg (including 'real' ones such as Michael Jackson, Stephen Hawking, Reagan) to interrogate the boundaries between people, machines and the environment, and propose a postmodern 'curriculum of possibility'.]

Lather, P. (1991) *Getting Smart: feminist research and pedagogy with/in the postmodern*. London: Routledge. [Rather wordy book: long on discussion of what postmodernist feminist educational research could look like; short on convincing examples. But at time of writing, the main book on the subject.]

Lather, P. (1993) Fertile obsession: validity after poststructuralism, *Sociological Quarterly*, 34, pp. 673-693. [Playful, but difficult, exploration of postmodern versions of validity. Uses notions of rhizomes and deconstruction.]

Luke, C. & Gore, J. (Eds) (1992) *Feminisms and Critical Pedagogy*. London: Routledge. [Collection of papers under the banner of poststructuralist feminism. Focuses on the multiple and contested nature of women's identities and implications for educational research.]

MacLure, M. & Stronach, I. (1993) Jack in Two Boxes: a postmodern perspective on the transformation of persons into portraits, *Interchange*, 14, pp. 373-384. [Two portraits of the same teacher, written by different researchers. Looks at the notion of a 'life' as a textual product, and raises questions about qualitative research methodology.]

MacLure, M. (1994) Language and Discourse: the embrace of uncertainty, *British Journal of Sociology of Education*, 15, pp. 283-300. [Review essay dealing with postmodernism and discourse, and implications for educational research.]

Winter, R. (1991) Postmodern Sociology as a Democratic Educational Practice? Some Suggestions, *British Journal of Sociology of Education*, 12, pp. 467-481. [Says yes to postmodernism for its anti-authoritarian impulses, but no to its reflexive tendencies (sound of branches being sawed again). Action research is the remedy which will reconnect postmodernism to practice, in the name of democracy.]

References

Baudrillard, J. (1988) *Selected Writings*, M. Poster (Ed.). Oxford: Polity Press.

Britzman, D. (1995) The Question of Belief. Writing Poststructuralist Ethnography, *International Journal of Qualitative Studies in Education*, 8, pp. 233-244.b

CARE (Centre for Applied Research in Education) (1994) *Coming to Terms with Research: an introduction to the language for research degree students*. Norwich: CARE, University of East Anglia.

Deleuze, G. & Guattari, F. (1988) *A Thousand Plateaus: capitalism and schizophrenia* (trans. B. Masumi). London: Athlone Press.

Derrida, J. (1974) *Of Grammatology* (trans. G.C. Spivak). Baltimore: Johns Hopkins.

Foucault, M. (1977) *Discipline and Punish: the birth of the prison* (trans. A. Sheridan). Harmondsworth: Penguin.

Jameson, F. (1984) Postmodernism, or the Cultural Logic of Late Capitalism, *New Left Review*, 146, July-August, pp. 53-92.

Lather, P. (1991) *Getting Smart: feminist research and pedagogy with/in the postmodern*. London: Routledge.

Lather, P. (1993) Fertile Obsession: validity after poststructuralism, *Sociological Quarterly*, 34, pp. 673-693.

Lather, P. (1994) Textuality as Praxis. Paper presented to AERA, New Orleans, April.

Luke, C. & Gore, J. (Eds) (1992) *Feminisms and Critical Pedagogy*. London: Routledge.

Lyotard, J.-F. (1984) *The Postmodern Condition: a report on knowledge* (trans. G. Bennington & B. Masumi). Minneapolis: University of Minneapolis Press.

Mulkay, M. (1985) *The Word and the World: explorations in the form of sociological analysis*. London: Allen & Unwin.

Skeggs, B. (1991) Postmodernism: what is all the fuss about? *British Journal of Sociology of Education*, 12, pp. 255-267.

Spivak, G.C. (1974) Translator's preface to J. Derrida, *Of Grammatology*. Baltimore: Johns Hopkins.

Stronach, I & Morris, B. (1994) Polemical Notes on Educational Evaluation in the Age of 'Policy Hysteria', *Evaluation and Research in Education,* 8, pp. 5-19.

Winter, R. (1991) Postmodern Sociology as a Democratic Educational Practice? Some Suggestions, *British Journal of Sociology of Education,* 12, pp. 467-481.

First published in *Educational Action Research*, Volume 3, Number 1, 1995

PART 2

Praxis and Partnership in Action Research

This section contains four research reports which focus upon the nature of collaborative second order and individual first order action research, and in particular the practical and ethical dilemmas and tensions which need to be managed and resolved. What shines through each article is the authors' intelligent commitment to thinking 'outside the box' of everyday taken for granted assumptions, their commitment to growth in themselves and others, and their willingness to challenge existing orthodoxies in order to seek improvement.

In her article, 'Inhabiting Each Other's Castles: towards knowledge and mutual growth through collaboration', Bridget Somekh provides an insightful analysis of the sometimes problematic relationships between the university and the institutions it seeks to serve and support, using the metaphor of a castle to illustrate both the strength of the individual cultures, practices, discourse, and value systems and the difficulties of collaborating across boundaries. The article addresses three interdependent questions fundamental to all collaborative research enterprises. These concern: i) perceived power differentials ii) appropriate epistemologies and iii) change processes. Using a pupil autonomy with microcomputers (PALM) project as a case in point she shows in meticulous detail the multiple realities of 'academics' and 'practitioners' well defended different conceptions of knowledge. She describes the ways in which she tried to establish a relationship of researchers as equal partners in carrying out action research into their own practice as well as that of others; to negotiate what 'counts' as knowledge through co-construction; and to ensure that it was the intention and belief of both parties that they would change as a result of the collaboration. Ultimately, she found that lack of a common discourse substantiated the differences between the two constructions of reality and she points to this as an important constraint on the building of collaborative work which would cause the drawbridges of both castles to be lowered and access to new understandings to grow further.

Jean-Claude Couture uses a different but equally powerful metaphor to discuss individual action research 'co-researcher' relationships between teacher education students and their 'instructors' in one Canadian university. 'Dracula as Action Researcher' exposes a 'Teacher Identity Research Project – Students Speaking Back to the Program' as, 'saturated with contradiction and disruption'. Couture describes how his initial enthusiasm for the project turned to cynicism of his role which he likens to that of Coppola's Dracula (predator), in which he gradually anaesthetises the students (victims), establishes a covenant for reflective conversation. Through this he complies with the university in inviting, beguiling and then consuming their stories and experiences for its own knowledge purposes. He likens this to Dracula being carried around Europe by his 'hired dupes'. The issue of partnership, as Somekh also observes, is not simply technical. In the case of students over whom tutors have undeniable power, it is essential to build an ethical contract which is understood and agreed by both parties. If not, what hope have we that the classrooms of the 21st Century will reflect not exploitation of the learners but their liberation and emancipation, described so long ago by Lawrence Stenhouse as:

> *the intellectual, moral and spiritual autonomy which we*
> *recognize when we eschew paternalism and the rule of*
> *authority and hold ourselves obliged to appeal to judgment.*
> *Emancipation rests not merely on the right of the person to*
> *exercise intellectual, moral and spiritual judgment, but upon*
> *the passionate belief that the virtue of humanity is diminished*
> *in man when judgment is overruled by authority. (Stenhouse,*
> *1979, p. 163)*

The third of the articles in this section elaborates upon Couture's notion of responsibilities, moving it from metaphorical rhetoric to morally driven action. In 'Reflection and Action Research: is there a moral responsibility to act?', Christine O'Hanlon wonders aloud whether research – in this case that submitted for PhD examination – should result in some change, some motivation, a moral responsibility to act on the new knowledge. She claims that change in the person conducting the research is what makes their research educational, adopting the Aristotlelian ethical stance that 'there can be no science without demonstration'. She concludes, therefore, that all researchers need to engage in personal reflection as part of their research process. Such reflection eschews traditional notions of 'objectivity' which, she believes, result in distorted and certainly partial rather than impartial, accounts. O'Hanlon describes the Habermasian (1974) notion that there are at least three ways in which we know and understand the world – the *technical* (which generates instrumental knowledge which defines our means of control of nature); the *practical* in which the main concern is validation of subjective interpretation; and the *emancipatory* through which people are released from taken for granted activities, customs, assumptions. She argues, like others before her, that the first two are limited and limiting forms of reflection and that it is the last which must form the basis for research which leads to change. This ethical dimension of action research brings theory and practice together, such that 'the validity of any abstract theory must be in its 'praxis', defined by Aristotle as, 'practice with morally committed action which is morally informed'.

O'Hanlon's powerfully argued article reminds us that neither research nor the researcher can ever be neutral and argues convincingly for a new consideration of research being transformational for the researcher as well as for those who might be involved in or receive the research results. The theme is strikingly similar to that raised by Somekh in the first article in this section, and illustrated further in the final article. In, 'Defining the Field of Literature in Action Research: a personal approach', Kath Green writes of her research into improving her own practice as a supervisor of practitioner action research projects – the only example of 'first order' action research in this section. In a fascinating analytical narrative which will be an encouragement to all those undertaking research into their own practice, she writes of the implications of her early intuitive adoption of an 'eclectic' approach within a concern for wholeness and a focus upon a particular context for her use of literature. Extracts from her personal journal will resonate with readers of this book —a feeling of being 'swamped' by reading, the occasional wish that her initial focus had been sharper, or even that she had undertaken a theoretical study. Significantly, her concerns to maintain the integrity of her approach led her to reject the traditional notion, even within many action research studies, of a special 'literature review' section, but rather to allow the relevant literature to be an integral part of her personal research journey and consistent with the 'fundamentally exploratory' nature of action research. As a result, she sometimes 'stumbled upon' literature that deeply affected her thinking, and found herself engaged by literature which was often outside the field of action research which helped her find 'new ways of looking at the familiar'. Her central argument is that justifications for her choice of literature could only come after it had been read and made its contribution to the development of her thinking. She provides fascinating examples of her then newly discovered relationships with chaos theory, anarchic thinking, feminist theory and the work of Richard Rorty on the power of story, Mark Freeman on autobiography and Paul Ricouer on discourse. Green concludes by describing how her research has influenced her thinking about her practice – a perfect example of what O'Hanlon claimed was a necessary condition for action researchers.

There is a sense, then, in which each of the articles in this section illustrates the uniqueness of action research and the common drive among action researchers to develop work which is relevant to themselves and others, which is genuinely emancipatory and which makes a difference to the quality of teaching and learning.

References

Stenhouse, L. A. (1979) Research as a Basis for Teaching, in L. A. Stenhouse (1983) *Authority, Education and Emancipation.* London: Heinemann Books.

Habermas, J. (1974) *Theory and Practice* (trans. J. Viental). London: Heinemann.

Inhabiting Each Other's Castles: towards knowledge and mutual growth through collaboration [1]

BRIDGET SOMEKH

It is far more important, for appreciating the human condition, to understand the ways human beings construct their worlds (and their castles) than it is to establish the ontological status of the products of these processes. For my central ontological conviction is that there is no 'aboriginal' reality against which one can compare a possible world in order to establish some form of correspondence between it and the real world. (Jerome Bruner, 1986, p. 46)

Bruner uses the story of the eminent physicist, Heisenberg's, visit to Kronberg Castle to illustrate the way in which we construct our worlds. Heisenberg's science was grounded in experimental method. His 'uncertainty principle' is posited on the notion that the accuracy and replicability of experimental results is of paramount importance in research, despite being inherently problematic. He assumed an 'ontological reality', yet he found that Kronberg Castle had a different meaning for him as soon as he was told that it was 'Hamlet's castle':

As scientists we believe that a castle consists only of stones, and admire the way the architect put them together ... None of this should be changed by the fact that Hamlet lived here, and yet it is changed completely. Suddenly the walls and the ramparts speak a different language. The courtyard becomes an entire world, a dark corner reminds us of the darkness of the human soul, we hear Hamlet's 'To be or not to be'. Yet all we really know about Hamlet is that his name appears in a thirteenth-century chronicle. No one can prove that he really lived here. (Heisenberg, 1924, as quoted in Mills, 1976, and Bruner, 1986, p. 45)

This article attempts to present a critical analysis of a form of collaborative research undertaken by teachers in schools and myself and colleagues at the Centre for Applied Research in Education of the University of East Anglia. It starts from the premise that researchers bring to the process of inquiry their own prior knowledge, values and beliefs, and that these, as much as any research data, construct their research outcomes. There are multiple realities, not just one. I am writing this article sitting, so to speak, in the castle of the academy, and presenting it to an audience who, on the whole, inhabit the same castle. But the article starts from the premise that the castle of the school has just as many turrets, secret passages and grassy courtyards, is as well defended by a moat and portcullis, and substantiates its own important questions about the nature of education and the human condition.

Between 1988 and 1990 I coordinated the Pupil Autonomy in Learning with Microcomputers project (PALM).[2] PALM was a two-year action research project in which around 100 teachers in 24 schools, (covering the full 5-18 age range) carried out action research into their use of computers as tools to promote autonomy in student learning. The schools were drawn from three local education authorities (LEAs), Cambridgeshire, Essex and Norfolk, covering a geographical area in a rough square with sides approximately 85 miles as the crow flies. Some schools were linked by main highways but others were in isolated rural areas with no major road links to the university or the other schools. The teachers were supported by a central team of a coordinator, three project officers, Jon Pratt, Erica Brown and Bob Davison, and a full-time secretary, Laura Tickner. During the last six months we were joined by an experienced qualitative researcher, Richard Davies, who assisted the central team with analysis and the writing of the final report.

I have written extensively about the PALM project elsewhere (Somekh, 1991a,b, 1993; Somekh & Davies, 1991). The teachers' research has also been published in 35 titles in the *Teachers' Voices* series (PALM, 1990/91). In this article my primary purpose is not to report on the work of PALM, but to use PALM as an example to illustrate the points I want to make about school/university collaboration.

I will address three questions:

In the collaborative relationship how do you deal with the perceived power differential construed by the educational community in school/university collaboration?

What might be appropriate epistemologies to underpin collaboration in school/university relationships?

How does each partner in these relationships change as a result of the process? What does each partner contribute to the process?

In the Collaborative Relationship, How Do You Deal with the Perceived Power Differential Construed by the Educational Community in School/University Collaboration?

In PALM, first and foremost I wanted to establish a relationship of *researchers as equal partners*. Initially I saw this in terms of the outsiders (myself and colleagues in the central team) carrying out action research into our roles as facilitators of research (what Elliott, 1988, p. 165, calls 'second order action research'). At the same time, however, I wanted to provide the teachers with support in acquiring competencies in using computers in their teaching, so there was a teaching as well as a researcher component to the outside facilitator's role. This was essential because many of the teachers made it a condition of their participation in PALM that we should support them in learning how to use computers.

I included the following features in the design of the PALM project (stated or unstated) with the aim of reducing the power differential between teachers and members of the university:

(1) The three project officers were teachers 'on loan' from their normal jobs in the three participating LEAs for the duration of the project. They did not have, initially at least, the status of a member of the university. At the end of the project teachers often commented that it had been very important to them that 'Jon (or Erica or Bob) was a teacher'.

(2) Although the overall research focus of the project had been chosen by myself and was specified in the contract I had signed with the sponsors, the teachers had as much control as possible over their own research. With the support of myself and the project officers:
(a) teachers decided on their own specific research questions;
(b) they decided what data they needed and collected it;
(c) they analysed their data;
(d) they wrote up their research;
(e) their writing was published;
(f) they contributed to the meta-analysis of their own and each other's writing in order to generate theories from the work of the project as a whole;
(g) they presented their work at local teachers' meetings and, in some cases, at national conferences;
(h) they and their schools were named in both oral presentations and written publications by the university-led team, unless they wished to remain anonymous (NB we did not adopt the practice whereby the university partner is fully named, Bridget Somekh, and the teacher partner referred to by first name only, Jean); and
(i) in the writing of the university-led team, teachers' publications were listed fully in the references in the normal way, with author, title, date, place of publication and publisher or, in the case of an unpublished text, the address from which it can be obtained.

(3) Our working relationship was governed by a written Code of Confidentially which was intended to ensure equality between the partners. It contained the following clauses:

1. It is understood that the use of any evidence or data collected by teachers will be fully negotiated with the individuals concerned.

2. It is also understood that the discussions of formal or informal meetings remain confidential to participants in the meeting until they have given permission for more general release (but see 3 below).

3. It is understood that students will have the same rights as teachers to refuse access to data that they have provided (e.g. notes taken of interviews with them).

4. Pupils' anonymity will normally be safeguarded at all stages of the research. Individuals will be mentioned by name only with their prior agreement or, where appropriate, with that of their parents

...

9. Wherever possible PALM teachers will share the outcomes of their investigations, first with their school and cluster teams and with the central team, then across the participating LEAs, and finally more widely where appropriate.

10. All reports produced by teachers, will be published under their names in order to give full credit to them for their work. All such reports will be subject to negotiation with the sponsor and the three LEAs. The central team will assist teachers with this work as and when required. (Extracts taken from the PALM Code of Confidentiality, 1988)

These were useful strategies, but I cannot pretend that they solved all the problems. First of all, the operation of power in the project was a great deal more complex than the literature might lead us to suppose. Much of the writing about the relationship between teachers and university faculty members in collaborative projects starts from the assumption that there is a status differential in which the university partner has a higher status arising from his/her perceived depth of knowledge, research expertise, higher salary and national or even international reputation. This is an over-simplification.

There are a number of preliminary points to be made.

Those who work in universities in the UK are by no means certainly in a job that is of higher status than that of a school teacher; their salaries are rather lower than those of teachers and the word 'academic' is frequently used as a term of abuse by the media, politicians and the public to suggest out-dated ideas, unrelated to the conditions of something called 'the real world'.

Education faculties in universities in the UK are generally considered to have a lower status than other faculties, partly because education is not regarded as a discrete academic discipline, and partly because their main business has traditionally been seen as teacher training rather than research.

Those who work in education departments in universities in the UK have nearly all come into their job straight from teaching in schools; the route into academia via a full-time research degree and a period of post-doctoral study has never been the norm for teacher-educators, and since the mid-1980s accreditation of teacher training courses has been dependent upon faculty having 'recent and relevant experience' of teaching – i.e. on their going back to teach in schools for a term or an equivalent period of time every five years.

Since 1980, education in the UK has been subject to more and more control by central government; part of this centralisation of power has been the introduction of computers into schools through a range of more or less coercive strategies, ranging from offers of 'matched' funding which triggered parental pressure to collect money to earn the grant, to the incorporation of computer use into the mandatory National Curriculum; this had the effect of casting the university-led team in PALM in the role of supporters coming to the aid of teachers who needed to respond to the demands of government.

Schools in the UK, at the time of the PALM project, were under LEA control, but the trend was towards them being given greater control over their own budgets; there was growing administrative autonomy for schools and no tradition of control over schools by the university.

Universities in the UK, at the time of the PALM project, were wholly responsible for initial teacher training; however, a Master's degree is not regarded as necessary for promotion within the profession and only a minority of teachers in the UK have studied to Master's level.

The University of East Anglia (UEA) has a reputation among teachers in the region for supporting teacher research and many of the PALM schools had one or two teachers on their staff who were unusual in having studied on a part-time basis for research-based Masters' degrees at UEA.

All this means is that, while it is clear that being a member of university staff *does* confer a certain status in the eyes of the education community in the UK, there is plenty of ammunition available for those who resent that status and wish to be defensive or confrontational in their relations with members of the university. By way of illustration, here is an example of an individual effectively exercising power to obstruct PALM's work.

In each school, in order to establish a genuine collaborative partnership we had to negotiate with the teachers concerned. This normally came as a second stage, following an invitation from the headteacher (principal) or an LEA inspector. It happened that we had been invited to work in this particular middle school (age range of students, 9-13) by the headteacher. By 1988, the long-running industrial dispute between teacher unions and the British government over pay and conditions had largely abated. However it had a long-term effect in some schools where the headteacher had come to be seen as supportive of government policy 'against' the staff. In this particular school the head's actions in promoting government policy on teacher appraisal, the previous year, had been regarded as sufficiently provocative for 'withdrawal of good will' to be still continuing: e.g. all teachers left the building for the whole of the dinner hour, instead of being available to talk to students or run lunch-time clubs, as is the tradition in the UK. When Bob Davison and I visited the school to negotiate with staff how they wanted to be involved, the tone of the meeting was highly emotionally charged as this extract from field notes makes clear:

> *One member of staff had a very strong concept of research in the scientific tradition and repeatedly asked us how we were going to prove that an improvement had taken place as a result of the project's work. Again and again she said 'I don't see any point to doing it' and this was echoed by other staff. She appeared to be unprepared to listen to rational argument. I used three deliberate strategies to break through and make contact with her [including] explaining clearly that there are at least two research traditions which have long standing academic credibility ... At one point when she contrasted academic research with the kind of research that we were proposing, I cut in and made the point very emphatically that the word 'academic' could not be used only to describe the scientific tradition ... It was interesting at this meeting, that the symbolic cakes were largely left uneaten, people ate cheese and bread and the little hoops but almost nobody ventured into the more substantial cream cakes. (Field notes, 7 February 1989)*

Here is a case of one teacher securing our exclusion from the school (save for a fairly unproductive link with one other teacher) by leading what amounted to a concerted attack upon the project's aims and methodology. To do this, she used the internal politics of the school, as well as the status of scientific research, to give her leverage. One might go further and say that the act of excluding the PALM project from working with the staff was itself an exercise of power which demonstrated the staff's rejection of the authority of the head. This leads naturally to my next point.

The operation of power within the PALM schools themselves was just as complex as the operation of power between teachers in schools and the university-based team. Our relationship with teachers had to be 'hooked on' to the existing spider's web of their relationships with colleagues. We often became pawns in the operation of power within the school. Teachers with responsibility for computer use saw us as a mechanism to bolster their influence over colleagues. Headteachers saw us a means of injecting energy and commitment into their staff, individual teachers saw us as a way of advancing their careers or giving their teaching a new focus, secondary school heads of English departments saw us as a way of gaining leverage over the budget for computer resources in the school, and so on. In each case, we had to make a decision about whether we could allow ourselves to be used in this way. Whatever we decided to do – whether it was action or non-action – had moral and political implications within the school.

The concept of power, which underpins this analysis of relations between teachers and the university-led team in the PALM project, is based on the work of Lukes (1974), particularly upon his 'three-dimensional view' of power. This rejects as too simple both the 'one-dimensional' behavioural approach which relies upon the analysis of decision-making in situations of observable conflict, and the 'two-dimensional' approach which recognises, in addition, the exercise of power through excluding some issues from public debate (Bachrach & Baratz, 1962) and the 'mobilisation of bias' through the structures and value systems of the organisation (Schattschneider, 1960). Lukes's 'three-dimensional view' takes account of a whole host of subtle ways in which power is exercised consciously or unconsciously by individuals within organisations and the organisation as a whole. These include the exercise of power over another 'by influencing, shaping or determining his very wants' (Lukes, 1974, p. 23), and the recognition that 'an apparent case of consensus [may not be] genuine but imposed' (ibid., p. 47). But perhaps the most important idea which I take from Lukes is the recognition that all means of analysing power are 'evaluative': 'Each arises out of and operates within a particular moral and political perspective. Indeed, I would maintain that power is one of those concepts which is ineradicably value-dependent' (ibid., p. 26). I understand this to mean, that in attempting to redress the power differentials manifested in the relations between insiders and outsiders in PALM, we were exercising moral and political judgement. However, the extent to which we were able to analyse accurately the power relations, *which we became part of* in working with teachers in their schools, must remain doubtful.

In every case, the analysis itself and the decisions made on the basis of that analysis, formed part of the action research of the university team member. We explored the effectiveness of different strategies:

Sometimes exercising overt power ourselves in order to 'free up' a teacher to resist the covert power of professional norms and institutional traditions. For example, without demands and deadlines set by us teachers tended to see their research as 'for them' and therefore of less importance than grading students' books which was 'for the students' and therefore expected to take precedence.

Frequently resisting the expectation that we would take control, allocate tasks and operate as research managers of teacher-research-assistants. By this I mean that we repeatedly resisted teachers' requests to 'Tell us what we have to do'. Instead, we had the difficult, but ultimately much more rewarding, task of giving them the confidence to take control of their own research with our help and support. We needed to exercise leadership without creating dependency.

Sometimes exercising covert power. For example, Bob Davison was asked in one school to work with a deputy head (senior teacher-administrator) who was computer-phobic. We were told by the teacher who was leading PALM work, that if we could get this deputy head to have a computer in her classroom, without the support of another adult, it would be a major step forward. Bob was able to persuade her to allow some students in her class to evaluate a piece of mathematics software for him and, once it was established that the computer came into her room in the charge of these students, he was able gradually to persuade her (empower her?) to make educational judgements about the value of this software as a tool for students' mathematics learning.

Sometimes using our perceived status and interpersonal skills to raise the status of individuals who we wished to play a key role. For example, on one occasion Erica Brown and I spent a day in St Helena's School in Colchester (a large high school) talking to teachers, listening to their concerns, and suggesting that they should talk to Elaine Griffin who was the teacher leading PALM work in the school. She later wrote that our visit and discussions, 'stimulated staff into a very receptive mood' (Griffin, 1990).

The exact nature of the collaboration between the teachers and the university-led team in PALM evolved during the life of the project. Initially, in designing the PALM project I was influenced by John Elliott, who had directed the Teacher–pupil Interaction and the Quality of Learning Project (TIQL) in which I had worked as a teacher–researcher during 1982-84 (see Ebbutt & Elliott, 1985). His approach to this kind of collaboration is best summarised in a article in which he gives an analysis of five different possible outsider–insider relations, the last of which, 'The outsider as reflective teacher–educator. The insider as reflective teacher', describes the approach he himself adopts:

The two educational practices overlap in the following ways. The kind of reflective inquiry the teacher is engaged in constitutes the teacher educator's concept of an educationally worthwhile process of professional learning. In fostering such learning, the teacher educator advises teachers on the methods and processes they can employ to collect observable data, to analyze it in the light of alternative perspectives, and to critique their own biases. What the teacher educator judges to be the best methods and processes will depend on his or her 'second-order action-research' into the problems of facilitating the professional learning of the teachers involved. And a dialogue with those teachers about their perspectives of the facilitation strategies will constitute an integral part of the 'second-order action-research' process. In this context, teacher-insiders also become outsider-facilitators of the teacher educators' professional learning. (Elliott, 1988, p. 165)

At first I saw the relationship as one in which the outsiders (myself and colleagues in the central team) would carry out action research into our roles as facilitators of the teachers' research. However, the appointment of teachers with no prior experience of action research as members of the university-led team made this model inappropriate. Although I did not immediately perceive this, my colleagues Erica Brown, Bob Davison and John Pratt instinctively adopted much more of the role of collaborative partners with teachers in their research. This did not preclude them from also acting as facilitators and, throughout the two years, they and I carried out second-order action research into our roles as facilitators of the teachers' research. In terms of the project design, it was not a total switch from one role to the other, rather it was a movement along a continuum towards a more equal collaboration. The shift in their relationship with teachers was in part brought about by their strong sense of their inexperience as action researchers, and their perceived need to understand how to carry out action research in the classroom by doing it. They could not facilitate something of which they had no first-hand experience (it is worth noting that this is also likely to be true of many university researchers). In part, though, it was due to the teachers' desire to work in a full partnership. If the project officer adopted the typical facilitator's role of questioning, encouraging and supplying resources there was too much of a sense of being watched, and there was an erosion of honesty. Moreover, this role led to a reduction in the level of intellectual challenge for both parties in the partnership. There was too much holding back and too much introspection – consequently, too little learning about the substantive research focus (effective computer use in classrooms). Gradually the university-led team, myself included, moved towards a more genuine partnership, participating with the teachers in their research into the use of computers as tools for teaching and learning – while attempting to be as sensitive as possible to the dangers of becoming over-controlling of the research and/or inducing dependency upon us rather than autonomy in the teachers.

In the end, the power differentials perceived by all participants in PALM could only be tempered and reconstructed into a partnership of equal researchers by each partner taking equal power in the research process. This required us not only to recognise the differences in 'the ways we constructed our worlds (and our castles)' but to recognise the need to respect, and learn, from each other – in terms of Bruner's metaphor, to inhabit each other's castles. Collaboration is always fraught with difficulties and complete equality is probably impossible to achieve in any partnership. Setting aside these inevitable limitations, the following elements of our research process demonstrate our attempt to achieve the ideal of equality between teachers and the university-led team in PALM. As far as possible:

> We addressed each other's research questions with as much seriousness as our own;
> in discussions, we asked real questions to which the questioner did not know the answer (rather than the university partner asking questions designed to lead his or her teacher partner along a predetermined conceptual path);
> both partners acknowledged honestly the gaps in their knowledge;
> both partners openly shared their knowledge and beliefs, without claiming 'an aboriginal reality' for their particular 'construction of the world' (Bruner, op. cit.);
> both partners expected to learn from working together.

It is not easy to keep to these precepts and we did not achieve them all, all of the time. However, their importance, in particular the importance of the emphasis they place upon honesty, is confirmed by other writers reporting on various kinds of collaborative partnerships. Interestingly, it seems that honesty is often only achieved after the expression of anger. It seems almost as if the layers of conventional role behaviour have to be stripped away through raw emotion before the partners, conscious of the socially constructed nature of their status differential, can forge a more equal relationship. Convery (1993, p. 137) describes how the anger he felt at reading a paper by his academic supervisor on teacher-thinking jolted him out of his sense of 'intimidation' in the face of 'the confident authority of the professional research community'. He continues, 'This provoked me into productive dissent and I found I could write freely and critically'. Early in the PALM project Dawn Fuller reacted in fury to something Jon Pratt had written about her work. At the time this was a traumatic event for them both, but it undoubtedly contributed to the depth of their subsequent collaboration and may have been a factor in the quality of her action research (Fuller, 1991). Schindler (1993), writing about his relationship with his 13-year-old students, describes how a powerful emotional outburst on his part, followed by the students frankly expressing their anger in written responses, provided the essential conditions for equality of respect. He writes, 'In a sense I had fallen from a throne. But this fall gave access to a new quality in my relationship with the students'. Plummer et al (1993) provide a particularly good example of how easily each partner in a collaboration can slip unwittingly into routines of institutional roles and relationships, thereby generating an intense sense of betrayal and frustration in the other. And of how honesty about the experience can ultimately strengthen the relationship and make it one that is more nearly a partnership of equals. It is difficult to illustrate the power of this article (written as a series of letters) with a single quotation, but perhaps this comes near to it:

> *Many thanks for sending me your 'rage' notes and letters. The interesting thing for me to look back on (after we have already talked a little about it) is how, for me, slipping (accidentally) into 'tutor' mode constitutes a sort of unequal relationship and this leads to a 'holding back', for fear of hurting. That is a worry because it opposes 'caring' and 'honesty'. I suppose I am aware of the pain tutors can cause by rejecting a student's work when they impose their own conceptions rather than working out from where the student is 'at'. You are therefore showing that what I take to be 'caring' can be experienced as 'paternalistic' and patronising. I wonder how to avoid this bind ... (Ibid., p. 311)*

What Might Be Appropriate Epistemologies to Underpin Collaboration in School/University Relationships?

Epistemology is the basis upon which research methodology 'establishes the ontological status of the products' of research (Bruner, 1986, p. 46, quoted at the opening of this article). A simpler way of putting this is to say that epistemology defines what 'counts' as knowledge. The way we go about seeking for knowledge – our research methodology – is defined by the nature of the knowledge we believe ourselves to be seeking. There is more than one construction of the world, which means that there is more than one way of deciding upon what 'counts' as knowledge.

Any discussion of school/university collaborations must begin by acknowledging that the castle of the academy and the castle of the school have different tests for truth when evaluating the products of research, and are, therefore, inclined to approach methodological issues from different points of view. They not only want to find out different kinds of things through their research, they want to go about their research in different ways. Of course, this is oversimplified. To pursue the metaphor, there is more than one castle in the academy: for example, there are those who have a concept of what Bruner (1986, p. 46) calls an 'aboriginal reality' and are concerned to establish the validity, reliability and generalisability of their research outcomes in terms of that reality; and there are those who have a concept of 'constructed realities' and are concerned to observe interactions, collect perceptions and use these to generate grounded theories about particular 'constructions' or individual 'cases' through the exercise of 'theoretical sensitivity' (Strauss & Corbin, 1990, pp. 41-47).

The epistemology which underpins action research methodology is distinctive in that it rejects the notion that knowledge can be de-contextualised from its context of practice. We live in a world of action, a world in which the nature of existence is shaped by perceptions, and this strongly suggests that knowledge constructed without the active participation of practitioners can only be partial knowledge. To an extent, this is because researchers who are not part of the action-context have a tendency to oversimplify their analysis and assume a simplistic cause–effect relationship between phenomena and events. In a paper in which he applies the theory of scientific realism to educational research and evaluation House (1991) argues that 'events are the outcomes of complex causal configurations, which sometimes cancel each other out'. He goes on to say that, 'the teacher possesses specific causal knowledge built on inferences made over a period of time from different sources and focused on particular students and the concrete conditions of the classroom' (pp. 8-9). He argues that this gives teachers special insight when it comes to the interpretation of the social reality of the classroom.

Practitioners are also essential to the process of knowledge-construction because they have the power to confirm or refute decontextualised theories, either unintentionally or by a conscious exercise of power, at the moment when an attempt is made to implement them. In this fact lies the key to understanding the long history of failure to apply the findings of educational research to schools and classrooms. Giddens provides an explanation of how and why individual agents exert this influence in his analysis of two kinds of generalisations and their interdependence. He argues that:

> *Generalizations in the social sciences, 'tend toward two poles*
> *... Some hold because actors themselves known them – in*
> *some guise – and apply them in the enactment of what they do*
> *...'*
>
> *Other generalizations refer to circumstances, or aspects of*
> *circumstances, of which agents are ignorant and which*
> *effectively 'act' on them, independent of whatever the agents*
> *may believe they are up to ...*

*The first [kind] is just as fundamental to social science as the
second, and each form of generalization is unstable in respect
of the other. (Giddens, 1984, p. xix)*

The methodology of action research, which takes account of the need to
integrate the construction of knowledge with its enactment in practice, is
more likely than other research methodologies to recognise and take
account of this 'instability' of generalisations (or social theories), because
it deals explicitly with the integration into practice of the two kinds of
generalisation that inform our actions. This is the feature of action
research which underpins the quality of its impact upon practice.

These writings of House and Giddens provide me with theories to
underpin what I have come to understand through the process of
carrying out action research in partnership with teachers: that in
collaborative action research, practitioners' analyses and interpretations
should be given *at least equal credence and status* with those of their
'outsider' partners from the university, and if possible precedence over
them.

In order to illustrate what the castle of the school looks like in
practice, I now want to quote the final passages from two of the PALM
teachers' publications. After more than 18 months as action researchers,
albeit very much as part-timers whose research was carried out over and
above their full-time work as teachers, these passages indicate the
knowledge that 'counted' for them.

From *From Lascaux to Archimedes*, John McGowan (1991, p. 27)

[John McGowan was the Head of Art and Design at Arthur Mellows
Village College, an 11-18 comprehensive school with approximately
1200 students, situated six miles north of a large city. When the school
joined the PALM project, the Art Department acquired a British-made
Archimedes computer.]

*Supporting Curriculum Development
of Information Technology in Art and Design*

*Classroom based curriculum development has been a central
issue in PALM work over the past two years. One of the
persistent feelings I have had at every stage of the project has
been the desire to find someone who has 'done it before' and
can help to short-circuit the learning cycle. On the rare
occasions when the expert has been found, the lesson
delivered, it is still vital to re-learn the processes for oneself,
for the teacher to acquire his own mastery. Making mistakes,*

Bridget Somekh

getting lost is just what will happen to the student; the teacher needs to have that experience to recall.

It seems to me at this stage, that it is more important to find appropriate applications for the use of computers than it is to worry about software/hardware and user competence. Short and intensive courses will do much to help teachers gain confidence in their own capacity to handle the new technology but applying their expertise to the classroom calls more upon the skills of the teacher as curriculum planner.

As computer design skills become a regular experience for our students, in the primary school and in other areas of the curriculum, so these notes will, in a short while, seem like writings about the cave paintings of Lascaux. We will have to re-evaluate the usefulness of treating all our first years as novices.

From *I Like to Read: computers and childrens' reading*, Jean Edwards (1991, p. 20)

[Jean Edwards taught at Gladstone Primary School, an inner-city primary school with 420 students, situated in an area populated almost exclusively by British Pakistani families. 90% of the students were Urdu/Punjabi speaking Muslims.]

Postscript

Despite all this has autonomy taken place? Are there signs of autonomy developing? What has happened to these children during this period?

They have entered a tunnel – warily at the narrow end, traversing the pitfalls and treasures and emerged into the daylight, larger, stronger, wider and far more confident, ready to enter a new tunnel with eagerness and anticipation.

From all this research, it is apparent that children are supporting each other and relying on each other's knowledge and respecting the other's innate ability, cooperation and self-reliance as their joint learned skills. They have helped each other to a common goal despite the massive hurdle of speaking and operating in a different language.

The computer becomes a third person in a relationship with a life of its own: with foibles and problems like anyone else, which the children accept. Like any other child, it often feels off-form!

The autonomy lies in the developing relationship between the children using the computer as a catalyst. The activities created an atmosphere in an insular, escapist world where divisions have to be made, creating a sub-culture where different rules apply and control is available over the ultimate goal and the paths to it.

These two passages tell us quite a lot about the constructed reality of these two teachers. In one sense they are very different, since the focus of the first is almost entirely upon teaching, how teachers learn, and the teacher's role as a 'curriculum planner', while the focus of the second is upon the children's social development and their relationships with each other and with the computer. But they also have much in common. I would suggest that both passages:

   assert the authors' learning in terms of a broad statement of values and beliefs, rather than a list of outcomes or conclusions;
   signal that they have been generated from a study of practical, everyday problems;
   are aspirational in tone, in the sense that the writer seems to be clear about the way forward from this point and how to build upon the work done;
   are written in straightforward language, using a compelling metaphor which appeals directly to the imagination of their readers;
   indicate a view of learning as a process of experimenting, overcoming problems, learning from mistakes and developing self-reliance, in which peers and teachers help most when they understand the problems involved;
   suggest that the authors are realistic about their own shortcomings, particularly in relation to their perceived lack of expertise in using computers (Jean Edwards's piece is not explicit about this, but I am assuming that the anthropomorphic passage about computers 'feeling off-form' indicates a wry smile about her own inability to make computer-use a trouble-free experience for the children);
   indicate that their authors' have reflected in depth on major educational issues (in one case, how teachers learn, in the other, the nature of autonomy) and have developed coherent theories which they feel confident they can operationalise.

In reporting this knowledge, the teachers' concern seems to be to pass on to other teachers the powerful and/or useful understandings which have become an integral part of their practice as a result of undertaking their research. No use is made of the devices frequently used by members of the academy to support their findings (e.g. quotations from other writers whose findings concur with theirs, accounts of research methods used, technical discourse creating a sense of critical distance from the text, multi-layered qualifications couching each statement in exactly the right degree of tentativeness). In this sense teachers may (wrongly) appear to be unconcerned with establishing the 'validity' of their findings.

In reality, the PALM teachers were deeply concerned with establishing the trustworthiness of their research knowledge. But I deliberately use the concept of 'trustworthiness' to replace the concept of 'validity' because it signifies that the teachers made their judgements of trustworthiness on the basis of different sets of criteria from those members of the university use to judge validity. The moat and portcullis of the castle of the school are of a different kind. The first set of criteria – there are many, not just one – relate to testing out ideas in practice (see Altrichter et al, 1993, p. 77). The second set of criteria relate to the degree of resonance between the action research knowledge and the experience of other teachers. In the case of the PALM project, in which around 100 teachers participated, this included the degree of resonance between their own action research knowledge and that generated and reported by other PALM teachers. As Richard Davies says, in a document that summarises the PALM research findings:

> *A teacher expresses an opinion, makes an observation, represents an experience. ... What is written by one teacher may be recognised subjectively by others. A kind of working validity is found in the subjective recognition of one's own experiences in the experiences of others in broadly similar contexts (the context in this case of teachers, schools, micros, PALM, the shared historical epoch, etc.). The subjective character of this 'validity' is reduced in proportion to the size of the consensus or the number of people who recognise their own experience in the accounts of others, What one has is a kind of vernacular triangulation conferring shared significance (or common meaning) which becomes itself a form of valid generalisation, or knowledge of sufficient confidence to support change. (Davies, 1990, p. 3)*

Sumara & Luce-Kapler (1993), building upon Bruner's concept of constructed realities and a range of recent post-modernist writing's, use 'the writerly text' as a metaphor for collaborative action research itself. A readerly text is one which proceeds according to well-established conventions, enabling the reader to 'become 'immersed' in the comfort of a given plot', whereas a writerly text is one in which 'at no point can [the reader] relax and let the text determine and govern our experience ... it forces us to more explicitly and deliberately *write* while we [are] *reading*' (ibid., p. 389). Sumara & Luce-Kapler see collaborative action research as requiring both partners to engage fully and actively in the problematics of the research, rather than one adopting a more comfortable and passive role akin to that of the reader of a readerly text. While agreeing with this as an illuminating metaphor for the collaborative action research *process* I would like to extend it to throw light upon practitioner *reporting* of action research.

Whatever the research methodology, research is concerned with constructing knowledge and making it widely available through some form of publication. But there are particular problems in practitioners reporting research which they have generated through an integrated research-action process. This is not knowledge which exists fully in a decontextualised form. The trustworthiness of practitioner action research knowledge can only be partially established by the text in which the research is reported. Its authenticity in the eyes of its practitioner–author lies in its effectiveness in practice and the way in which it resonates with his or her past experience. This kind of action research report requires a 'writerly reader', one who will approach the text with an expectation of collaborating with the author in the construction of knowledge. It appeals to the prior experience of the reader and to his or her passionate engagement with the issues it raises. Therefore, the reader of a practitioner's action research report is required to engage with it *as if it were data* and construct further knowledge through a kind of action research with the text. The difficulty is that such reports usually appear deceptively easy to read and we are used to being 'readerly readers'. The power of the writing is destroyed when it is subjected to critical appraisal on the basis of the criteria normally applied to academic texts. (For a more detailed discussion of these issues, see Somekh, 1993.)

How Does Each Partner in These Relationships Change as a Result of the Process? What Does Each Partner Contribute to the Process

By now, a moderately 'writerly' reader will have realised that the three questions addressed by the article are interdependent, with the result that I have already said a good deal about the third while attempting to answer the first and second. My exploration of the question about perceived power and status strongly suggests that true collaboration is only possible if there is an *intention and belief* that both partners will make an equal, but different contribution to the action research process, and each will change as a result of the collaboration; and my exploration of the epistemological question strongly suggests that the quality of action research depends upon the school/university collaboration being a genuine partnership in which both parties contribute equally.

Change for each individual in the partnership arises from understanding that, in collaboration, both contributing and learning become a single process. This is what it means to inhabit each other's castles. Nevertheless, each castle retains its integrity and continues to belong to one member of the partnership. In other words, collaboration is about celebrating difference and strengthening one's own sense of identity; and at the same time it is about developing knowledge and understanding of the other so that movement between the two castles is pleasurable, challenging and mutually empowering.

I want to illustrate this through an analysis of how our collaboration dealt with the problematic issue of discourse.

In our discussions with teachers in PALM there was always a tension over discourse. The word 'research' itself was a problem. It seemed to signify to teachers of the 11-18 age-range that the project would be engaging in something alien to their experience. It was unclear what connotations they brought to the word, but these probably included 'difficulty', 'abstraction', 'impracticality' and 'something which is done in laboratories'. Most of all, though, the word simply lacked familiarity, it was not part of their professional discourse, it belonged to the discourse of the academy. A clear illustration that familiarity was the key lay in the fact that many of the primary teachers did *not* find the word problematic, and this seemed to be for no better reason than that they were accustomed to refer to their students as undertaking 'research' in topic work. (There is a tradition in British primary schools of organising younger students' learning around a multi-disciplinary exploration of a topic or theme over an extended period of time, see Barnes, 1993.)

Although there were some differences in the particular manifestations of the problem, the language we used was a frequent source of division between the teachers and the university-led team. Primary and secondary teachers alike had difficulty with research terminology such as 'data' or 'data analysis', and with the terminology for certain abstract concepts such as 'autonomy'. As a result we had to decide whether to use these terms, or to replace them with non-specialist terms, such as 'inquiry' for 'research', 'evidence' for 'data', or 'taking responsibility for one's own learning' for 'autonomy'. However, none of these terms was an exact equivalent, and in addition to their defined meanings being slightly different, they carried with them different connotations in terms of the status of the activity we were engaging in. Those very terms that alienated the teachers were those that would give the project status in the eyes of the academy.

Through discourse human beings construct their castles. More than this, discourse makes up the fabric of the building, defining the questions which can be asked, the nature of 'what counts as true' and the accepted ways of establishing 'truth'. As Foucault says:

> *Each society has its regime of truth, its 'general politics' of*
> *truth: that is, the types of discourse which it accepts and*
> *makes function as true; the mechanisms and instances which*

> *enable one to distinguish true and false statements, the means*
> *by which each is sanctioned; the techniques and procedures*
> *accorded value in the acquisition of truth; the status of those*
> *who are charged with saying what counts as true. (Foucault,*
> *1972, p. 131)*

The problem for the PALM school–university collaboration lay in the way in which the different discourses of the two groups structured the power relations between us. The language we used continually confirmed our traditional roles, in such a way that it did not merely indicate the power differential, it served to re-create it. Moreover, since our combined endeavour was research there was no possibility of meeting on a limited common ground from which considerations of educational knowledge, values and beliefs were excluded. But the 'problem' was productive. The strength of the collaboration lay in the continuous challenge to both partners resulting from discourse confrontation.

The aim of the university-led team was to give each group access to the discourse of the other. We recognised that the discourse of the academy was well-honed to certain kinds of analytical thinking and we deliberately introduced some of its terminology in our discussions with our teacher–researcher partners. Although we felt the need to *adapt* our own discourse when talking to teachers, we felt that it would ultimately be patronising to *restrict* it, so we attempted to compromise by learning to move from one discourse to the other, as fitted the circumstances and the individuals concerned.

One serious limitation resulting from the discourse gap was that teachers were excluded from reading much of the academic literature on student learning – in the sense that they found these books inaccessible. We were not able to do a great deal to change this, particularly as the teachers were undertaking their research alongside their full-time work as teachers, without any time set aside for data collection, analysis or writing, let alone reading. But we made a small inroad into the problem by putting together a pack of key readings on autonomy in learning and using these to promote discussion about some of the major issues raised by the research.

The inaccessibility of academic texts and our own awareness of modifying our language when talking to our teacher partners, tended to create a sense that the discourse of the academy was more extensive than that of the school, but of course this was not the case. The two were different, and inescapably they implied differential status for the two user groups, but neither was more extensive or in its way more exclusive than the other. When, towards the end of the project, my university colleague Richard Davies joined the team, he had to try to get inside the discourse of the school in order to establish his credibility with the teachers.

Our understanding of the importance of the discourse of the school in constructing the teachers' view of the world was the first step in reducing the ability of the discourse differential to confirm and strengthen the latent inequalities in the collaboration. More than this, by working together over a two-year period we challenged the settled assumptions of both discourses. In the university-led team, we abandoned the notion that writing consists in empowering individuals to 'find their voice', and began to experiment with producing texts in different voices, appropriate to our different audiences of teachers, officers of the LEA and central government, and university researchers.

Neither group was able to escape from the fact that our experience and the process of our knowledge construction was systematised by different patterns of discourse, but we began to have the power to move consciously from one to the other. Teachers adopted selectively from the language and concepts of the academy and vice-versa. Progress was tentative, but deliberate. At the end of the Introduction to The Archaeology of Knowledge, Foucault writes:

> *... rather than trying to reduce others to silence, by claiming that what they say is worthless, I have tried to define this blank space from which I speak, and which is slowly taking shape in a discourse that I still feel to be so precarious and so unsure. (Foucault, 1974, p. 17)*

He is referring to the book he is embarking upon writing (or just finishing, since introductions are frequently written last). His enterprise is to create a new discourse whose meanings will be free of the power structures of any previous human constructions of the world. Our enterprise in PALM was more concrete, and less ambitious, but also concerned to resist existing power structures. Perhaps I can indicate the sense of disorientation and powerlessness which sometimes resulted from shedding *familiar speech patterns in which our thinking was located* by quoting an extract from Foucault's metaphor for his own more literary venture. It comes from further down the same page:

> *Do you think that I would keep so persistently to my task, if I were not preparing – with a rather shaky hand – a labyrinth into which I can venture, in which I can move my discourse, opening up underground passages, forcing it to go far from itself, finding overhangs that reduce and deform its itinerary, in which I can lose myself and appear at last to eyes that I will never have to meet again. (Ibid., p. 17)*

But the strength of the collaboration lay in *our possession of two discourses.* By depending upon each other we could speak persuasively to a much wider audience. Teachers could present our work orally to meetings and conferences of other teachers; and academics could present our work at academic conferences. In the same way, we could direct our writing to different audiences and draw each other's work to the attention of those who otherwise would probably not have given it credence. For example, in the space of four academic articles I was able to quote at length from the work of seven teachers, refer more briefly to another five, and give an overview of the work in three schools, as well as providing full references for all 35 studies in the Teachers' Voices series (Somekh, 1991a,b; 1993; Somekh & Davies, 1991). Likewise, PALM teachers referred in their writing to the ideas of their university-based colleagues, and implemented our ideas as well as their own in their teaching.

In the PALM project we found evidence that teachers focused more easily on issues relating to the management of learning than on learning itself. They began by establishing what they wanted students to learn, but then much of their energy went into planning how to organise activities which they believed would lead to learning. Often, superficial signs of organisational breakdown were interpreted as signs of learning failure. For example, on one occasion a student who did not appear to be participating actively in group discussion was assumed by his teacher to be failing until the tape-recording of the discussion showed that his interventions were crucial to the group achieving the task they had been set (Tooth, 1989). On another occasion, students asked to work collaboratively on producing a newspaper were assumed by their teacher to be getting nowhere with the task when they did not settle to work within five minutes; whereas evidence from observation and student interviews later showed that the group had needed time to discuss their ideas and reach agreements before embarking on a collaborative endeavour (Moon, 1991). For many teachers, PALM action research was a process of discovering that learning did not necessarily follow from good classroom management. Equally, the reality of the classroom continually reminded members of the university-led team that learning in school was a social activity. It could not be the *only* focus of the teacher's attention. It must take its place alongside other goals such as socialisation and the motivation of students.

In PALM we also found that teachers were concerned primarily with researching their own classrooms. Although they enjoyed reading each other's writing and assisted with meta-analysis of the body of writing as a whole when specifically asked to do so at the PALM conference, they did so with the aim of applying what they learned in their own teaching. By contrast, the university-led team members were concerned to make sense of phenomena which we observed across a number of classrooms. The opportunity to work as research partners with teachers in a large number of schools over a two-year period enabled us to carry out research into teaching, but we were researching *with* the teachers and not *on* them. I began working on PALM at a time when little was known about the way teachers approached the use of computers and an important outcome of my research was the model of the pattern of teacher development in computer use set out in Table I. While it has all the usual limitations of models, this is of direct practical use in planning teacher professional development programmes in computer use.

In most cases, teachers:

begin with a concept of the computer as tutor, assuming that its role will be to replace the teacher as a kind of machine-tutor;

move to a concept of the computer as neutral tool, assuming that its role is similar to that of a pencil, and that it should be used to carry out the same learning tasks their students would have undertaken without a computer, but to do them more efficiently;

and in a few cases, teachers:

come to see computers as cognitive tools which enable them to set new kinds of learning tasks which their pupils could not attempt before. So, for example, they find they are able to teach the interpretation of graphs more explicitly and at greater depth because the drawing of the graphs has been completed quickly with the aid of the computer and this has created a new teaching opportunity.

Table I. A model of the pattern of teacher development in computer use.

School–university action research collaborations provide a means of overcoming the credibility gap between the castle of the school and the castle of the academy. They bring together the two kinds of understanding – both essential to educational improvement – which Eisner (1991) calls 'educational connoisseurship' and 'educational criticism'. The private world of the individual classroom, is placed in the context of other classrooms, in other schools; the patterns of practice across the education system can be explored by meta-analysis of action research in many individual classrooms. Teachers and their university-based partners each play a different part in this joint enterprise.

Without such collaborations, it is almost certain that teachers (consciously or unconsciously) will continue to exercise their considerable power to resist the advice and exhortations of researchers in the university. Locked in their own discourse they *cannot* be persuaded by voices constrained by a different discourse. Put another way, ethnographers, such as Jackson (1968) and Smith & Geoffrey (1968), and sociologists such as Willis (1977) have documented the power of normative socialisation to enable organisational routines and cultural role-play to dominate what happens in schools. According to Doyle's work (1979a,b; 1983), learning is often not the central motivating force: instead, teachers' needs, such as keeping students well motivated and on-task, are traded against students' needs, such as knowing exactly what the teacher expects in order to be sure of gaining good grades. In this way, teachers' intentions to provide the best possible education for their students can be unintentionally subverted. School–university collaborations appear to be able to generate the cross-classroom knowledge of trends of practice and the within-classroom practical wisdom (Elliott, 1991, p. 53), which together enable teachers to overcome some of these systemic problems.

Discourse is the most problematic issue in school–university collaboration because it substantiates the differences between the constructions of reality through and in which each partner lives and works. Language is not the only component of discourse, but it is rooted in the other larger educational issues of what 'counts' as knowledge, and how we decide that knowledge is sufficiently trustworthy for us to act on it. Educational development often appears to be blocked by a lack of mutual understanding between teachers and university researchers of each other's discourses. The PALM action-research collaboration between teacher-researchers and a university-led team of researcher-facilitators began to establish such an understanding. We need many many more collaborations of a similar kind. Although his tone is rather tentative, and his viewpoint displays the bias of the university researcher of the period (in assuming that we need to establish a common language rather than learning to celebrate difference), this builds upon what Jackson was saying as far back as 1968:

> *The descriptive terms derived from observational studies may provide a language of educational criticism that will be useful to insiders and outsiders alike. When teachers and researchers begin to talk the same language, as it were, the possible benefits that each may derive from listening to the other will be greatly increased. At present teachers in particular lack an effective set of descriptive terms for talking about what they do. As a result, they often must fall back on clichés and outworn slogans when called upon to describe their work. Perhaps such a state of affairs is inevitable. Perhaps by the time a set of critical terms has become common among teachers is has already hardened into clichés. But the need for a fresh and vibrant language with which to talk about educational affairs seems apparent. (Jackson, 1968, p. 176)*

Notes

[1] This article was first presented at the symposium, The Many Faces of School/University Collaboration, at the Annual Meeting of the American Educational Research Association, New Orleans, April 1994.

[2] PALM was funded by the National Council for Educational Technology, a quasi-autonomous body funded by the Department of Education and Science of the British government.

References

Altrichter, Herbert, Posch, Peter & Somekh, Bridget (1993) *Teachers Investigate their Work*. London: Routledge.

Bachrach, Peter & Baratz, Morton W. (1962) The Two Faces of Power, American *Political Science Review*, 56, pp. 947-952.

Barnes, Rob (1993) Keeping track of topic work, Educational Action Research, 1, pp. 397-410.

Bruner, Jerome (1986) *Actual Minds, Possible Worlds*. Cambridge: Harvard University Press.

Convery, Andy (1993) Developing Fictional Writing as a Means of Stimulating Teacher Reflection: a case study, *Educational Action Research*, 1, pp. 135-152.

Davies, Richard (1990) Shared Perspectives, unpublished mimeo, available from PALM Project, CARE, University of East Anglia.

Doyle, Walter (1979a) *The Tasks of Teaching and Learning in Classrooms*, R&D Rep. No. 4103). Research and Development Center for Teacher Education, University of Texas at Austin.

Doyle, Walter (1979b) Classroom tasks and Student Abilities, in P. L. Peterson & H. J. Walberg (Eds) *Research on Teaching: concepts, findings and implications*, pp. 183-209, in National Society for the Study of Education. Berkeley: McCutchan.

Doyle, Walter (1983) Academic Work, *Review of Educational Research*, 53, pp. 159-200.

Ebbutt, Dave & Elliott, John (Eds) (1985) *Issues in Teaching for Understanding*. London: Longman for the SCDC.

Edwards, Jean (1991) *'I like to read': computers and children's reading*. Norwich: PALM Project, CARE, University of East Anglia.

Eisner, Elliot W. (1991) *The Enlightened Eye*. New York: Macmillan.

Elliott, John (1988) Educational Research and Outsider–Insider Relations, *Qualitative Studies in Education*, 1, pp. 155-166.

Elliott, John (1991) *Action Research for Educational Change*. Milton Keynes: Open University Press.

Foucault, Michel (1972) *Power/Knowledge: selected interviews and other writings, 1972-77* (ed. by Colin Gordon). Bury St Edmunds: Harvester Press.

Foucault, Michel (1974) *The Archaeology of Knowledge*. London: Tavistock Publications. (First edition in French, 1969, Editions Gallimard.)

Fuller, Dawn (1991) *Committed to Excellence: a study of children's learning using desktop publishing programs*. Norwich: PALM Publications, CARE, University of East Anglia.

Giddens, Anthony (1984) *The Constitution of Society*. Cambridge: Polity Press.

Griffin, Elaine (1990) *By Hook or by Crook: putting IT into the curriculum.* Norwich: PALM Publications, CARE, University of East Anglia.

House, Ernest R. (1991) Realism in Research, *Educational Researcher*, 20(6), pp. 2-25, 25.

Jackson, Philip W. (1968) *Life in Classrooms.* New York: Holt, Rinehart & Winston.

Lukes, Steven (1974) *Power.* London: Macmillan.

McGowan, John (1991) *From Lascaux to Archimedes.* Norwich: PALM Publications, CARE, University of East Anglia.

Mills, Gordon (1976) *Hamlet's Castle: the study of literature as a social experience.* Austin: University of Texas Press.

Moon, Vince (1991) *Making the News: group work and autonomy using microcomputers.* Norwich: PALM publications, CARE, University of East Anglia.

PALM (1990/91) *Teachers' Voices Series* (35 titles). Norwich: PALM Project, CARE, University of East Anglia.

Plummer Gill, Newman, Kerry & Winter, Richard (1993) Exchanging Letters: a format for collaborative action research?, *Educational Action Research*, 1, pp. 305-314.

Schattschneider, E.E. (1960) *The Semi-sovereign People: a realist's view of democracy in America.* New York: Holt, Rinehart & Winston.

Schindler, Gerd (1993) The Conflict, *Educational Action Research*, 1, pp. 457-468.

Smith, Louis M. & Geoffrey, William (1968) *The Complexities of an Urban Classroom.* New York: Holt Rinehart & Winston.

Somekh, Bridget (1991a) Pupil Autonomy in Learning with Microcomputers: rhetoric or reality? An Action Research Study, *Cambridge Journal of Education*, 21, pp. 47-64.

Somekh, Bridget (1991b) *Teachers Becoming Researchers: an exploration in dynamic collaboration*, RUCCUS Occasional Papers, 2, pp. 97-144. University of Western Ontario, London, Ontario.

Somekh, Bridget (1993) Teachers Generating Knowledge: constructing practical and theoretical understanding from multi-site case studies, in C. Day & P. Denicolo (Eds) *Research on Teachers' Thinking: understanding professional development.* London: Falmer Press.

Somekh, Bridget & Davies, Richard (1991) Towards a Pedagogy for Information Technology, *Curriculum Journal*, 2, pp. 153-170.

Somekh, Bridget (1994) The Implications of Requiring Student Teachers to 'Evaluate the Ways in Which the Use of Information Technology Changes the Nature of Teaching and Learning, available from the author at CARE, University of East Anglia, Norwich NR4 7TJ, UK.

Strauss, Anselm & Corbin, Juliet (1990) *Basics of Qualitative Research: grounded theory procedures and techniques.* Newbury Park: Sage.

Sumara, Dennis J. & Luce-Kapler, Rebecca (1993) Action Research as a Writerly Text: locating co-labouring in collaboration, *Educational Action Research*, 1, pp. 387-396.

Tooth, Chris (1989) Observation Notes, internal document of the PALM project.

Willis, Paul (1977) *Learning to Labour*. Aldershot: Gower.

First published in *Educational Action Research*, Volume 2, Number 3, 1994

Dracula as Action Researcher

JEAN-CLAUDE COUTURE

What I am attempting to excavate in this article is my resistance to being positioned as an educational practitioner who attempts to build institutional intelligibility and improvement in a university action research project. In the fall of 1993, as I entered the project 'Teacher Identity Research Project – Students Speaking Back to the Program', I grew increasingly aware of the action research project as saturated with contradiction and disruption. I was appointed (anointed?) to 'get the feedback' of student teachers about the teacher education program at the University of Alberta, Edmonton. Initially I thought that this represented an opportunity to do real participatory, activist research. I recall the invitation to the student teachers – 'talk back to the program and make a difference!' The student teacher who was my co-researcher was enthusiastic about having an impact on the teacher education program. Our working relationship promised to be a vigorous way of interrogating the teacher education program. Yet as a middle-aged graduate student from a conservative small town, I found the research becoming more about us as co-researchers than about the teacher education program. To employ the words of Michelle Fine, the 'tensions at the hyphen of consultant-activity-researcher are numerous, the gains of being in the change – for knowing, 'eavesdropping,' gathering varied points of view, and being able to orchestrate conversations around multiple stances – are enormous'.[1]

The difficulties in living at the hyphen connotes for me a space that resists intelligible speech. It is a series of multiple locales where, as deconstruction suggests, contradictions and ruptures live side-by-side. For action research, deconstruction can be deployed, as Lather suggests, to 'demonstrate how a text works against itself'.[2] In a re-reading of the action research project I wish to call up Caputo's sense of deconstruction as an attempt to show 'how the dice are loaded, how the game is fixed, how the play has been arrested before it starts'.[3] To playfully express the difficulty of living in multiple locales I have given our teacher education action research project the title: 'Dracula in search of teacher identity'.

I wish to preface this strategic re-reading by drawing on Foucault's sense of the control over life being achieved through the positive or productive management of discipline that sees power dispersed or 'invested' through bodies.[4] Increasingly popular over the last few years in the teacher education program has been the push towards 'reflective practice' where teachers share stories and experiences that constitute and give shape to their teacher identity. What I read into this teacher education program is the process of probing into the silence that belongs to the Other. I see my action research in a way that Spivak might, as 'the colonization of the Other'.[5] Using Spivak, might teacher identity and reflective practice be an 'epistemic violence' that is expended to incorporate – to feed on the stories and experiences of student teachers? This is the larger question that emerges from the action research we undertook.

Partly as parody, and at some risk I'm sure, I wish to offer a re-reading of the student teacher as a nomadic wanderer and the university as Dracula.[6] I use here Grossberg's sense of the nomad as a subject who wanders 'through ever-changing positions and apparatuses'.[7] The student/nomad represents the alterity or difference that feeds the university. It is through the appropriation of difference, that reflective practice, autobiography, and other trends in teacher research manage to carefully incorporate alterity.[8] The university, for its part, acts as the apparition that invites its clients (victims) to join the project of reflective practice – in search of the transcendental signifier of (salvation) teacher identity.

In this re-reading of teacher identity I admit to my complicity. As a graduate student I am a colonizer of student-teachers' souls – just as Renfeld collected souls for 'the master' in Coppola's Dracula. From these souls Renfeld, extracted life. I too extract life from the loathsome ones – the undergraduates. (As budgets decline for universities, are the lords of the castle swooping down to feed on the villagers below?)

The secret of Dracula's power is the gradual anesthetization of the victim. Dracula draws blood to nourish himself in the somnambulant state of the Other's sleep. Are these the moments of the invested gaze in reading student journals? Is mine the gaze of the *Dracul*? As a teacher I am uncomfortable reading and 'marking' student journals. Am I a predator as I scan through 'memories of lived experiences' and 'personal anecdotes'? Perhaps there is a reminder of Baudrillard here – in the hyperreal simulacra, if we move quickly enough, there are no identities only 'amnesia' (where stray voices once were). Student stories and experiences are appropriated and absorbed in the simulacra of academic journals and conferences. Anesthetization and amnesia are important features of life in both the *Dracul* and the simulacra. So I wonder: Does the university's predatory incorporation of alterity of the student/nomad serve anyone else outside of the academy? How does reflective practice in the postmodern condition avoid being nothing more than one of the micro-technologies of surveillance that Foucault wrote about?

For three months I have worked with Jim (not his real name) on a project at the University of Alberta. Our conversations were initiated by the institutional interest in what improvements might be made to the teacher education program at the university. One of Jim's first journal entries reads as follows:

I really believe in one on one counselling. You know, everyone of those students I've had ...

I'd like to sit down with them individually ... but there's no time for that. I don't know if it's the boards, or whoever sets up the timetable ... it just doesn't occur.

Are these the naive dreams of the uninitiated (virgin) student teacher? Certainly the fanciful call for 'individual counseling for all kids' would give dyspepsia to any school trustee in the land. As an experienced (certainly not a virgin) teacher, what am I to make out of Jim's innocent sensibility? Yet Jim and I share with other teachers in Alberta what a recent province-wide survey found of our local contradictions:

We can't do it all. We need help and support, especially from parents.

Increased double income pressure to survive is switching more and more of the responsibility to teachers. We are becoming parents and social workers.[9]

Of course none of this is new. As I talk with Jim, I am struck by the way our language conflicts and mediates, how our subject positions shift as we process language around this dead smelly thing called 'teacher identity'. Our conversations talk over the project – time and again we reminisce about local situations and contradictions, over the impossibilities that are constructed around tropes of 'teacher excellence'. Perhaps sincerity escapes us as our conversations, like sand dunes, move through the desert and cover over our silences that we choose not to reveal. I wonder: can we really speak?[10] Yet our conversation make us as subjects, capable of experiencing the experience of doing something called 'action research'. The project still breathes.

Jim suddenly raises the issue of his homosexuality. After two weeks in the school Jim is aware that many students know 'his secret'. There is a community of submerged Others who know. Jim wonders: 'Is being gay part of teacher identity? Is this knowledge worth counting as identity? How might the students and teachers respond to him? Should he stay alone in a classroom with male students?' What can I say, what can anyone say?

My journal entry following our conversation:

Jim is privileged in this conversation – I have only the general sense of a 'societal response' (that is typically polite but ambiguous). Jim and I flounder, we awkwardly talk about the need to appreciate the 'context' of the school and community. There is a sense of urgency in inviting in the social backdrop of meaning – given by the social milieu that cannot be ignored.

As Kemmis reminds us, we need to situate reflection beyond the psychological domain – the social dimension that is continually changing needs to be considered in a pivotal way.[11] This pivot of course is language. As we puzzle through the dilemma of 'coming out' I am aware that there is a meaning within the middle spaces that Deluze describes [12] – as we try to apprehend what *might* happen, what *might* be 'sensible'. I do not want to give advice, Jim does not ask for it. We keep talking, aware that the silence needs to be covered over. Perhaps in the way Deluze describes, we are called forward by the conversation that has emerged:

One opens the circle a crack, opens it all the way, lets someone in, calls someone, or else goes out oneself, launches forth.[13] One launches forth, hazards an improvisation. But to improvise is to join with the World, to meld with it.

Jim talks of his location, 'caught in a bind between being seen to encourage a student (to come out) and being insensitive, pushing the student away'. Jim describes how he has developed 'gaydar' (after radar) – a way of seeing (detecting) 'gay' individuals. My journal entry that night:

'Gaydar' – is this what Donna Haraway meant by the 'situated knowledges' in her Manifesto for Cyborgs? Pushed to the margins and fabricated by the patriarchy – the woman, the gay, the Other, is constituted and reconstituted both in response to and resisting, the privileged position of the hetero society. Perhaps Jim is both 'given his politics' and resists within it.

Sutured into each of us, perhaps, is the central repressive apparatus of the institutions that retain their resistance to polymorphous sexuality. Foucault might see our conversation, our tormented wringing of hands over 'what to do', as the effects of power.[14] Meanwhile, Jim and I struggle in the master's gaze.

So what of the possibility of working with teacher identity in action research? What I have argued here is the inherent danger of the university's incorporation of alterity. That this project is undertaken framed as a reflective, participatory action research is problematic. As John Willinsky reminds us, we must be aware of how text constitutes our reality, how text 'writes out a response' for us.[15] The text of teacher reflection as already inscribed upon or given to the student teacher by the university. The university acts much as does the *Dracul* – to invite, to beguile, and to finally consume for its own purposes. (I recall the university's invitation to the student teachers, 'get involved – you can make a difference!') Essential to the seductive power of the *Dracul* is the covenant, the bond between prey and predator. The university invites the student teacher to 'share' and 'reflect' on their stories and experiences. As Dracula, the university inscribes upon the student-teacher Ahab's notion of the covenant; 'I do not order ye: ye will it'.[16] Thus power is invested in Jim and I. So here I sit listening to Jim's predicament that is his; as a teacher with a secure teaching position to go back to after my graduate work, and as a heterosexual middle-aged male with three children, I cannot suffer the same questions that Jim does.

The problem of complicity within postmodern action research practice is one I live with 'in the hyphens'. I cannot avoid my hyphenated subjectivity and location. My work with student teachers continues. Jim continues this semester in the last round of his practicum. He confided one day, 'I'm not sure why I work so hard at teaching ... I want to make things better. Or maybe I've always wanted to be a good boy'. Is this the ethic that calls us forward? Jim and I, as 'good boys', continue to be drawn into the teacher preparation program. The *Dracul* always feeds on the 'good' virgins. We continue to resist its colonization of our lives, we sense its performative power and its ever-present ability to 'write our responses for us,' as Willinsky might suggest.

Drawn back to Coppola's film, I am reminded of Dracula's smirking face as he is carted around Europe by his hired dupes (read 'grad students'). For me, Coppola's image was what was needed to reveal my complicity as an action researcher. The camera closes in on Dracula, one who lives in the hyphen between living-dead. I see the guile in his smile – I look into the eyes of the *Dracul* as it looks back at mine; I see the danger in continuing to go on, yet realize – 'how can I resist?'

Notes

[1] Michelle Fine (1992) *Disruptive Voices*, p. 229. Ann Arbor: University of Michigan Press.

[2] Patti Lather (1991) *Getting Smart: feminist research and pedagogy with/in the postmodern*, p. 82. New York: Routledge.

[3] John D. Caputo (1987) *Radical Hermeneutics*, p. 197. Indianapolis: Indiana University Press.

[4] Michael Foucault (1978) *The History of Sexuality, Volume 1* (trans. R. Hurley), pp. 151-152. Harmondsworth: Penguin.

[5] Gayatri Spivak (1988) Can the subaltern speak?, in Cary Nelson & Lawrence Grossberg (Eds) *Marxism and the Interpretation of Culture*, p. 284. Urbana: University of Illinois Press.

[6] See also Ziauddin Sardar (1992) When Dracula meets the 'Other': Europe, Columbus and the Colombian legacy, *Alternatives*, 17, pp. 493-517.

[7] See 'The in-difference of television', *Screen*, 28(2), pp. 28-48.

[8] I am indebted to Jan Jagodinski for his 'Postmodern allegories and the politics of difference: Hollywood's incorporation of alterity', unpublished manuscript, University of Alberta, 1992.

[9] Teacher views on educational issues, *Edmonton Public Teachers' Local*, 37, October 1992.

[10] This is the question raised by Elspeth Probyn (1990) concerning the subaltern in 'Travels in the postmodern: making sense of the local', in Linda Nicholson (Ed.) *Feminism/Postfeminism*, pp. 177-189. New York: Routledge.

[11] S. Kemmis (1985) Action research and the politics of reflection, in D. Boud et al (Eds) *Reflection: turning experience into learning*, pp. 139-165. London: Routledge & Kegan Paul.

[12] Gilles Deluze & Clare Parnet (1987) *Dialogues*, p. 22. New York: Columbia University Press.

[13] Gilles Deluze & Felix Guattari (1991) *A Thousand Places*, cited in Kenneth Gergen (Ed.) *The Saturated Self*, p. 218. New York: Basic Books.

[14] Ibid. [4].

[15] Cited in Don Gutteridge (1992) The search for presence: a reader-response to postmodern literacy, *Our Schools Our Selves*, 4, p. 91.

[16] This ironic calling forth to the Other is employed by Patricia Williams (1990) *The Alchemy of Race and Rights*, p. 34. Cambridge: Harvard University Press.

First published in *Educational Action Research*, Volume 2, Number 1, 1994

Reflection and Action in Research: is there a moral responsibility to act?

CHRISTINE O'HANLON

This article is prompted by a recent examination procedure I was involved in with a PhD student. The student had written his thesis in the confidence that a conceptual analysis of his subject was the aim of his thesis, and that his writing and investigation was the product and ultimate end of his research, because it bestowed upon him the much coveted title of PhD. I was concerned about his new found knowledge and its' effects upon him. Did the investigation not confer on him some change, some motivation to act on his knowledge, some responsibility to take action in relation to his findings? The student was surprised by my line of questioning and resisted my demands. In fact, the other examiner involved in the viva-voce later asked me the purpose of the queries. This led me to examine my insistence on asking 'What action would emerge from the research and how had it changed the views or values of the researcher?' I had assumed that the process of doctoral research changed the student through the process of the investigation and as a result of changed perceptions would give the researcher a moral justification to act. Yet my assumption was germaine to the student and the other examiner. Is not research an educational process of discovery? Is not the PhD a journey of investigation which brings with it new or re-perceived knowledge? Is not the new perspective on the subject researched, primarily the property of the researcher, the writer or the student in the case of an MPhil or PhD, and does not new intellectual property bring new responsibilities with it?

One of the primary requisites for undertaking research for a higher degree is that it contributes new knowledge to the field of study, and that it is an original investigation of some kind. The word original implies uniqueness, differentiation from previous work in the field, and personal attribution. The research undertaken should be one person's specific contribution to the field through their own personal choice of – what, when and how to research. Each person in their individual experience of life, in their genetic inheritance and in their personal and cultural predispositions, has a unique way of thinking about whatever matters to them in their lives. Researchers too, have an individual and particular way of viewing the subject to be researched, the means of researching it and the data to be interpreted during the research process. They have a personal view of the situation. As an educational process, the person's view of the subject under research, should be expected to change during the process of researching. The researcher's understanding of the subject after investigation at doctoral level will invariably deepen and become more complex and meaningful and may lead to a changed perspective on the subject which unconsciously motivates subsequent action in an innovative or novel direction. The research may also consciously direct the graduate to specific new forms of acting because of his/her new awareness and determination to make an impact on static or unproductive educational contexts. Such change in the person is what makes their research educational. It can provide a personal confidence and certainty related to theories and ideas, which forms a platform for planned and effective action. Action based on educational change which results from the research process is a form of voluntary action or 'proairesis'. Aristotle argues that:

> No-one deliberates about things which cannot be changed ...
> there can be no science without demonstration ... (Ethics, Book
> 6, Chapter 5)

In doing research, in deliberating about information and data accumulated in the research process, one is in fact changing one's self. The demonstration of that change is in subsequent action. Actions demonstrate any personal change or transformation which has resulted from the 'science' of research. The actions demonstrate in some way a change in the researcher, as well as a different view of the researched 'situation'. Perhaps the research process has changed the person so profoundly that they are conscious of this change and therefore become aware of the changes in their choice of action and how it has affected their personal values and judgements. Is there, (or should there be?), a conscious connection between 'reflexivity' and the educational potential of the research through personal changes in values and reasons for action?

Knowledge Reflection and Action

One would hope that the PhD endeavour would lead to the students' awareness of their personal transformation and an impetus for action to effect and realise the potential of their research findings in the real world i.e., to really make a difference to society. Should not the student be conscious and aware of their potential to make deliberate choices, to actively demonstrate the power of their educational transformation? PhD students and other researchers need to engage in personal reflection to understand themselves in relationship to the world and to deliberate about or reconstruct their values in relation to everyday situations, which constantly demand their judgements for action. In conceptually reshaping the research situation they are therefore involved in a reflexive research dimension. It may happen that traditional notions of objectivity encourage students to detach themselves from the situation they are researching, therefore the final thesis rather than a true objective account becomes a distorted account, without any recognition of inherent subjective bias. Once a reflexive component enters the research process it brings about a transformation of the student's understanding of their practical and individual potential influence. Yet because reflexivity is a personal activity, no one else can understand it, except when it is consciously or deliberately shared. Therefore reflexivity itself is invisible until the student takes action, and through that action e.g. a speech act, the student exposes his/her thoughts, perceptions, values and attitudes. Dewey (1933) explains reflection as:

> *Active, persistent, and careful consideration of any belief or*
> *supposed form of knowledge ... it includes a conscious and*
> *voluntary effort to establish belief upon a firm basis of*
> *evidence and rationality. (Dewey, 1933, p. 9)*

In doing research, researchers discover new information which they consciously reconstruct to form new beliefs or personal theories. The personal theories thus derived, are personal constructs which require re-working and revision in reflection, for deeper understanding or for further articulation and communication to the wider research or educational audience. Dewey's definition implies conscious and deliberate focusing of the mind on a 'belief' or 'form of knowledge' to bring about secure understanding based on the evidence of our experience. He brings in the notion that this process is founded upon 'rationality'. Belief is to be established on a basis of reasoned ideas or facts. The secure meaning for the thinker emerges from the reasoned connections between different aspects of the new information. It comes from the intentional effort of the learner to discover specific connections in experiences or in information received, in order to improve his/her own certainty. This is achieved through a reflexive understanding.

For Habermas (1974) reflection is a process which frees the human mind in its' purposeful intention. However, is not 'purposive intention' a synonym for planned action? Habermas links the concept of reflection to a questioning of experience which brings with it a certain freedom from unchallenged assumptions and new perceptions. He sees the reflective process to be a form of investigatory activity of the social and moral environment which leads to enlightenment and emancipation.

Habermas was interested in different ways of validating a person's knowledge. He showed that the search for knowledge was guided by self-interest. This supports the view that each person in seeking 'truth', values and holds what they find of personal worth or what meets their personal needs. In researching for a higher degree students are normally free to choose the – 'what', 'when', and 'how' to research, and what evidence to include in the study. The evidence chosen for inclusion in the thesis may have a personal significance and value to the student, although this is not always admitted in all research contexts, because it is subjective and not conventionally admissible. As reflexive evidence it is seen to be interpretive and therefore subjectively biased unless otherwise explained; it is not always admissible evidence because it lacks objectivity. However, if we explore the world through our interests as Habermas suggests, then in an educational process the exploration of the personal domain needs to be acknowledged and explicated. We can understand this by further examining the three ways in which we come to know and understand things about the world, through the technical, the practical and the emancipatory interest.

1. The *technical* interest is generally pursued through the empirical and analytical sciences. It generates instrumental knowledge which defines our means of control of nature, which includes social and educational contexts.

2. The *practical* interest is in the form of interpretations of social life. It is generally pursued through the interpretative or hermeneutic sciences. Its' main concern is the validation of subjective interpretation.

3. The *emancipatory* interest is aimed at releasing people from taken for granted activities, customs and assumptions. Habermas sees the content and form of our thinking as social constructions, which links our interest to our experience. The emancipatory interest is founded upon the critique of culture and social life. We use our critical faculties to reconstruct what history and our culture and experience have already constructed for us. We critique the existing situation to reconstruct new forms of thought and social action.

As part of the process of emancipation it is –

> ... in the power of self-reflection that knowledge and interest
> are one. (Habermas, 1972, p. 314)

Habermas recognises the basic human precept that knowledge is sought on the basis of self-interest. What we think that we know to be in our interest is something that we must question through our critique of the social world through its' investigation, and our dialogue and discourse within it.

What is important for the present argument is the understanding that the *technical* interest leads to a certain kind of action. This form of research looks for patterns that exist in the environment from which rules for action can be formulated. For example if we find in the course of investigation that certain laws guide children's learning , then we can create a set of rules to be followed to promote children's learning. When these technical methods are used, the product will conform to the 'eidos', the intentions and ideas outlined in the original objectives. Predetermined hypotheses are verified or disproved.

With respect to the *practical* interest, the interpreter, or in this argument the student/researcher, applies his/her own traditional taken for granted values to his/her own situation and in so doing, comes to understand it better. The implication is, that the subjective or personal experiences of the research process are part of the constructed meaning which should be recorded in the research report. The self reflection/reflexivity about the effects of the process personally on students, their feelings, reactions, and responses to other research participants are part of the hermeneutic process of developing understanding. It is the hermeneutic process which changes the perceptions of the persons involved, primarily the researcher, but also the research participants and all those who contributed to the process in some way. This may include a reader or examiner of the thesis, who through questioning the evidence, its analysis and conclusions, has provoked the writer to reconsider aspects of the interpretations which at first appeared to be uncontentious.

The *emancipatory* interest is a state of autonomy or for Habermas – 'independence from all that is outside the individual'. It is only in self-reflection that understanding emerges and liberates one from dogmatic dependence. He believes it is a fundamental human interest which is implicit in all that we communicate to each other, particularly in speech and language. This interest generates critical theories which explain how coercion and control, deception and manipulation operate to inhibit freedom. But these theories must, he believes, be validated through self reflection and authentic insight. The emancipatory interest is concerned with the improvement of social conditions and contexts, by means of the use of autonomy and responsibility to enable people to take control of their own lives either individually or collectively.

What does this mean for research? For one thing, with the practical interest there is the danger, in the process of making-meaning that we may be deceived about the true nature of the 'researched' situation. The researcher must, to be emancipated, be freed from 'false consciousness', s/he must be involved in activities which recognise and expose constraints to freedom in the educational context which is being researched. It involves some form of praxis (practical action), which is also political action, because it aims to transform the existing, or as

Habermas puts it, 'ideologically frozen relations' of dependence. It involves going beyond the accepted traditions in education, to discover what supports the cause of autonomy and responsibility. It uncovers the true nature of social/educational interactions that must be transformed for the sake of deeper and newer understanding.

This view of educational research is based upon critical analysis for the purpose of the transformation of educational practices, the educational understandings and educational values of those involved in the process. It also aims to transform the social and institutional structures which provide the frameworks for their action.

Yet, in making this connection to action, Habermas did not see that knowledge generated by individual critical reflection was in itself sufficient for social action. He believed it was necessary to engage in discursive processes through which participants in the (research) situation come to an authentic understanding of their situation. This understanding is facilitated by a form of 'practical discourse' during which decisions are taken by participants about taking action which is seen to be appropriate to the moral context of the research. We are not given any practical advice about how the discourse could be organised or directed. It may be a process of listening and responding to -children and adults involved in the educational contexts researched, or to collegial discussion of students following a similar research course in an institutional situation. It is also a process which requires the principal actors or researchers to articulate their understanding of the evidence as it presents itself to them. In the discourse within the research process the communication between participants and the reconstruction of meaning is the basis of the transformative or emancipatory interest. The discourse should ideally proceed on democratic principles agreed upon by participants and re-negotiated as necessary in the development of personal reflexivity and self-actualisation. The discursive context requires the development of democratic procedures and the recognition of moral issues related to existing authority and hierarchical structures which threaten traditional forms of discourse while at the same time creating new discursive practices at all levels of education.

Practice/Theory Relevance?

Practice need not be represented as the opposite to theory. Theory can be defined as abstract ideas situated in disconnected or context-free generalisations, while practice can be defined as acting in the tangible reality. In viewing theory and practice as oppositional concepts we are overlooking much of educational practice that is not obviously connected to specific situations, and depends upon abstract ideas for innovation and change. There is a danger of over-simplifying the situation by viewing theory as non-practical and practice as nontheoretical, because it overlooks the reflective activity of those who engage in educational practice and their natural need to theorise about it. All practice takes place against a conceptual framework which structures and guides its' activities, either tacitly or consciously in the action in the real world.

Carr (1987) asserts that practice may at times be independent of theory, if the practitioner knows how to act, but is however, unaware of the ethical disposition of the criteria within 'educational' activities. A practice is therefore only educational when it occurs in an ethical awareness. In his words therefore:

> *The educational character of any practice can only be made intelligible by reference to an ethical disposition to proceed according to some more or less tacit understanding of what it is to act educationally. (p. 166)*

This suggests that an educational act is informed on a moral or ethical level. If action or practice is unreflective without a moral educational purpose, it is action taken independently of educational theory. What does this mean if we apply this argument to the conduct of research which is justified as an educational practice? Research may be based on educational theory but it will not be intelligible unless or until it is situated in a moral awareness or reflexivity which includes reference to action or the 'how to' realise the theory in a practical context. To become theoretical in an educational endeavour like an MPhil or PhD, the student needs to show the ability to ground the theory in a practical situation which will inform action both for the researcher and for the reader. Otherwise, it will make interesting but futile reading because there will be no relationship to the tangible reality from purely theoretical and abstract research, unless the author indicates what it could be, and clarifies its significance, and its potential for social and educational change. The meaning of the word 'theory' is not solely the preserve of academics and intellectuals writing in an abstract manner 'about' education, it is also the researcher's personally constructed intentions for action based upon principles reconstructed through research evidence.

Theory is not produced by a group of 'intellectuals' or experts who claim the right to generate valid knowledge. In educational research a wide range of techniques, methods and procedures are used, which allows researchers to define their own forms of valid knowledge, and present them as educational theories. When educational practitioners submit automatically, uncritically or unconsciously to another's perceived superior theory they are disempowering themselves and denying their own experience-based craft knowledge. This may be one reason why teachers and other educational professionals learn much from case studies because they experience them more closely and immediately than general and more abstract theories of knowledge emanating from research. Case studies make a bigger impact on practitioners and are identifiable to them through their own experiences which are often echoed in their case records recorded in the thesis.

Elliott (1989) like Carr, in his analysis of educational practices emphasises the importance of the ethical dimension in 'action research' or in reflective practice. In the practice personal values are realised in concrete forms of action and this necessarily involves a continuous process of practitioner reflection. The realisation of value is ultimately a matter of personal judgement in specific situations, and is infinitely open to reinterpretation. In reflective practice, practitioners continually re-interpret their own beliefs and values in the process of reflection *in* and *on* action. Elliott asserts that:

> *Within ... educational inquiry, theoretical abstraction plays a subordinate role in the development of a practical wisdom grounded in reflective experiences of concrete cases.*

He makes it clear in the relationship between theoretical abstraction and practical reflection (leading to practical wisdom) that practical wisdom is superior to theoretical abstraction. This is not a universal principle that I personally would corroborate, because it depends on the purpose of the theory. The issue is not the superiority or inferiority of one position to another, rather it is the inter-relationship of the two, and the validation of theoretical abstractions in their practical applications. In action research, for example, the practical investigation is deliberately aimed to improve educational practices. However, in other forms of research the aim is more to add to the knowledge of the educational community in some way. Investigation may be carried out via the analysis of literature or via theoretical analysis which may never suggest the implications for action or practice. Although a necessary precondition of action research is a felt need to initiate change or to innovate, which sets the scene for action, it is a profound disappointment to witness research for higher degrees, which has little personal impact on the researcher, except as a purely intellectual exercise for the purpose of an award. What I am expressing goes beyond a simple attack on indulgent intellectualism. I am moving to the view that research which is 'outsider' research or, which is purely speculative and based on abstract ideas, is difficult to validate except through argued personal convictions often disguised as 'rational' argument. The subjective view is too easily disguised as an objective view through the use of language conventions which make the words appear to be impartial and detached.

I am expressing the view that the validity of any abstract theory must lie in its' 'praxis' or practical potential, as defined by Aristotle, *which is practice with morally committed action which is morally informed.* Educational practices are not simply the implementation of rational accounts of what practice is recommended to be in hypothetical and abstruse situations. Educational practice which includes research is 'practical philosophy' with a focus in action. It is a 'science' which creates knowledge about how to promote the 'educational good' through morally right action. Such knowledge can only point generally in the direction that practical actions ought to take. It cannot predict the success of the practice in advance, because of the influences implicit in its implementation in different situations. It necessitates a form of reasoning in which informed choice and judgement play a crucial role. It is a means of deciding not so much how something is to be done as a rule, but more what factors ought to be considered in different circumstances, by proceeding in a deliberative and conscious manner. Through a form of deliberation and reasoning the student can decide between different ways of achieving the same ethical end, or of possible alternative means of reaching different ethical ends. It is a means of resolving the many inevitable moral dilemmas, which arise in the reconstruction of educational practices through research.

We must demonstrate, I believe, in educational research at higher degree level,which is predominantly concerned with teaching and learning, that we have attempted to achieve an acceptable form of *phronesis* or 'practical wisdom' which is the virtue of knowing the appropriate ethical principles which apply in specific educational contexts. Without *phronesis* much of what passes as research and theory becomes simply a personal and intellectual indulgence and good practice becomes indistinguishable from technical interests. I believe we need to challenge the student to acknowledge the practical opportunities and limitations of their thesis at doctoral level. They need to be challenged about their reflexive contributions to the research and their implications for personal and professional changes in action.

In the argument developed in this article, action is implied as a result of the change brought about by the involvement of the researcher in new forms of understanding. The educational transformation of learners or researchers changes their view of reality which in turn changes the way they interact with that reality. Perhaps the original problem I outline in page one is not so much a question of why there is no implicit imperative to action through research, but more a question of why there is no *intention* for deliberate or conscious action? However, the emergence of a moral responsibility to act may only be possible in *critical* research contexts. Therefore one must ask the reader if it is an 'assumption' on my part to ask that all educational researchers should consider the moral responsibility to act? How can we influence the world as a result of a process of altered consciousness, or how do we validate the true meaning of the investigation in the real world if we do not embrace the moral imperative to act intentionally as a result of educational research? Action research through the use of the concept of *action*, deliberately makes it an intention and primary research focus.

References

Aristotle (1955) *The Ethics of Aristotle.* Harmondsworth: Penguin Books.

Carr, W. (1987) What is an Educational Practice? *Journal of Philosophy of Education*, 21, pp. 163-176.

Dewey, J. (1933) *How We Think.* New York: Heath.

Elliott, J. (1989) Educational Theory and the Professional Learning of Teachers: an overview, *Cambridge Journal of Education*, 19, pp. 81-102.

Habermas, J. (1972) *Knowledge and Human Interests*, trans. J. Shapiro. London: Heinemann.

Habermas, J. (1974) *Theory and Practice*, trans. J. Viental. London: Heinemann.

Defining the Field of Literature in Action Research: a personal approach

KATH GREEN

Background to the Project

For the past few years I have been engaged in an action research project which began with the very broad question: How do I improve my practice as a supervisor of practitioner action research?

This has involved me in exploring both my role as a supervisor, and my learning as a supervisee. The exploration of my role as a supervisor has been carried out in two specific contexts, namely, the supervision of final year action research projects at both undergraduate and masters levels. The exploration of my learning as a supervisee has been carried out in the context of my own PhD studies in relation to this project.

In this article I want to focus on just one of the issues emerging from my research, namely, that of defining the field of literature in an action research study. In the sections that follow I shall begin with a brief outline of the exploratory and personal nature of my inquiry and then examine the implications of this for defining the field of literature from which I might draw in providing the intellectual support for my inquiry.

I shall discuss the way in which I have reviewed and reported on the literature during the course of my inquiry. In doing this, I want to challenge some of the traditional notions of what constitutes a literature review including challenges to the notion of subject disciplines, disciplinary boundaries and the ways in which, as action researchers, we construct and use knowledge.

The Exploratory Nature of My Inquiry,
Including a Concern for Wholeness and Focus on Context

I have always been attracted to forms of research which are fundamentally *exploratory* for the simple reason that they do not attempt to predetermine the central issues before the start of any inquiry. Therefore, I deliberately began my inquiry without any pre-conceived notions of what the substantial issues were likely to be and also rejected the notion of looking through a particular lens – sociological, psychological etc. My experience of engaging with previous action research projects (see, for example, Green, 1993) led me to feel confident in beginning merely with an intuitive feeling, coupled with a certain level of confidence that the exploration of this area of my practice would be both intellectually stimulating and educationally worthwhile.

At the outset of my inquiry I recognised that I did not have a clearly defined focus for my work but I also knew that I wanted to avoid making early decisions about the nature of that focus merely in order to give the study a false kind of clarity in its early stages. Whilst I recognised that in many other areas of research, an early and clear definition of focus might be considered an important starting point and one which should certainly be grappled with well before any empirical work begins, my current work did not fit this mould as I felt there was a requirement for it to be essentially *exploratory* in nature. It was important to me that *all* the emerging issues about exploring, understanding and improving my practice as a supervisor were kept central to my thinking. I did not want to artificially narrow the focus just so that I would have something more 'manageable' for PhD purposes.

At this early stage, it was most encouraging to have a supervisor who could live comfortably with uncertainty and who could recognise and support my need to keep the focus fairly loosely defined. He encouraged me to 'go with the flow' of my own intuitive feelings and resisted any temptation to tie me down prematurely with the sort of structures that might well have made my emerging thesis more predictable and 'safe' and made his own role as a supervisor decidedly more comfortable.

As my work has progressed, the methodology of my inquiry has itself become the subject of my inquiry, raising serious issues for both myself as a researcher and for my understanding of the support I offer for the professional development of the practitioners with whom I work.

In my view, a fundamental aspect of action research is its concern with context. Action research is always concerned with the particular. Its generalisations come from understandings about the way a very particular context can be recognised and explored and about the nature of the professional judgements made in response to those explorations. Of course, the outcomes of action research are not in the form of neat generalisations that can be applied across a variety of different classrooms because its whole rationale is based on the uniqueness of particular classrooms and the uniqueness of particular teachers, children and learning situations. It is this recognition of the uniqueness of each learning situation that, I believe, lies at the heart of action research.

Whilst action research does not attempt to produce results that are immediately transferable to other teaching situations, that does not mean that it can have no effect beyond its particular context. In my view, it is the understandings of the complexities of the particular situation and the recognition of the different ways in which the familiar can be interpreted that is the aspect that is so readily transferable to other situations. Whenever I read good quality action research, I gain particular insights and confront particular issues that immediately raise questions about my own classroom practice. I am encouraged to see my own practice with new eyes and offered the possibility of developing new ways of working in my own particular context.

To What Extent Does My Exploratory Approach to the Research have Implications for My Approach Towards Finding Relevant Literature?

In considering the field in which my study would be located, I knew at an early stage that I wanted to draw on ideas from a number of areas, although the identification of those areas was to emerge slowly as I grappled with the emerging issues. From the start, an eclectic approach seemed to be the best fit for researching my practice as a supervisor. Interestingly, this commitment to an eclectic approach was more intuitive than intellectual in the early stages. Sometimes I identified emerging issues and then turned to the relevant literature. At other times, literature from a variety of sources supported me in identifying the issues by making me see my practice in a new light. During this study I have felt both committed to and somewhat unnerved by the eclectic approach I have adopted. At one point I reflected in my journal:

> *I think I started with just an intuitive feel that the eclectic approach would be better and that it fitted my way of looking at things and trying to understand them. Over time, it has developed into a stronger sense of it being more theoretically sound. (Journal 1, p. 44)*

Clearly, the adoption of an eclectic approach, my concern for wholeness and a focus on the particular context will all have serious implications for the way in which I relate my work to 'the literature'.

What is the Body of Literature in
Which My Work is to Be Located?

I began by thinking that my work would, of course, need to take account of the current literature within the field of action research and I would need to position myself within that tradition. However, beyond that body of literature, the question arose as to where else I would be turning for intellectual support and sustenance? At the outset of my study I did not really know the answer to this question and certainly did not want to be forced into arbitrary decisions in those early stages. From the start, this led to feelings of insecurity which are all too apparent in some of the early entries in my personal journal.

One reads:

Feeling swamped by reading

I don't want to artificially structure and focus reading but sometimes I wish I was just looking at power relationships in tutorials with respect to the work of Foucault

Sometimes I wish I was doing a purely theoretical study – the reality of practice keeps crashing against the theoretical perspectives

BUT on balance I like what I'm doing. I'm trying to understand the whole untidy business of supervising action research even if it does feel like treading treacle on some days! (Journal 1, p. 144b)

I was eager to make use of theoretical insights from any discipline provided it helped to illuminate some area of my practice although there was, of course, a risk that I would open myself to the charge of superficiality.

What Counts as Relevant in
Relation to the Literature to Be Consulted?

A traditional way of defining *relevance* in relation to the literature is to define the boundaries of the field in which the literature is located and to read as widely as possible within that field. In my exploration of a wide range of PhD theses I have found that the field is often very tightly defined so that the candidate can read all the literature within that boundary and become an expert within that particular field. This approach is, of course, entirely appropriate where the focus of the study needs to be tightly defined at the outset.

However, this approach did not seem to fit the particular type of inquiry I was engaged in. Having started out by saying that I did *not* want to predetermine the issues and narrow the focus prematurely, it was important that I avoided adopting precisely this predetermined type of approach in relation to defining the field of literature that might best inform my inquiry. It is this notion of *what might best inform the inquiry* that I see as problematic and, therefore, open to debate.

After one tutorial discussion with my supervisor at which we discussed my use of the literature I was concerned about an implied view that, whilst some of the sections of my thesis would necessarily be deeply personal, the literature relating to my work would somehow need to be presented in a more distanced and depersonalised way. Over the years I have been influenced by many feminist writers who have acknowledged the importance of the subjectivity of the knower in relation to the acquisition of knowledge. In particular, my early work on women returners to primary teaching (Green, 1994) was influenced by writers such as Oakley (1981) and Finch (1984) and my more recent work by those such as Code (1991), Lather (e.g. 1986), Stenstad (1988) and Benhabib (1992).

Thus, in my reflections after the above discussion, I wrote:

> *I'm not sure about this. Why can't I talk about my engagement with the literature in a more personal way? It certainly felt very personal when I found it. Does academic have to be distanced and de-personalised? Maybe it has to be more distanced, more reflective but perhaps not more de-personalised.*

I continued:

> *My engagement with the literature has felt very personal. I have responded to the literature in terms of how it has affected my thinking, how it has helped me to see things in new ways. It is that very personal engagement with the literature that I want to keep hold of. I don't want to do a distanced and measured review of the literature according to some pre-defined boundaries. Surely, what I am saying is that what moves my thinking on is the literature that is important to me, the literature that really touches me in a very personal way.*
>
> ...
>
> *Generally, I find myself exceedingly bored by the standard literature review so I don't want to do it. I don't want to review literature because it's there, I want to review it because it affected my thinking and I want to show the reader how it affected my thinking. I'm sure I could produce the standard literature review but I don't want to – that would feel too much of a cop-out. I certainly want to argue why I haven't trod the*

> *standard path. Is this unreasonable? (Journal entry, 9 July*
> *1996)*

In reflecting on the above journal entry, it seems to me that one of the central issues in terms of relating my work to the literature is that of exploring how I might decide what literature is relevant in terms of moving my inquiry forward. Indeed, it was the bringing together of these two themes, defining the field of literature and the personal response to literature that moved my thinking forward.

Personal Relevance in Relation to the Literature

I wanted the literature which I reviewed to be defined in terms of *its relevance to me personally*. I wanted to report on the literature that had really made a difference to my thinking. I wanted to show how I have used the literature to support me in exploring new ideas and to reveal new ways of looking at different aspects of my practice. Of course, there is a danger that this could result in engagement with the literature at a somewhat superficial level unsuited to work at PhD level. Yet, surely, the danger of superficial reading of the literature is a real one in *any approach* to defining a field and not one peculiar to an eclectic approach.

Another important issue for me is the location of 'the literature' within the thesis. My view is that my reading of the literature has been an important aspect of the development of my thinking at every stage of this inquiry. The literature that felt most relevant necessarily changed as my thinking developed, and as new issues emerged from the data and from my personal reflections. If one of the strengths of action research is that it is fundamentally exploratory, allowing the main issues to emerge slowly over time rather than focusing on predetermined issues, then this must have serious implications for both the use of literature and the way in which it is presented. My view, therefore, is that the literature needs to permeate each chapter of the thesis rather than being predominantly bound within any kind of literature review and this view is one that is now more commonly accepted within the action research tradition.

It is the literature that *excites, that challenges, that opens up new lines of thinking* which is the literature I feel committed to reviewing. I want, in writing up my thesis, to try to share with the reader some of the excitement I have experienced as I have engaged with new ideas and new ways of looking. I want to show the reader how I have responded to particular texts in the same way as, in writing about my practice, I want to show how I have responded to particular students. Whether this approach leads to engagement with the literature at a level deemed suitable for PhD work I must leave my examiners to judge.

What Does it Really Mean to Locate
the Literature in Which the Study Will Be Framed?

When I reflect on the literature that has really made a difference to my thinking, I am reminded about some of the ways in which I became aware of its existence. If I am really honest, I would have to say that the literature that has most *deeply* affected my thinking has rarely appeared as a result of my many systematic searches in the library. Interestingly, some of it I have merely stumbled across while browsing in the library or while trying to locate something else. During the course of this inquiry, I read and reviewed much literature in the fields of action research and supervision but found that these were not the areas that provided the richest intellectual support for my thinking.

Indeed, many of the references to literature that I have found most influential have originated from chance conversations with colleagues and friends, as well as from the more structured conversations with supervisors. I am constantly struck by how little of the literature that has affected me most deeply has come from my systematic approaches to finding it.

Interestingly, I have found that it has often been the literature outside the field of action research that has really engaged me and raised important issues about the nature of action research and this literature has often been more stumbled across than systematically located. However, in a sense, I would argue, this seems to fit with some of the basic principles which underlie the processes of action research.

In using action research to develop my practice, I am often searching for new ways of looking at the familiar. My everyday practice can become so routinised, so familiar, that it becomes difficult for me to see it with new eyes. I often need to step outside it and look from a different angle in order to gain fresh insights. Likewise with the literature: in order to find fresh ways of looking I need to step outside the familiar explanations, the familiar body of literature, and view my practice from a different perspective. As I reflect on the whole inquiry process, I am struck by the fact that it has often been the casual conversations with colleagues and friends that have put me in contact with interesting ideas and literature, often outside my own field of action research. The real resources for my learning during this inquiry have rarely come from traditional ways of finding them.

So What Might Be a Different Way of
Locating the Literature and Justifying My Choices?

My central argument is that the justifications for my choice of literature can only come *after* the literature has been read and has made its contribution to the development of my thinking. I will try to illustrate my view on this with a few specific examples, although I realise that,

Kath Green

given the constraints of space for this brief article, my attempt to do this may open myself to the very charges that I am wishing to avoid: namely, either that of superficiality or the charge (so often laid at the door of postmodernism) that somehow 'anything goes'.

Chaos and Complexity, Anarchic and Feminist Thinking

I knew very little about chaos and complexity theories until I began having conversations with a colleague about how we each tried to make sense of the way our personal practice developed. I talked about my unhappiness with some of the seemingly neat systematic models presented in the action research literature. It always looked so predictable, so controlled. That was not how I felt my practice developed. For me, it was all so much messier. I always have this feeling that I never actually solved problems but that it was more a question of revealing and coming to understand increasing layers of complexity. The development of my practice certainly did not fit any of the traditional models of neat spirals and cycles I found in the action research literature. My colleague, a thoughtful and original thinker with a strong scientific background, told me about his interest in chaos and complexity theory, and this opened up an exciting new world where I felt, almost immediately, that I could make some interesting connections with the more complex and inter-related models being presented.

In my view, teaching is a messy, complex activity with many inter-related strands. Indeed, it is this constant inter-relatedness that is so much part of what I recognise in any aspect of teaching. When looking at my practice and trying to understand it, I have always felt the need to keep the notion of 'wholeness' central to my thinking. It is the whole picture that is the abiding metaphor. As I engage in action research on my practice I may want to 'zoom in' in order to examine some aspect of my practice in detail but I need to keep 'zooming out' in order to keep a check on the whole. So I could relate to the way that Briggs shows:

> ... dynamical systems imply a holism in which everything influences, or potentially influences, everything else – because everything is in some sense constantly interacting with everything else. (Briggs, 1992, p. 21)

I can also relate strongly to the notion of sensitive dependence on initial conditions – the so called Butterfly Effect – where a small incident can have vast long term effects (see, for example, Gleick, 1987). Whilst Briggs states that, somewhat paradoxically, the study of chaos is also the study of wholeness, he also argues that:

> ... the most fertile area of chaos study lies along the ferociously active frontier that has been found to exist between stability and incomprehensible disorder. (Briggs, 1992, p. 21)

This work has much in common with the way in which I have located and used the literature. It does not fit some pre-determined mould. Very particular events happen – i.e. I read a particular text – and some of these events may have a profound effect on my thinking which, in turn, sends ripples through the whole of my inquiry. It changes the inquiry as it has changed me. Whilst another text might have had a different effect at that particular time, I will never know what that would have been for I am changed in the process of reading and move on to the next event or text as a different person. Yet, despite this fairly obvious insight, there appears to be little recognition of the possible effect of the order in which texts are read on the understandings developed by the reader and the subsequent development of any inquiry. In the early stages of the inquiry, the limitless possibilities of my own personal development somewhat frightened me. Only when I accepted the infinite variety of possibilities in front of me and stopped thinking in terms of trying to experience it all, in a desperate effort to exert some kind of control over my own development, could I relinquish the shackles of trying to read the right things and thus allow myself the freedom to go with the flow of my own development. For, as Briggs argues:

> *The question is, shall we inhabit a world shaped (as we have long believed) by lifeless mechanically interacting fragments driven by mechanical laws and awaiting our reassembly and control? Or shall we inhabit a world – the one suggested by fractals and chaos – that is alive, creative, and diversified because its parts are unified, inseparable, and born of an unpredictability ultimately beyond our control? (Briggs, 1992, p. 180)*

Personally, I have found Paul Feyerabend's work *Against Method: outline of an anarchistic theory of knowledge* (1975) both imaginative and challenging. His view that theoretical anarchism is more likely to encourage progress than what he terms law-and-order alternatives, and that the only principle that does not inhibit progress is 'anything goes' are stimulating starting points for anyone grappling with issues of methodology, particularly where the research is exploratory. Feyerabend reminds us that most developments in science have occurred because people either decided not to be bound by obvious methodological rules or because they unwittingly broke them. Whilst scientific method has been very rule bound, the major leaps forward in science have been as the result of someone being prepared to go against the rules and challenge the orthodoxies of the day.

These ideas also linked with some of my reading of the feminist writer Gail Stenstad's work. In an article entitled 'Anarchic thinking' she explores the notion of atheoretical feminist thinking, as being:

> *thinking which goes beyond conventional boundaries, deviates*
> *from expected goals and methods, and is not accounted for or*
> *predicted by any theory. This thinking will be, in a word, un-*
> *ruled or anarchic. (Stenstad, 1988)*

She emphasises the need to distinguish anarchic thinking from merely
sloppy or chaotic thinking and argues that the thing which keeps
thinking moving on is unresolved tension. In anarchic thinking, the
tensions are deliberately maintained and the tendency to try to settle for
one explanation is resisted. She, in common with other feminists, argues
the need to do more than confront patriarchal thinking in its own terms,
but also to think in ways which break the rules, ways which deny to
patriarchy the right to set a standard for feminist thinking (Stenstad,
p. 88). Stenstad argues that whilst anarchic thinking is rule-less it is
nevertheless precise and careful for, she emphasises, 'anarchic thinking
is not sloppy thinking' (Stenstad, p. 88).

In considering what sets anarchic thinking in motion she draws on
the work of Heidegger in saying that anything which deeply concerns us,
touches us in mind and heart, provokes thinking and goes on to argue
that:

> *Persistence in questioning, working and playing with*
> *ambiguities, being alert for the presence of the strange within*
> *the familiar, and allowing for concealment or unclarity in the*
> *midst of disclosure are four elements of anarchic thinking*
> *which stand out as particularly significant in this respect.*
> *(Stenstad, p. 89)*

I liked the emphasis she places on the way in which persistence in
questioning is important as our responses engender further questions
thus ensuring that our thinking remains in motion. For:

> *To deliberately maintain fluidity in thinking is to resist the*
> *tendency to settle for one explanation, one voice. (Stenstad,*
> *p. 89)*

This line of thought connects with my beliefs about the nature of action
research which seems to me to be more a constant process of asking
further and more interesting questions about practice, rather than some
kind of neat problem-solving process.

Another of the interesting tensions identified in Stenstad's anarchic
thinking is that between the familiar and the strange.

> *One of the things that theory building seeks to do is to make*
> *the strange familiar, to tame it and place it in its proper slot in*
> *the totality. Anarchic thinking, on the other hand, takes note*
> *of the previously unnoticed or unheeded strangeness in what*
> *is familiar. (Stenstad, p. 89)*

Again, this seems, to me, to connect with my views about the sort of unfamiliar reading that might support action research. I have felt the need to read outside the familiar texts in order to see the familiarity of my practice with strange eyes for, as Stenstad argues:

> *The effect of this making-strange is to decenter the familiar,*
> *the taken-for-granted, the true, the real, etc. .... The previously*
> *unthinkable becomes thinkable. (Stenstad, p. 90)*

These ideas also connected, for me, with Lorraine Code's fascinating book *What Can She Know? Feminist Theory and the Construction of Knowledge* (Code, 1991) where, in discussing her view of knowledge as a social construct validated through critical dialogue, she defines the knower with reference to a view of subjectivity which is based on a 'personal relational' model. Her work gave me the confidence to tackle the 'writing up' of my thesis in a way that would fully acknowledge my intuitive understandings, the deeply personal aspects of my learning and the strong 'feelings' dimension which runs as a thread through every chapter of my thesis. Code challenges the positivist view that any attempt to claim a legitimate place for emotion in the creation of knowledge is some kind of surrender to subjectivism and insists on the recognition that it is emotion that can often prompt investigations:

> *Emotion and intellect are mutually constitutive and sustaining*
> *rather than oppositional forces in the construction of*
> *knowledge. (Code, 1991, p. 47)*

In drawing on the work of Carol Gilligan (1992) who challenged traditional definitions of 'maturity' by emphasising the tensions between notions of autonomy and interdependence, and between claims of impartiality and of particularity, Code argues that 'the traditionally autonomous, impartial moral agent is a seriously flawed character' (Code, 1991, p. 108).

Some of my personal concerns about the tension between, on the one hand, the questioning of the traditional and somewhat totalising notions of scientific authority and, on the other, its subsequent replacement with various and sometimes extreme forms of relativism are addressed by Harraway when she asserts:

> *I, and others, started out wanting a strong tool for*
> *deconstructing the truth claims of hostile science by showing*
> *the radical historical specificity, and so contestability, of every*
> *layer of the onion of scientific and technological*
> *constructions, and we end up with a kind of epistemological*
> *electro-shock therapy, which far from ushering us into the*
> *high stakes tables of the game of contesting public truths, lays*
> *us out on the table with self-induced multiple personality*
> *disorder. (Harraway, 1991, p. 186)*

She talks of *situated knowledges* which promise 'more adequate, sustained, objective transforming accounts of the world' yet she emphasises that the practice of seeing 'from below' requires as much skill as those traditional 'techno-scientific' visualisations. For Harraway:

> *The alternative to relativism is partial, locatable, critical*
> *knowledges sustaining the possibility of webs and connections*
> *called solidarity in politics and shared conversations in*
> *epistemology. (Harraway, p. 191)*

She emphasises the partial nature of the knowing self and argues for the kind of practice:

> *that privileges contestation, deconstruction, passionate*
> *construction, webbed connections, and hope for*
> *transformation of systems of knowledge and ways of seeing.*
> *(Harraway, pp. 191-192)*

All these ideas make many connections with my views about the nature of education in general and action research in particular and have proved a rich resource in intellectual support for my inquiry.

Influences of Individual Writers:
e.g. Richard Rorty, Mark Freeman and Paul Ricoeur

In the next section I continue to support my earlier arguments by outlining – again somewhat briefly – examples of specific writers and particular texts that I feel have made a significant contribution to my inquiry.

Richard Rorty's 'Contingency, Irony and Solidarity'

In the process of trying to articulate my beliefs about the nature of my own educational values, and in engaging in debates about universal and relative values (Green, 1997), I was struck by Connor's view that there can be no choice possible between absolutism and relativism for:

> *it is impossible to choose plurality without making an absolute*
> *commitment to the absolute desirability of plurality; just as it*
> *is impossible to imagine any absolute value ... which would*
> *not have in principle to be vulnerable to the kind of*
> *relativising critique with which the last couple of decades have*
> *made us familiar. (Connor, 1993, p. 48)*

I can well remember reading Richard Rorty's *Contingency, Irony and Solidarity* (1989) and finding that his ideas provided me with much food for thought. Rorty sketches the figure whom he calls the liberal ironist as someone who thinks cruelty is the worst thing we can do, and who also faces up to the contingencies of his or her own most central beliefs and desires. This certainly had an appealing ring to it. I liked the way individuals are seen as taking more responsibility for their own moral decisions rather than following a set of rules laid down either by a religion or some agreement on 'human essence'. It seem to me, that it is only by accepting personal responsibility for decisions about what counts as a moral way forward that we are able to protect ourselves from those who may want to abuse their power.

Rorty's emphasis on the power of story as the means of communicating important ideas in philosophy seems, at one level, to be a statement of the obvious and yet I wonder why it was that this one central idea sparked off so much fruitful thinking about my own ideas on the writing up of action research projects. Rorty argues that we need to develop increased sensitivity to others so that we do not marginalise them:

> *The process of coming to see other human beings as 'one of us' rather than as 'them' is a matter of detailed description of what unfamiliar people are like and of redescription of what we ourselves are like. (Rorty, 1989, p. xvi)*

Rorty sees this task as one for journalism, ethnography and the novel, with the recognition of a turn against theory and toward narrative. It would amount to a recognition of what Rorty calls the 'contingency of language' – the fact that there is no way to step outside the various vocabularies we have employed and find a metavocabulary which somehow takes account of *all possible* vocabularies, all possible ways of judging and feeling. Despite some of my strong reservations about Rorty's work (particularly in relation to his elitism together with the complete and somewhat surprising absence of any reference to his *own* personal story), I found that this work stimulated much fruitful thinking about my own practice and, in particular, has prompted me to develop my use of stories in my own teaching situation and to look at the theoretical underpinnings of that work.

Understanding Autobiography: Mark Freeman and Paul Ricoeur

Throughout the period of my engagement with this project I have been struck by the importance of my personal biography in relation to my current work. In trying to understand myself as I am now, I have been forced to look back and to attempt to trace the origins of some of my own current beliefs. Time and time again, issues that I have been dealing with in the context of my research have made me uncover and examine some of the earlier and major influences on my development as a person. I have also been struck by the parallels I found in my work with students as they, too, have had to grapple with aspects of their own personal biographies as they struggle to understand themselves as teachers.

In looking at this aspect of my work I have had to engage with some of the central ideas in autobiographical work. How do I come to understand myself? What are the processes by which I review my life to date and pick out significant incidents? What makes a life event 'significant'? Why choose some events and not others?

In this process of coming to understand myself I have engaged with issues in the literature of autobiography. A starting point for my own thinking in this area was Mark Freeman's particularly interesting and stimulating book *Rewriting the Self: history, memory and narrative*. In this, he defines 'rewriting the self' as the process by which one's past and, indeed, oneself is figured anew through 'interpretation' seeing *explanation* and *understanding* as different 'moments' in the process of making sense of the human world (Freeman, 1993, pp. 3-4).

In engaging in interpretative work where the object of our work is ourselves, we are, of course, placed in a very different situation from our normal attempts at interpreting the world. Freeman argues that, because what we are interpreting is our own past 'the history of our words and deeds' then, inevitably, these pasts are inseparable from us as interpreters.

Thus, when we seek to interpret ourselves we are:

> *interpreting precisely that which, in some sense, we ourselves have fashioned through our own reflective imagination.*
> *(Freeman, 1993, p. 5)*

and, in doing so, our starting point:

> *will not be lives as such but the words used to speak them.*
> *(Freeman, p. 7)*

Of course, these texts of our lives are deeply problematic in that they will inevitably be *recollections* of experience. This, again, raises the whole question as to what extent these recollections might be regarded as 'mere fictions', resulting in a consequent belief that we, too, are ultimately fictions. Clearly, 'the self as fiction' is not a new idea and fits Derrida's view that there is no world apart from language. Freeman suggests that, if we question the very notion of the 'true past' there to be discovered we would, as Derrida would argue, concentrate on the study of the multiple texts of our lives rather than constantly worrying about what exists outside those texts.

Freeman goes on to raise the question that, if both our lives and the stories we tell about them are socially constructed to the extent that we cannot 'step beyond the discursive order inherent in one's own culture' then how will we ever be able to do anything new. In doing so, he argues for the need to both understand and rewrite ourselves, reminding us of Bakhtin's powerful words:

> *The better a person understands the degree to which he is*
> *externally determined, the closer he comes to understanding*
> *and exercising his real freedom. (Bakhtin, 1986, quoted in*
> *Freeman, 1993, p. 24)*

There are certainly strong connections here with my attempts to understand my own biography in that it has largely been through gaining a fuller understanding of the extent to which I was socially constructed that I have been able to free myself to make – at least to some extent – free choices about how I really want to be.

Freeman tells us how Augustine talks of being 'constructed' as a child in accordance with the expectations of others with the result that 'he was living a narrative that others wrote'. This phrase 'living a narrative that others wrote' seemed to make some powerful connections for me in terms of understanding my early years. My journal entry at this point in my reading includes the comment:

> *Yes! I had strong sense of this as a child. I was expected to fit*
> *the mould prepared for me – constructed by others to their*
> *design. (Journal 3, p. 76)*

I carried the phrase 'living a narrative that others wrote' around in my head for several days and began to relate it to some of my understandings of my early history. I had a very strong sense as a child of being expected to fit a mould prepared for me and constructed by others to their own design (particularly in relation to my upbringing as a Northern Ireland Protestant). I constantly felt that I needed to escape this prepared script in order to begin to live out a life chosen by me, rather than one written for me.

In exploring some of these ideas on the nature of development I turned to a collection of essays by Paul Ricoeur entitled *Hermeneutics and the Human Sciences* (Ricoeur, 1981). Ricoeur sees the features of discourse in terms of an internal dialectic between event and meaning. He sees speaking and writing as alternative yet 'equally legitimate modes of the realisation of discourse'. In writing, the text is distanced from the conditions of spoken discourse through characteristics encapsulated in Ricoeur's key notion of *distanciation*. Written discourse is, by its nature, addressed to an unknown audience where the shared reality of the speech situation does not exist.

In a chapter on 'meaningful action considered as text', Ricoeur suggests we can use the methodology of text interpretation as a paradigm for interpretation in general in the field of human sciences. He goes on to apply criteria of what a text is to the concept of meaningful action. This involves, first, a kind of objectification of meaningful action which is equivalent to the fixation of a discourse by writing. Secondly, action is autonomised by becoming detached from its agent and developing consequences of its own. Thirdly, meaningful action has an importance which goes beyond its relevance to its initial situation and, fourthly, human action, like a text, is an 'open work' which is addressed to a range of possible readers.

Ricoeur goes on to argue for a fresh approach to the relation between explanation and understanding in the human sciences using the paradigm of reading. He sees validation, not as verification but rather as an argumentative discipline. He also emphasises that, while there is always more than one way of reading a text, that should not imply that all interpretations are equal. He argues that the:

> *logic of validation allows us to move between the two limits of dogmatism and scepticism (Ricoeur, 1981, p. 213),*

for:

> *in arguing about the meaning of an action I put my wants and my beliefs at a distance and submit them to a concrete dialectic of confrontation with opposite points of view. (Ricoeur, 1981, p. 214)*

Ricoeur identifies four stages in this process of development and, it seems to me, that these make important connections with some of the key processes of action research. In the *recognition* phase, we see the disjunction between the existence we were living and the one we might. We ask ourselves what was inadequate about this previous text of our life. In seeing what we do *not* believe we engage in the process of *distanciation* whereby we are able to separate self from self. By distancing ourselves from our former self we are more able to cope with the loss of self involved. We can then engage in the process of *articulation* where we can attempt to define the difference between the old self and the projected self and clarify the direction in which we should proceed. The final phase of *appropriation* is one whereby we act on our new understandings and projections. This phase is clearly crucial and again, it seems to me, that it mirrors the action in action research. For, as Freeman states:

> *knowledge without action is perhaps even more tragic, and certainly more painful than the most profound ignorance. (Freeman, 1993, p. 43)*

These texts have raised important issues for me not only in relation to understanding my own biography but also in the connections I found between my understanding of action research and Ricoeur's notion of 'meaningful action considered as text'.

Stepping Outside the Boundaries

In the above, all too brief, account of my personal responses to some of the literature that I feel has informed my inquiry I hope that I have been able to give a enough of a 'flavour' to illustrate the main thrust of my argument. Clearly, feminist and anarchistic methodology, the ideas of Richard Rorty and literature on autobiography are not to be found within either the action research literature or the literature on supervision. It has been the challenge of stepping outside these areas that has been the most fruitful aspect in the development of my thinking during this journey of personal and professional development.

Indeed, I would want to argue that good action research *demands* that we show a willingness to step outside our usual frames of reference, that we question our habitual ways of seeing and that we constantly seek out fresh perspectives on the familiar. Clearly, the above brief account of the way in which I have stepped outside my familiar boundaries is deeply problematic in that, in trying to give a 'flavour' of my engagement with these ideas, I am only too conscious that I have dealt with them here in a fairly superficial way. Hopefully, the fuller engagement with these ideas within the chapters of my emerging thesis will present a different picture.

I believe that there are two central issues concerning the identification of 'the field of literature' in which any action research study is located. The first relates to the timing of the decisions about appropriate literature to be consulted and its subsequent identification. The second relates to the way in which a claim is made that the literature is, indeed, appropriate.

In some ways, it would seem fairly straightforward to argue that in any research which is fundamentally *exploratory* there will be a need to see that literature is identified in an ongoing way as issues emerge, rather than being identified at the outset as is the case in many, less exploratory, studies. In addition, however, if literature which helps to illuminate, which challenges thinking and which encourages practitioners to see their practice in a new light is seen as a major resource for their research then, surely, its identification can only occur *after* the reading. How could one know *what* literature will challenge before the challenge has occurred? Clearly, it could then be argued that by using an eclectic approach and drawing on literature from a variety of fields that the academic rigour of the study becomes questionable. I would agree that there is a risk that by merely following personal interests and motivations this could result in a 'pick and mix' approach to reading literature where the resulting thesis merely skates across the surface of a variety of ideas never holding one long enough to do it justice.

My response to this problem in relation to action research would be to say that, just as decisions about the issues that are to be the focus of the study can only be made whilst the study is in progress, so decisions about the academic rigour of the candidates engagement with reading can only be made after the case has been argued. In a traditional study, an 'expert' in the area would be able to look at the list of references and make a decision about whether the works consulted could be regarded as adequate and appropriate for the focus of the study – albeit with the proviso that the candidate would need to engage with that literature in a suitably rigorous way.

In the sort of identification of literature to which I have referred, decisions about its adequacy can only be made in light of *the use made of it*. Did the chosen literature support the candidate in achieving sufficient academic rigour in the presentation of their work. The case needs to be argued, but after the inquiry has been completed rather than before the event.

The way in which these ideas have influenced my role as a supervisor of student action research could well be the focus of a future article. Suffice it to say, at present, that I am constantly looking for literature which will genuinely engage and excite a particular student. It seems to me that it is only when students become genuinely absorbed and excited by their reading that they begin to seek out further literature in order to critically engage with it rather than to adopt a superficial 'secretarial' approach of merely summarising the work of others or, worse still, merely 'raiding' it for suitable quotes with which to 'sandbag' their work.

As a primary teacher, I always knew that if I wanted children to develop as lifelong, critical readers then one of the most skilled contributions I could make was the seeking out of particular texts that would engage and excite a particular child. More recently, I have often wondered why it took me so long to subject my practice as a university lecturer to the same set of values. Only when students find literature that genuinely engages them and supports their own intellectual growth will they go willingly to the library to seek out new texts to challenge their thinking on a wider range of issues.

Knowledge about our practice as teachers is something we construct rather than find and it cuts across traditional disciplinary boundaries. It seems to me that action research would be strengthened by encouraging researchers to draw on *any* literature that supports them in seeing their practice with fresh eyes, in challenging the assumptions they bring to their practice, and in helping them to both articulate and critique the values they bring to their practice. In conclusion, in reflecting on my approach towards defining the field of literature and justifying those choices, it seems to me that the qualities of openness, the willingness to engage with the unfamiliar, the friendships across subject boundaries are all as important as the more systematic skills required for the traditional library search.

Acknowledgement

Earlier versions of this article were presented at British Educational Research Association Annual Conference, 1997, 11-14 September, University of York and at the Collaborative Action Research Network International Conference 17-19 October 1997, hosted by Kingston University at Watford.

References

Benhabib, S. (1992) *Situating the Self*. Cambridge: Polity Press.

Briggs, J. (1992) *Fractals: the patterns of chaos*. London: Thames & Hudson.

Code, L. (1991) *What Can She Know? Feminist Theory and the Construction of Knowledge*. London: Cornell University Press.

Connor, S. (1993) The Necessity of Value, in J. Squires (Ed.) *Principled Positions: postmodernism and the rediscovery of value*. London: Lawrence & Wishart.

Feyerabend, P. (1975) *Against Method: outline of an anarchistic theory of knowledge*. London: Verso Edition.

Finch, J. (1984) It's Great to have Someone to Talk to: the ethics and politics of interviewing women, in C. Bell & H. Roberts (Eds) *Social Researching: politics, problems, practices*. London: Routledge & Kegan Paul.

Freeman, M. (1993) *Rewriting the Self: history, memory and narrative*. London: Routledge.

Gilligan, C. (1992) *In a Different Voice: psychological theory and women's development*. London: Harvard University Press.

Gleick, J. (1987) *Chaos*. London: Heinneman.

Green, K. (1993) Diary Writing in a Mathematics Education Class, in G. Plummer & G. Edwards (Ed.) *Dimensions of Action Research: people, practice and power*. Bournemouth: Hyde Publications.

Green, K. (1994) Celebrating Experience, in S. Galloway & M. Morrison (Eds) *The Supply Story*. London: Falmer Press.

Green, K. (1997) What Counts as 'Better' Practice? Supporting Students in Improving Their Practice by Drawing out the Value Dimensions, *Educational Action Research*, 5, pp. 31-41.

Harraway, D. (1991) *Simians, Cyborgs and Women: the reinvention of nature*. London: Free Association Books.

Lather, P. (1986) Research as Praxis, *Harvard Educational Review*, 56, pp. 257-277.

Oakley, A. (1981) Interviewing Women: a contradiction in terms, in H. Roberts (Ed.) *Doing Feminist Research*. Boston: Routledge & Kegan Paul.

Ricouer, P. (1981) *Hermeneutics and the Human Sciences* (trans. and ed. by J.B. Thompson). Cambridge: Cambridge University Press.

Rorty, R. (1989) *Contingency, Irony and Solidarity*. Cambridge: Cambridge University Press.

Stenstad, G. (1988) Anarchic Thinking, *Hypatia*, 3(2), Summer.

First published in *Educational Action Research*, Volume 7, Number 1, 1999

PART 3

Action Research
for Change

This section will enable the reader to explore issues surrounding the role of public service professionals as agents in bringing about a more just and equitable society and the place of action research as an aspect of this role. Such issues need to be faced by anyone concerned with the vocational pd development of public service professionals in liberal democratic societies that acknowledge there are many different ways in which human beings can flourish.

Melanie Walker's contribution questions whether it is appropriate to develop professionals independently of the pursuit of social justice in societies where different communities of people embrace incommensurable visions of the good life and compete with each other for scarce resources to enhance and maintain their sense of well-being. Such communities often appear to be at enmity with each other. In this context she argues that there can be no 'singular essentialist narrative' of professionalism because the idea of a 'common good' can no longer be taken-for-granted. Even the idea of social justice as a means of providing citizens with equal rights of access to a consensual vision of the good life is rendered problematic. One of the major issues in developing professionals as agents in bringing about a more just society in pluralistic democracies is that surrounding the meaning of social justice. For Walker the process of professionals attempting to change the social order to better realise their commitment to social justice as a professional ideal must involve continuous reflection not only about the means they use but also about the nature of the ideal itself. Hence, her view that action research must be central to the process of professional development, inasmuch as this form of research involves joint reflection about both ends and means, and a refusal to separate them as discrete objects of enquiry; one a focus for philosophical investigation and the other for empirical research.

Walker's contribution to the construction of a new discourse of professionalism around social justice issues highlights the significance of attempts by action research theorists to reconstruct the relationship between knowledge construction and knowledge use in the form of practical philosophy. She very clearly demonstrates how this new discourse challenges taken-for-granted assumptions about 'expert knowledge' as a basis for justifying the authority and autonomy of professional practitioners to decide what is in the interests of the communities they serve and how best to provide for them. The boundaries between the expert knowledge of professionals and the commonsense everyday knowledge of the communities they serve, between the processes of professional knowledge production and professionals use of that knowledge, between university-based professional educators and professionals operating in the field of practice, can no longer be sustained in societies characterised by the competing and conflicting interests of the diverse communities they consist of. Professionals can no longer pretend that their expert knowledge is neutral with respect to whose interests it serves. Hence, the importance of a professional development process that involves critical self-reflection about the ideological structures that shape the construction and use of professional knowledge.

Walker's attempt to reconstruct the role of the public service professional in contemporary democracies gives an important place to Said's call for professionals to 'speak the truth to power'. She employs, somewhat controversially as she acknowledges, the metaphor of the 'subaltern' to articulate a role that works 'alongside' rather than 'on behalf of 'the communities served, that positions itself across 'the boundaries' in ways which 'transform the status quo and interrupt privilege'. In the latter part of her article Walker provides us with accounts of action research projects that position public service professionals in these ways. One of these accounts is based on Victor Valla's article on the response of Brasilian health and education professionals to their government's incapacity to deal with the demands of urban communities for appropriate forms of healthcare and education.

Valla describes the failure of authorities to gather and disseminate data that would enable professionals to make an adequate diagnosis of the complex health and educational problems that confront particular communities at the local level. In response he proposes and illustrates processes whereby service professionals engage communities in a) creating data-banks that enable them to diagnose the problems they confront, and b) in formulating, testing and comparing different 'solutions' to these problems. This role as a facilitator of participatory action research may have the consequence in some societies, as Valla points out, of positioning professionals as transgressing the presumed prerogative of the state with respect to who steers the provision of services. It is an example of the role conflict and tension that Walker identifies as a characteristic of professionals who position themselves across the traditionally defined boundaries. However, Valla's article resonates also with that of Peter Posche in this section, suggesting that the tensions and conflicts he and Walker talk about may be transitional moments in the evolution of societies. Posch argues that many states in advanced industrial societies are beginning to realise that they have little option but to devolve more responsibility and power for effecting solutions to problems in society to the local level. The growing complexity and individualisation of contemporary societies means that central governments have decreasing capacity to solve the problems that confront their members in everyday life. In this context they begin to delegate more responsibility and power and this provides a context for the emergence of action research as a means of effecting this social transformation.

Posch articulates a rationale for transforming traditional cultures of teaching and learning in educational institutions to prepare students for participation in solving the 'unstructured' and complex problems of every-day living that present themselves at the local level in advanced industrial societies. A greater delegation of power and responsibility to communities themselves to effect their own solutions implies a greater emphasis on the construction of 'local' as opposed to universal 'knowledge' Posch argues. It then becomes an important part of the teacher's role to foster a learning process that enables students to participate with their community in the construction of local knowledge that can be used by them to improve the well-being of its members. Like Valla, Posch see's active participation in knowledge construction by communities at the local level as indispensable to improving their capacity to solve the problems of every-day living, and professional practitioners as having a central role in collaborating with communities to undertake this action research process.

The final article in this section demonstrates the contribution non-western cultures and traditions can make to the development of a methodology for action research in pursuit of greater justice in society. Arphorn Chuaprapaisilp describes and explains how two forms of Buddhist meditation aimed at promoting mindfulness can help public service professionals develop a more reflective consciousness of their role and the social forces that shape and condition their practices in often contradictory and paradoxical ways. He claims that Buddhism offers concrete procedures for disciplining reflective practice in ways that offer an assurance of objectivity and protection against personal bias that is consistent with a commitment to overcome human suffering. In doing so he challenges the western assumption that the active pursuit of human values is inconsistent with the process of constructing valid knowledge and opens a space for action researchers in the public service professions to practically demonstrate that they can help to construct valid knowledge in the pursuit of greater social justice within society.

Subaltern Professionals:
acting in pursuit of social justice

MELANIE WALKER

This article begins with a 'story' – a story about the professional life of a nurse working in a rural clinic in Kwazulu-Natal, one of the nine regions comprising post-independence South Africa. At issue, in this recounting of selected aspects of her professional life, is what it means for Zanele Ncama to be a 'professional', including what opportunities and support might be available to her for professional growth.

Zanele Ncama's story

At the clinic in Ezingolweni, a rural village near Port Shepstone in Kwazulu-Natal, 12 nurses battle to get through wave after wave of patients and the emergencies which punctuate the day. Patients get to the clinic at 4.00 am to be first in the queue when the doors open at 7.00 am, and through the day the queue snakes right out of the yard. Each nurse sees about 70 patients a day, and patients usually wait 3-4 hours for a nurse. Once their turn comes, finally, the busy nurse can only spare them a few minutes.

This clinic is where nurse Zanele Ncama works. Here the nurses get by with the most basic equipment. There are no patient trolleys or wheelchairs, and when the bus drops off a patient too sick to walk down the hill to the clinic, he is collected in a wheelbarrow. The clinic lacks many essential medicines, so patients needing those that are not in stock have to travel another 25 km to the hospital.

Zanele sees patients in a large room where there are only curtains for privacy. She grabs a cup of tea and a sandwich at about 1.00 pm, but apart from that there is no chance to take a break all through the day. Nearly all the cases she sees are caused by conditions of poverty. Most are mothers bringing their babies, dehydrated from diarrhoea, and children with burns and injuries they sustained when they were left unsupervised. Others have scabies from malnourishment, and a young boy has a gash on his head after being hit with a bottle. With each case she gives a few words of advice, preventing infection and giving advice about nutrition. Most of the patients she treats; other cases needing more specialised care she refers to the hospital. The clinic also delivers babies.

A doctor comes every two weeks from the nearby hospital, and when the nurses need advice they can phone him. Today, though, the phone is out of order, so they cannot call for an ambulance or order extra drugs. Today, Zanele has made time to counsel a bereaved woman whose mother was killed a few days before. The area has been racked by violence and this has taken its toll on the health services. Zanele explains how the nurses used to take it in turns to work night duty, and to keep the clinic open for emergencies. However, the nurses finally decided to end the night duty the previous week, when a young woman who had been shot was brought in by two young men and a policeman. While she was being treated, the gangsters who had shot her came bursting in to kill her, but were repelled by the men inside. 'It's very hard for nurses working here', says Zanele.

She has been at the clinic for 7 years, and for all her experience and 5 years of training she has a salary of R2800 of which R240 a month goes on transport. She leaves home at 5.30 am, catches a bus and then a minibus taxi and gets to the clinic by 7.00 am. With a 17 month-old baby to care for, she gets up at 4.30 am. She employs a childminder to look after her baby during the day. The baby is usually asleep when she leaves in the morning and when she gets home, so the weekends are the only time to spend with her child.

At 4.00 pm the clinic closes but because she has a wait between the taxi and the bus it takes her 2 hours to get home.

Another frustration for Zanele is the lack of opportunities and career paths. Further education courses are available only in cities and they are very expensive. She would have to leave her family and live in Durban for a year if she wanted to study further. 'If I have aspirations they are not in nursing. They would be to go into something else.'

She was given no choice when she was sent by the Kwazulu government to Ezingolweni 7 years ago to pay back a year's study loan. She would like to get a job in a clinic nearer her home, but she has been trying for many years and a transfer has not been possible. She also feels she cannot leave the clinic because there is no one to replace her.

At the end of her day, Zanele Ncama is too exhausted even to watch TV. (Adapted from a report in *Business Day*, 14 November 1995.)

Reworking my Text – I

When I set about writing this article, I had thought initially to include both the stories of Zanele Ncama and Linda Strydom as a concrete way of highlighting their differences in a socially unjust society. Thus, the personally experienced professional lives of Linda and Zanele are deeply saturated by the social. I include Linda Strydom's story in this reworked account to emphasise further the importance of forms of professional development and professional knowledge that extend into these broader social issues in order to challenge the status quo.

I wish further to address a point raised in one of the discussion groups at the conference, namely that Zanele's story could only have been told by a woman and as such her professional life is deeply gendered. Setting Linda's story alongside/against Zanele's confirms this (for example, the separation by the professions of the private and public), but shows too that Zanele's story could only have been told by a black rural woman. Moreover, Linda Strydom's opportunities for her own professional development, while clearly of personal benefit, seem not to have raised issues of inequality for her (is she even aware that they exist?).

At issue is not whether Linda is a 'good' or 'bad' nurse, she and Zanele both seem to care for their patients, but the ways in which the prevailing status quo maintains privileges based on race, rather than seeking to transform it. The point is to avoid premature fixing of professional identities but to understand these as constructed, fractured and shifting, held together by multiple tensions and dilemmas.

Linda Strydom's story

With its pristine passageways and gleaming white floors, Universitas Hospital in Bloemfontein looks like the model of what a hospital should be. Against this ordered background, nurse Linda Strydom blends in perfectly. She holds complete control in Ward 3B, the pulmonary and medical ward. Everything runs like clockwork – she knows exactly how many seconds the lift takes to get to her floor, and so the pattern of her day begins. Strydom has all the high-tech equipment she needs, and never runs out of medication. She can bring her two babies to the hospital's 24 hour crèche, and is expecting her third child. She lives 10 minutes from the hospital and travels by car.

After doing 2 years at university and getting a diploma from the Free State Nursing College, she came to Universitas, where she has been for 15 years. When she had each of her babies she worked night shift because it was quieter and easier to take breaks to feed her baby. Later she would leave the baby to play in the crèche during the morning while she went home to sleep, in peace.

At the age of 26 she wanted more, and with the supportive network of the hospital it was easier to study further. When she embarked on a midwifery course, she got a month's leave and the children stayed at the crèche all day, where they had stimulating, attentive care-givers. The many courses she attended enabled her to rise through the ranks. Now

34, she has been a chief professional nurse for 3 years: 'We have everything here. The matron encourages us if we want to study, and we have the university and the nursing college right here'. Her position now involves supervising the ward. She does not want to go further up the ladder because this would take her away from hands-on nursing, which she loves.

Her day starts at 6.50 am and finishes at 4.00 pm, except on Fridays when she finishes at 1.00 pm. Supervising a ward of about 30 nurses and 25 seriously ill people, from AIDS patients to heart disease patients, her day is very busy. Each patient needs a lot of time and care. Between the endless rounds of doctors' visits, taking blood samples, giving out medicines and injections, giving instructions to the kitchen on special diets, checking that all the medicines needed are in stock, she still takes time to talk to each patient. Talking to patients is the only way she can pick up social problems like abuse at home, and pass this information on to the social worker.

A domestic worker with AIDS talked to her about her worries over what will happen to her 4 year-old daughter and her mother, who both depend on her, when she is gone. Strydom dispelled the fears of the woman's employer. The employer was afraid her children might contract AIDS by being near her, and Strydom's advice has meant the woman will keep her job.

With 15 years of experience and 4 years of education, she earns R3800 a month. After deductions she takes home R2800. The salary does not go far, but 'we get on with our middle class life – and we get to the sea every year'. She will never leave. She has the chance to work in a private clinic for R1000 a month more, but stays at Universitas because she finds fulfillment in working with patients from such varied backgrounds. 'Every day there is something else; there is never a day the same'.

At the end of her day, Linda Strydom sets off to attend a flower arranging course.

* * * * * *

So, what does it mean for Zanele Ncama (and indeed, Linda Strydom) to be a professional? What does professional development 'mean' for them where the gaps between haves and have nots in post-independence South Africa have hardly narrowed? What does it mean when the social and material context does not support Zanele Ncama's professional development, while encouraging that of Linda Strydom? While these stories set in a developing country with a hazardous history might be particularly stark, the issues and questions they throw into relief seem to me no less important where such gaps are less wide, or less obvious, or different. We can no longer pretend that the colonial margins are an exception.

Moreover, if we persist in our language of 'globalisation' and more astonishingly the 'global village', how can we subscribe to such language without also admitting that the so-called 'justice of the market' is integral to the 'globalisation' discourse. What, then, does this imply for the pursuit of social justice in the making of democratic communities? As Zeichner reminds us, 'in a democratic society, all children must be taught so that they can participate intelligently as adults in the political processes that shape their society' (1993, pp. 212-213). Yet for many children this simply does not happen, and it happens least of all for 'Third World' children (especially girls), or for ethnic minorities and immigrant communities (Zeichner, 1993).[1]

The central questions seem, then, to be broadly similar: is it useful or appropriate to construct professional development outside of the pursuit also of social justice, outside 'the hidden injuries of class, the hurts of racism – all those ways of thinking and feeling that are actually about enmity between communities of people ...' (Steedman, 1994, p. 62)? The idea of communities further suggests practices of mutual accountability, the individual-within-community, where a community is deeply imbricated in economic, political and cultural patterns, and the race, gender, class and other dynamics of the larger society.

The answer surely is 'No', professional development cannot be separated from notions of social justice, we cannot help but intervene at our own institutional sites. Action research is, then, a form of professional development which involves continuously shifting between trying to alter a social situation in ways which bring us closer to living out our democratic values, and revising what ought to be done, while simultaneously interrogating what we mean by social justice. In this we bring to the fore our values of social justice and reworked, non-bureaucratic, community-oriented notions of accountability, while also dealing with the practicalities of everyday work, what Noffke (1996, p. 1) describes as 'becoming practically critical'.

Problematising the 'Professional' in Professional Development

Over 20 years ago now, Stenhouse (1975) argued for the idea of 'extended professionalism', by which he meant 'the capacity for autonomous professional self-development through systematic self study, through the study of the work of other teachers and through the testing of ideas by classroom research procedures' (1975, p. 144). What I wish to explore first are discourses (not a singular essentialist narrative) of 'professionalism', for it seems to me that projects of/for professional development have no inherent meaning or taken-for-granted common good (even, or especially, those laying claim to being emancipatory). Equally, what it means for each of us to be a 'professional' seems to me to need some exploration before we begin to pronounce on our own self-development, as if being a professional is ahistorical, or intrinsically, or necessarily 'a good thing'. For example, in South Africa, recent public hearings of the Truth and Reconciliation Commission have revealed the extent to which state-employed doctors colluded in the torture of detainees by 'recommending' after examining victims that they were 'fit enough' for further brutal beatings (*Business Day*, 23 May 1996). On the other hand, at least one of those doctors, Wendy Orr, fought courageously and successfully to publicly expose and restrain the vicious physical assaults on detainees.

I am not arguing, however, that a macro radical political discourse in and of itself will make the necessary difference between what have been described as technical and emancipatory practices (see Carr & Kemmis, 1986). Teacher training in South African colleges provides a compelling example of a political discourse dislocated from a professional ethos in the wake of years of turbulence and oppression. The recent comprehensive National Teacher Education Audit of the 104 colleges reported depressingly that a high degree of politicisation apparent in most colleges had problematic effects for the still fragile culture of teaching and learning:

> *A 'victim culture' and atmosphere of fear and helplessness pervades many beleaguered colleges which are struggling to function in the face of student activism ... In a number of cases the elaborate security of the administration buildings is indicative of a state of siege in the college. As one vice-rector put it,'We come from a culture of resistance'. A culture of violence is pervasive. Many lecturers have been intimidated if they fail students. There are cases where lecturers and rectors have been chased out of their colleges and refused permission to return. Others have been physically assaulted by students ... The major focus of any college curriculum should be to foster professionalism. (Jaffe et al, 1996, pp. 109-110)*

The same study found that of the 500,000 students registered at colleges, 95% did not wish to be teachers!

What I rather wish to suggest is that professional development and the related discourse of 'professionalism' is neither essentially reactionary nor necessarily progressive, but socially constructed in specific geographical and historical contexts and struggles over education. It will be shaped not only by its own internal dynamic but in relation to other dominant discourses operating in the society at any time. It involves the production of 'official knowledge' (Apple, 1993), including the historical context, social practices and power relations that inhere in such knowledge, and of course the absence, silence or subjugation of other knowledges.

Thus, the discourse of professionalism in the Teacher Education Audit articulates with a democratic political discourse, and with a new thrust for accountability and responsibility where demands for redistribution are heavy, state funds limited, and decisions hard. In Stenhouse's case, he, of course, wrote in the context of a different political climate in the United Kingdom, and different discourses about education which made his storyline a democratic one at that time. Dislocated from these political conditions, the discourse of professional self-development may be read rather more conservatively. In a time of 'markets', 'free trade', 'globalisation', and 'the end of ideology', a 'professional development' discourse is more often focused on individual careers, individual self-advancement and on exclusion, far less often within a discourse of collective work, social justice and equity.

There are, then, multiple readings of professionalism and professional development available to us if we pay attention to history, politics, and the material contexts which shape different storylines and different possibilities for Zanele Ncama and many others across the globe.

Professional 'Expertise'

However, all professionals will have in common a usually taken-for-granted claim to 'expert' knowledge, as Said demonstrates:

> *I shall never forget the shock I received when in responding to*
> *my insistent question, 'What did you actually do in the*
> *airforce?' he replied, 'Target acquisition'. It took me several*
> *more minutes to figure out that he was a bombardier whose*
> *job it was, well, to bomb, but he had coated it in a professional*
> *language that in a certain sense was meant to exclude and*
> *mystify the rather more direct probings of a rank outsider.*
> *(1993, p. 63)*

Professional authority (or domination) resides in having professional knowledge in relation to those constituted as the objects of that knowledge; the professional therefore knows what communities need, apparently better than they do themselves. We then all operate with the best of intentions (this being part of our professional socialisation) in our desire to 'save' people (including, or especially from themselves).

A Historical Example:
the construction of professions in the USA

Geisler (1994) has produced a compelling account in which she explores the dominant assumption in the USA that 'professionals' are the sole guardians, controllers and repositories of 'expert knowledge' (witness also the outrage in the United Kingdom a few years back at the idea of unlicensed teachers, or the recent controversy amongst the South African medical fraternity about the employment of Cuban doctors, for which read, 'not properly trained'!) She maps how the modern professions arose in the second half of the nineteenth century. Prior to that, professions included only law, medicine and the clergy. But, with increasing industrialization and social complexity, the idea developed that professionals should be sheltered from the dictates of the market-place in order to serve the common good. In the words of R. H. Tawney:

> ... the essence of the latter [a profession] is that, though men [sic] enter it for the sake of livelihood, the measure of their success is the service which they perform, not the gains which they amass. (Quoted in Geisler, 1994, p. 71)

As Geisler points out, the bedrock of professionals' claim to public confidence came to be their expertise. Control of expertise could then also be used to justify social status in that such expertise took time and money to develop. Paralleling this was the emergence of US universities as credentialling institutions, as they took on the certification of professional expertise. Geisler notes that this in turn 'guaranteed academic professionals some lifetime jobs in universities and colleges ...' (p. 73).

A boundary was drawn between expert knowledge and common sense or everyday knowledge, knowledge production separated from knowledge use, and professionals stratified into academic and practitioner wings. The effect was 'the transformation of expertise into a formal culture at odds with everyday or indigenous culture' (p. 74); what was at stake was what was to count as legitimate knowledge, the effects of which we still argue today.

Moreover, the formal had the appearance of being 'impersonal' or 'neutral'. Not surprisingly, then, the definition of expertise came to exclude civic action, even though the early vision of social reformers had envisaged an integration of formal and everyday cultures. Daniel Coit Gilman, first president of Johns Hopkins, thus shifted his own position from one in which he saw the need to connect expertise to social reform, to arguing against it on two grounds. One was the university system's dependence on industrial (capitalist) support for its expansion. Secondly, he came to distinguish between 'investigation' of social conditions and 'agitation' to change them:

> The point of Gilman's distinction between investigation and agitation was not to condemn agitation, but simply to observe its inherently controversial nature and declare it unfit for professionalization ... Gilman recognized that abstract inquiry into the essential nature of man and society was sufficiently removed from the fray that it might yield a professional

> consensus; however, practical agitation was not so removed. If
> authority in the field of man and society was to be established
> at all, the friends of authority would have to settle for half a
> loaf – they would have to form rigorous communities devoted
> to investigation and interpretation, leaving agitation to fend
> for itself. (Haskell, 1977, p. 163, quoted in Geisler, 1994,
> pp. 76-77)

Practitioners in the field, however, could less easily make such a distinction when confronted with the vicissitudes of everyday life. This led in turn to a somewhat sceptical, even hostile attitude towards the authoritative, often abstract assertions of university professors and researchers working under rather more protected circumstances (Geisler, 1994).

Equally important has been the public recognition of the superiority of expertise; compare the influence of the medical profession and the pharmaceutical industry on how we understand our own bodies, and the effects on indigenous medical knowledge (which survives alongside but may be dismissed as 'superstition', 'old wives' remedies, and the like). Similarly, in the teaching profession in the USA, Gitlin et al (1992) demonstrate the moves to construct teachers as neutral in relation to social struggles; as having expert and thereby dominant knowledge; as legitimising university academic knowledge; and embedding maleness as the professional norm.

The effects are with us still, for, at the core of the emergence of the modern professions is a denial of the legitimacy of everyday knowledge and its replacement with formal or esoteric or academic knowledge. Action research, too, suffers from this tension between the esoteric and everyday, from who decides what counts as legitimate knowledge about education, and what counts as acceptable forms of academic research in the academy, about the privileging of research over action (see Sanger, 1995; Walker, 1996; Zeichner, 1993).

What is important about these historical accounts by Geisler and Gitlin et al is that they raise the question as to whose interests professionalisation serves when expertise works as a relation of domination? What is the nature of the power relations embedded in professionalisation and how do these power relations benefit some social groups and not others? Do academics enjoy privileged working conditions precisely because those working in schools continue to work within intensified work structures (Gitlin et al, 1992)? Where do women locate themselves in relation to patriarchal professional values, and the separation of the private and the public? What are the effects for those not middle class, nor white, nor first world, nor committed to values of neutrality and professional domination, or for those wishing to challenge the discourse of 'market justice'?

'Amateurs', not 'Professionals': speaking truth to power

My next move is a turn to Edward Said (1993) who offers hope, which I believe to be of central political importance. He argues for 'amateurism' to replace 'professionalism', by which he means:

> ... thinking of your work as an intellectual as something you
> do for a living, between the hours of nine and five with one eye
> on the clock, and another cocked at what is to be considered
> to be proper, professional behaviour – not rocking the boat,
> not straying outside the accepted paradigms or limits, making
> yourself marketable and above all presentable, hence
> uncontroversial and unpolitical and 'objective'. (1993, p. 55)

At the core of Said's argument is whether one approaches authority (whether at the level of government or any other professional hierarchy) as a 'supplicant' or as its 'amateurish conscience'. Clearly, the former avoids taking up a principled position, even knowing it to be the right one. As we acquire the expertise and specialised knowledge of our professions, says Said, we learn to speak the right 'language':

> You do not want to appear too political; you are afraid of
> seeming controversial; you need the approval of a boss or
> authority figure; you want to keep a reputation for being
> balanced, objective, moderate; your hope is to be asked back,
> to consult, to be on a board or prestigious committee ...
> someday you hope to get an honorary degree, a big prize,
> perhaps even an ambassadorship. (1993, p. 74)

Thus, he argues for 'amateurism', 'literally, an activity that is fuelled by care and affection rather than by profit, and selfish, narrow specialization' (p. 61), exemplified by someone:

> ... who considers that to be a thinking and concerned member
> of a society one is entitled to raise moral issues at the heart of
> even the most technical and professionalized activity as it
> involves one's country, its power, its mode of interacting with
> its citizens, as well as with other societies. (p. 61)

The basic questions then become: how does one speak the truth? What truth? For whom and where? Central to Said's call 'to speak the truth to power' is not an impossible and unattainable ideal, but paying attention to one's own individual performance, but not individualism, of course, as an ideological position or value.

Subaltern Professionals

At this point, therefore, I wish to construct the 'subaltern' (Spivak, 1988) professional who tries to work 'alongside', rather than 'on behalf of' non-professionals. They would migrate transgressively across boundaries, audiences and hierarchies and therefore face contradictory demands for accountability, from below as well as above, thereby challenging unexamined claims to professional authority' (Yeatman, 1994).

Reworking my Text – II

One of the issues raised in the plenary report back at the conference was my use of 'subaltern'. Was this just another fancy descriptor without any particular analytical vigour (or rigour)? Some associated subaltern with the army (one of the accepted dictionary definitions is that of a junior officer in an army). One of the participants felt concerned enough to write to me afterwards: 'The first association I get is of someone committed to implementing the decisions of the officer, whether those decisions are understood or not. An army functions on the principle that orders are to be followed not questioned, and I find that any term from that larger set of hierarchical terminology necessarily invokes the whole hierarchical approach to order and control'.

Now this was not the way I had intended the use of subaltern despite my rhetorical commitments to writerly texts! I had meant it as denoting inferior status, quality or importance (another accepted dictionary definition), picked up by post-colonial writers like Spivak (1988), who refers to subaltern classes, used synonymously with the notion of the 'people' or the excluded subproletariat. My purpose had been to use the one term (subaltern) to interrupt, persistently destabilise and interrogate the other (professional), to capture somehow the notion of professional work which overturns taken-for-granted assumptions of a professional as occupying a superior or privileged status. Rather, by jamming the two terms up against each other, I had hoped to draw attention to and understand the possibilities and choices inherent in professional work – of working to transform the status quo and to interrupt privilege.

Clearly I should have elaborated on my rather compressed notion in the address, nor should I have assumed audience familiarity with post-colonial writing. But, for me, subaltern is more than an empty descriptor, it works to describe an oppositional positioning for professionals working alongside people, not for them.

******

As practitioners, subaltern professionals may themselves occupy an in-between position in relation to academic knowledge and whose knowledge really counts, positioned as consumers rather than producers of expert knowledge. It is precisely this in-betweenness which can be positively reworked as a different set of power/knowledge relations – not in ways which deny the importance of expertise in the delivery of a quality service (Yeatman, 1994), nor in flattening or equalising of the differences between professionals and non-professionals, but rather 'in maintaining this differentiation while requiring both dialogue and accountability across it' (Yeatman, 1994, p. 50).

The competencies we then need as professionals must include the competence to cross borders, cultures and dialects, the learning and translating of multiple languages (the political, the everyday, the academic) [2] and the courage to transgress when faced with social injustices. Our aspiration will be not only to understand inequality but to act against it. How we practise our authority is then the issue, not what we claim or profess: if we believe in something, then we have to practise it (Horton & Freire, 1990; Yeatman, 1994).

But the forms of professional development we both advocate and participate in need also to pay attention to what Helsby (1995, p. 324) calls 'professional confidence', 'a belief in one's authority and in one's capacity to make decisions about the conduct of one's work'. The crucial point she makes is that where confidence is high, teachers and other professionals are more likely to adopt a 'writerly' approach to policy texts, that is interpret policy in such a way as to choose to resist or subvert it. Where confidence is low, professionals are more likely to take up a 'readerly' position and a passive, collusive role. The issue then is what conditions make possible professional development for a writerly rather than a readerly approach?

Reworking my Text – III

During my stay in the United Kingdom following the conference, I was fortunate to be able to spend some time in extended discussion with Mo Griffiths (whose I work I had cited in the address but whom I had never met personally). In the course of these discussions she alerted me to the writing of Robin Richardson. I subsequently bought a copy of his book *Daring to be a Teacher*, where I found a clear but not closed definition of 'oppression' which seems very useful in interrogating my own actions in pursuit of greater social justice. Richardson writes: 'when a system of interactions and transactions produces and distributes more benefits and scarce resources for some of its members than for others, and correspondingly more losses and advantages for some than for others, then that system is oppressive, its beneficiaries are oppressors, its losers are oppressed' (1990, p. 34). Richardson (p. 29) also argues that we have choices as to what stances we adopt, 'between accepting the status quo as unproblematic ("conforming"); or trying to improve it a little for the sake of a few individuals ("reforming"); or trying to smash or deny it ("deforming"); or trying to change it radically and at the same time to change ourselves ("transforming")'. I shall resist placing my own interpretive gloss on this, and leave professionals to decide where they have, do and will locate themselves in relation to these orientations. But, as Richardson also notes, we are likely to be both oppressed and oppressors at different points of our lives, and our own wishes will also be shaped not only by our own (good) intentions but also by sets of social and historical conditions of possibility. Thus, in my own experience, I have been limited to choosing reform at times, even though transformation remains a long-term vision, value and goal.

A further point emerging from the group discussions was the question as to whether the pursuit of social justice was only ever desperately earnest. Was there no place for joy in constructing a better life for all? Again, Richardson helps, this time by quoting Paolo Freire who argues that struggling for freedom is not merely a fight for freedom from hunger but also for 'freedom to create and to construct, to wonder and to venture' (quoted in Richardson, 1990, p. 32).

Transformation, then (and we need in our own action research studies to provide practical examples), involves making our societies less unequal and less unjust, it involves the transformation of individuals in their social worlds 'such that they have the energy and the expertise to build and defend structures and procedures of justice' (Richardson, 1990, p. 45).

There was a further concern with the metaphor of 'struggle' which some saw as overly (only?) militaristic. This concern I find harder to share. Even while acknowledging the awful violence done in the name of ideology, there are also instances of real gains by oppressed people through armed struggle, in the case of southern Africa a last resort anyway in the face of intransigent colonial and/or racist regimes.

My final move, then, is to turn to illustrative action research projects which pay attention to individual performance, to local struggles, and to praxis as committed, self-aware social action. They too are deliberately chosen, one from the North, two from the South; one a feminist account, one a cross-professional story, one about teacher education. They are examples, I think, of struggling strategically against local social injustice as a more pragmatic approach, less idealised than struggling for social justice for all, which may appear a hopeless quest.

Morwenna Griffiths, United Kingdom

The first study is by Morwenna Griffiths (1994), called *Autobiography, Feminism and the Practice of Action Research*.

Griffiths makes a case for action research that is both personal and political. Her agenda is quite explicit:

> *I believe that individual researchers should focus on*
> *themselves as individuals and as part of wider political*
> *structures. Actions should be directed at improving particular,*

> *local situations, recognising the broader, global repercussions.*
> *(p. 71)*

She aligns herself 'with those who consider that action research ... is a critical, political movement' (p. 72) and that 'reliable knowledge' must pay attention to 'politically situated perspectives' (p. 76). But, she also concedes that, 'This is easier said than done' (p. 71), and in practice 'the criticism and the politics could easily get lost' (p. 72). Griffiths then goes on to describe a collaborative project with a school teacher in which she attempts to put her own epistemological and political claims into practice, using the tools of critical autobiography and feminist theory. Like Valla, Griffiths claims that 'to be epistemologically sound, a method must be both critical and political' (p. 73), and adds to this, that it must also be personal, influenced here by the focus of feminist epistemologies on the subjective consciousness of the self.

Using her frames of individual experience, theory, reflection and rethinking, and perspectives of race, gender and class, she provides illustrative examples from her autobiographical writing. At the end she sounds a warning note – our social positions will materially shape our perspectives which are then always situated and partial (the world looks different from an affluent suburb in Constantia than it does from a tin shack in the squatter area of Khayalitsha; different from a comfortable London suburb than from under Waterloo Bridge), but we can learn from the stories of others and so improve 'one's own vision and practice' (p. 81).

Victor Valla, Brasil

The second action research account is by Victor V. Valla (1994), titled Popular Education and Knowledge: popular surveillance of health and education services in Brasilian metropolitan areas.

In his article, Valla explores the incapacity of Brasilian authorities to deal effectively with popular demands for education and health. He attributes this to the expansion of 'the neo-liberal program' in Latin America, signalled by plans to 'cut the fat from governmental programmes', or put another way, reducing funding for public health initiatives which serve the Brasilian poor. Valla outlines a context in which the minimum salary is one of the lowest in the world, working people have little leisure time given that they spend up to 4 hours a day travelling to and from work, and where research projects might be challenged by armed drug traffic groups whose reach extends year by year in the Rio De Janiero 'favelas'.

Valla then illustrates the crucial point that our liberation is bound up together in his discussion of the implicit relationship between the organised working class and health and education professionals as they try to deal with the problems of a new Brasilian and international political order. Valla seems clear about the political role of civil society (which would include professionals): it must monitor government action, including obtaining public data to create an alternative data bank, and introduce debate as to how popular sectors might resist the erosion of publicly funded programmes, as well as the dominant discourse of 'medicalisation'.

One possibility is joint projects between professionals and popular organizations, writes Valla:

> *On the one hand, the suggested relationship between professionals and popular groups necessarily questions the 'hegemony' of professional service delivery as the only place for making decisions and storing and releasing information. On the other hand, however, it is necessary to take care that this 'new' relationship does not reproduce the old hegemony in the new space 'outside' of the services. (p. 406)*

Clearly the latter would subvert community participation and social transformation.

Also to be wary of is any paternalistic move on the part of professionals to indulge the illusion of participation by the popular sectors. Rather, notes Valla, democracy:

> *... refers to a concept of participation which is essential for knowledge construction. In other words,* only with the participation of popular sectors *can one construct knowledge necessary for solving public health problems. (p. 408, my emphasis)*

Such popular participation also has a democratic political goal in that it constitutes 'a continuous process of formation of public opinion about the need for the universal provision of these basic services' (p. 409). Finally, Valla ends by warning professionals against assuming the superiority of professional discourse and knowledge over other forms. In support, he quotes Marilena Cahaui who problematises a taken-for-granted superiority of intellectual authority:

> *We are accustomed ... to supposing that the working population uses a limited perceptual and linguistic code (euphemism to avoid words such as 'inferior', 'poor', 'narrow'), since we use our own codes as paradigms: we are incapable of apprehending the difference of the other code, concise in words and expressive in gestures, marked by fatigue and by a relationship with work characterized by weariness. In other words the very way of designating space and time is determined by exhaustion. (quoted by Valla, p. 412)*

Teacher Education Reform Project, Namibia

The third example is taken from the work of the Teacher Education Reform Project (TERP) in Namibia, a project with whose teacher educators I was recently privileged to work. It is important to note that on independence in 1990, Namibia inherited a deeply racist and élitist education system from the colonial master, South Africa. Like apartheid education, it was fractured and segregated along ethnic lines, with the bulk of resources allocated to the white minority (5% of the population). But independence 'and its concomitant participatory liberation ideology brought the rhetoric of educational change to every walk of life in Namibia' (Howard, 1995, p. 3). This signalled a shift from authoritarian approaches and externally imposed expert knowledge, to a democratic pedagogy and knowledge creation in teacher research communities as 'the foundation for self-reliance and self confidence which enables each one to have, not just control over one's life conditions, but also the means to change them' (Howard, 1995, p. 3).

TERP, working closely with the National Institute for Educational Development, is thus using action research as a teacher development approach, and as a source of new knowledge through 'useful' research about the implementation of educational reform in schools and teachers' colleges (see Dahlstrom, 1995; Zeichner, 1996). Teacher education is seen as a crucial part of national reform, and teachers and teacher educators are to be fully involved in promoting change in Namibia. The new curriculum 'emphasises learner-centred, reflective, inquiring and productive methods in teacher education' (Dahlstrom, 1995, p. 285). The political commitment of teacher educators and student teachers to new social goals of equity, access, quality and democratic processes, and education goals of learner-centred education and lifelong learning are brought to the fore. The experience of doing action research flows out of this and the political experiences of teacher educators and teachers (many of whom had had to flee from South African army harassment to the SWAPO camp in Angola), and how it might translate into alternative educational practices.

This is not to say that reform and transformation are uncontested processes in Namibia, given the official policy of 'reconciliation' and the layers of ideological and professional power struggles (Dahlstrom, 1995). But teacher educators have begun to investigate their own practice 'which was unthought of only a few years back' (Dahlstrom, 1995, p. 287), and to find their voices as producers of knowledge about education. As Ken Zeichner, an international consultant to TERP, comments:

> *It was clear to me in observing these [action] researchers that*
> *all of them had experienced new insights related to their*
> *practices and that they all experienced some progress both in*

*understanding and in advancing the educational reform
agenda ...*

He goes on:

*... but I do not think that the experience of doing action
research created a commitment to the reforms. It merely
strengthened the commitment that was already present and
deepened participants' understanding of the meaning and
principles underlying them. (1996, p. 25)*

Closing Words

All of these projects satisfy, I believe, Iram Siraj-Blatchford's call for:

*... not simply 'practitioner action research' but rather an
action research pursued by organic intellectuals. A critical,
committed and reflexive process that recognises that we are
still involved in an ideological struggle where the new right
claims that the age of egalitarianism is over. (1995, p. 218)*

As importantly, they demonstrate that small-scale self-aware action, one
step at a time, does constitute accountable educational action for social
change, and a more useful way of thinking about the pursuit of social
justice than proffering grand or absolute claims about what constitutes
'emancipatory' action. The teacher working in a squatter community,
impermanent, violent and unstable, outside Cape Town (Tshego's story
in Orpen et al, 1995) equally struggles step by step as she shifts from rote
teaching to engaging her pupils by making learning materials ('we try
and make use of what we already have'), working with colleagues, and
struggling against despair ('sometimes one feels this is a hopeless
situation ...') as she tries to be more creative.

Moreover, such struggles demonstrate that we might recuperate a
language of practical hope in that professionals are equally key in any
construction of professionalism, however fragmented and multilayered
their agency might be (Giroux & McLaren, 1994). Practitioners in the
field in particular might use their 'hybrid' positioning to work for them
in constructing alternative discourses which problematise dominant
lines of power to ask whose knowledge and interests are at the margins,
and whose at the centre (Noffke, 1996).

In the end I believe the interests of our pupils, our clients or our
patients need to be at the centre of our professional work, in ways which
will involve us in more than simply conveying knowledge, but which
will help produce critical citizens able to participate in multiple
struggles for more appropriate ways of organising all our lives,
individually and collectively. Such moves would still be framed by a
strong determination not to gain at the expense of others; by small or

large oppositional struggles against social injustice and 'market justice'; and practised as a commitment to the liberation of all people in 'a dialectical relation to particularity, positionality and group difference' (Harvey, 1993, p. 108).

Finally, too, our clarion calls to social justice and democratic education do not mean that as professionals professing social justice concerns we can stand outside of power/knowledge relations (Harvey, 1993). Thus, argues Sue Noffke (1996), alongside terms like democracy and emancipation must come our examination of relations of privilege (including our own), supremacy and domination (including our own) and a recursive critique of what we do as professionals and its regulative and normalising effects in the control, management and production of 'disciplined', 'productive' citizens.

Acknowledgements

My thanks to Marie Brennan and David Hursh for helping me to get started, to Uta Lehman for advice in redrafting my complicated account, and to various participants at the Educational Action Research conference who pushed my thinking on. I would like to dedicate the paper to the staff of TERP in Namibia, and all Namibian teacher educators and teachers.

Notes

[1] How do we overlook the increase in the number of the poor from one in 10 to one in three under successive British Conservative Party governments; that one in five children in the USA, the world's richest country, live in poverty; when the United Nations describes 2 billion people in the world as 'marginalised'; when Tanzania spends $2 million on health and $5 million on servicing its debt burden, and when the logic of competition has replaced solidarity?

[2] I am grateful to Mo Griffiths for this conceptualisation of learning and using 'languages' to cross and transgress borders.

References

Apple, M. (1993) *Official Knowledge: democratic education in a conservative age.* New York: Routledge.

Carr, W. & Kemmis, S. (1986) *Becoming Critical.* Lewes: Falmer Press.

Dahlstrom, L. (1995) Teacher Education for Independent Namibia: from the liberation struggle to a national agenda, *Journal of Education for Teaching,* 21, pp. 273-288.

Dalstrom, L. (1996) Teacher Education for a Non-racist Society, paper presented at the Annual Meeting of the American Educational Research Association, New York, April.

Geisler, C. (1994) *Academic Literacy and the Nature of Expertise: reading, writing and knowing in academic philosophy*. New Jersey: Lawrence Erlbaum.

Giroux, H. A. & Mclaren, P. (Eds) (1994) *Between Borders: pedagogy and the politics of cultural studies*. London: Routledge.

Gitlin, A., Bringhurst, K., Burns, M., Cooley, V., Myers, B., Price, K., Russell, R. & Tiess, P. (1992) *Teachers' Voices for School Change: an introduction to educative research*. London: Routledge.

Griffiths, M. (1994) Autobiography, Feminism and the Practice of Action Research, *Educational Action Research*, 2, pp. 71-82.

Harvey, D. (1993) Class Relations, Social Justice and the Politics of Difference, in J. Squires (Ed.) *Principled Positions: postmodernism and the rediscovery of value*. London: Lawrence & Wishart.

Helsby, G. (1995) Teachers' Construction of Professionalism in England in the 1990s, *Journal of Education for Teaching*, 21, pp. 317-332.

Horton, M. & Freire, P. (1990) *We Make the Road by Walking: conversations on education and social change*. Philadelphia: Temple University Press.

Howard, L. (1995) Introduction, in *National Institute for Educational Development Summaries of Action Research Reports from the Postgraduate B-level Teacher Education Programme in Namibia*. Namibia: Ministry of Basic Education and Culture.

Jaffe, R., Rice, M., Hofmeyr, J. & Hall, G. (1996) *The National Teacher Education Audit: the colleges of education*. Auckland Park: Edupol.

Noffke, S. (1996) Research and Action: reconstituting the political in action research, paper presented in the symposium Reconstructing Educational Research in a Problematized Democracy at the Annual Meeting of the American Educational Research Association, New York, April.

Orpen, B., Colyn, W. & Wilson-Thompson, B. (Eds) (1995) *Teachers' Voices, Mathematics Education Project*. Cape Town: University of Cape Town.

Richardson, R. (1990) *Daring to be a Teacher*. Stoke-on-Trent: Trentham Books

Said, E. (1993) *Representations of the Intellectual: the 1993 Reith Lectures*. London: Vintage.

Sanger, J. (1995) Making Action Research Mainstream: a post-modern perspective on appraisal, *Educational Action Research*, 3, pp. 93-104.

Siraj-Blatchford, I. (1995) Critical Social Research and the Academy: the role of organic intellectuals in educational research, *British Journal of Sociology of Education*, 16, pp. 205-220.

Spivak, G. (1988) *In Other Worlds: essays in cultural politics*. New York: Routledge.

Steedman, C. (1994) Bimbos from Hell, *Social History*, 19, pp. 57-67.

Stenhouse, L. (1975) *An Introduction to Curriculum Research and Development*. London: Heinemann.

Tabachnik, B. R. (1996) Useful Educational Research in a Transforming Society, paper given at the Annual Meeting of the American Educational Research Association, New York, April.

Valla, V. V. (1994) Popular Education and Knowledge: popular surveillance of health and education services in Brasilian metropolitan areas, *Educational Action Research*, 2, pp. 403-414.

Walker, M. (1996) Transgressing Boundaries: everyday/academic discourses, in S. Hollingsworth (Ed.) *International Action Research and Educational Reform*. London: Falmer Press.

Yeatman, A. (1994) *Postmodern Revisionings of the Political*. New York: Routledge.

Zeichner, K. (1993) Action Research: personal renewal and social reconstruction, *Educational Action Research*, 1, pp. 199-219.

Zeichner, K. (1996) Educational Action Research and the Transformation of Teacher Education in Namibia, paper presented at the Annual Meeting of the American Educational Research Association, New York, April.

First published in *Educational Action Research*, Volume 4, Number 3, 1996

Popular Education and Knowledge: popular surveillance of health and education services in Brasilian metropolitan areas [1]

VICTOR V. VALLA

Introduction

The expansion of the neo-liberal program in Latin America is contributing to a decline in quality of the already precarious education and health services in the large cities, and thus sets challenges for those developing popular education programs. Policies such as 'cutting the fat from governmental programs' as well as the 'municipalization of basic services' result in grave consequences: the incapacity of municipal governments to deal with health hazards, either because state and federal governments do not pass the necessary funds or because the problems in question cannot be resolved on a municipal level – these are questions which must be faced in the fields of education and health. This article discusses the implicit relationship between organized sectors of the working-class population and professionals of education and health in the process of constructing knowledge to face these many problems in the new Brasilian international and national political setting.

During the period before the 1989 Brasilian presidential elections, the public health scene was already at risk, and the neo-liberal program implanted after Fernando Collor de Melo was elected only served to worsen the many problems afflicting the poor sectors of the Brasilian population. Many national health programs were cancelled, such as the anti-malaria program in the Amazon Valley, thereby transferring responsibility to poor, isolated municipalities. As in First-World countries, disseminating information on health became one of the principal policies of the Ministry of Health, although millions of

Brasilians had access neither to basic sanitary facilities, nor to eight years of primary education.[2]

Although, on the one hand, there exists an adequate methodological discussion about the channelling of public money in a privileged manner towards the industrial infrastructure to the detriment of collective consumption, nevertheless, on the other hand, the role of popular civil society [3] appears to be insufficiently analyzed. For example, it is necessary for popular organized sectors of society to pressurize the different levels of government so as to guarantee adequate investment in the basic services essential for better living conditions for the working population.

The Peruvian experience with its cholera epidemic indicated an apparently contradictory movement on the part of the organized popular sectors. On the one hand, there was the correct and necessary demand that the government should invest the public money needed to control the present epidemic as well as to prevent others by means of basic sanitation. On the other hand, because of the government's cold refusal to satisfy these demands, it was necessary for these informal organizations to assume tasks that, in fact, were the responsibility of the public sector (transporting and tending to the cholera stricken population, for example).[4]

The Peruvian experience demonstrates that in addition to restarting the debate about the validity of 'self-help' experiences in popular education, it is also necessary to introduce into Latin American societies practices of civil surveillance over government, and at the same time to begin a discussion about 'popular civil defense' on the part of the organized popular sectors.

Formulating the Problem as a Methodological Procedure

One of the basic characteristics of popular education is the selection of concrete problems and the effort to resolve them. To a certain degree, one could say that in the field of popular education the procedure is to formulate the problem and then to seek an adequate methodology for its solution. In this sense, the process is sometimes the inverse of that taught in university courses on methodology, where often a wide range of options are offered, which have little to do with the choice of a problem. For example action research is often considered adequate for those who are interested in political activity; not because it may be the only form of obtaining the information desired. In this sense, it is the problems that people actually face to guarantee their survival which provide the reference point for popular education.

In the immediate context under discussion here, the formulation of the problem lies in the field of epidemiological and sanitary vigilance, but in a wider sense it is called simply 'health hazards', which certainly includes infectious–contagious diseases, but also problems such as floods, fires, barren *favela* [5] hillsides and problems of basic sanitation.

What is being proposed as a starting point for discussion is the incapacity of the Brasilian public authorities to register and disseminate data on these health hazards, as well as to provide effective action against them in the large cities. Examples that can be cited in Rio de Janeiro include recent meningitis epidemics that were never registered; abandoning treatment at Municipal Health Centers by large numbers of sick citizens: the irregular distribution of water to residences in poor neighborhoods, frequently at intervals as long as a week. Diseases such as leprosy, dengue fever, malaria and cholera are already endemic in other cities or soon will be. At the same time, these very diseases, together with questions such as poverty, family background or malnutrition, serve as justifications for primary school failure or 'drop-out' which continue to afflict large parts of the popular sectors of Brasilian society. Nevertheless, the child is almost always blamed, while the responsibility of the public educational sector becomes a secondary aspect.[6]

Methodologically, an attempt is being made to use the image of a contradictory movement, when dealing with the question of health hazards: on the one hand, the need for the popular sectors to intensify their demands for more rigorous vigilance by health authorities towards these hazards; and, on the other hand, the need for the 'civil society' [7] to create forms of surveillance over government vigilance policy. The idea is to demand abundant, quality services, of course, but also to create data banks according to the civil society's view of the principal problems to be dealt with in public health and education.[8]

The discussion proposed is predominantly about public health, but the same methodology can be used for public education or public transportation, for example, what is being proposed is the mounting of civil surveillance over all of the services operated by the government. If, for example, the proposal were to be the policy of the public school system in a certain municipality, it would be necessary for popular sectors to gain access to the data that the State Secretary of Education possesses, and also the data that are in the hands of each school principal. What is at stake is the possibility of gaining access, questioning, interpreting and making public data which should be in the public domain, but which are frequently reserved for exclusive use by municipal administrations.

In the case of public health, various factors influence the availability of public data. Frequently it is even possible that the municipal authorities are incapable of obtaining the data necessary for adequate planning. Municipal and state elections are events that frequently lead to reluctance on the part of governmental authorities to make public the data they possess. The tourist industry also contributes towards the same result, since the budget for some Brasilian municipalities is in great part determined by the income generated by tourism. Thus, not making public, or underplaying, certain data about violence and epidemics are decisions that impede access by the public to adequate information. Another important factor is the poor attention given to epidemiological and sanitary vigilance as well as to basic sanitation in the university curriculum. This last point, together with the reduced investment in these fields, makes these activities secondary in comparison with other public health priorities.[9]

The above factors, together with the fact that Brasil's minimum salary is one of the lowest in the world (US$60.00, April 1993), indicates the possibility of disastrous consequences for many Brasilian municipalities in the near future.

Civilian Surveillance of the State and Alternative Forms of Investigation

As a result of the situation described above, several proposals have been made in the fields of popular education and public health in Latin America. Two of these proposals have their origin in Brasil and Argentina, and, to a certain extent, point in the same direction: participatory diagnosis (PD) and community epidemiology (CE). The former originated in the Leopoldina region, in the municipality of Rio de Janeiro, while the latter is taking place in the city of Córdoba.[10]

Although the two proposals indicate similar discussions of education and health, each gives a specific emphasis to a particular aspect. While PD emphasizes the need for popular civil society to create an alternative data bank and to develop the surveillance of health hazards, the CE proposal refers more to the need for the popular sectors to resist the idea that medical professionals services and medicalization (hospitals, sophiscated health equipment) are synonomous with health. In this way, CE proposes a day-to-day epidemiology developed by popular groups together with interested professionals. One could say that each proposal complements the other, in such a way that each one's emphasis is incorporated by the other. The two proposals have much in common. One possibility to be considered, for example, is that of a project being undertaken both by education and health professionals and by popular organized sectors of civil society.

Although such proposals may seem obvious, there are methodological questions to be faced. On the one hand, the suggested relationship between professionals and popular groups necessarily questions the 'hegemony' [11] of professional service delivery as the only place for making decisions and storing and releasing information. On the other hand, however, it is necessary to take care that this 'new' relationship does not reproduce the old hegemony in the new space 'outside' of the services. There is a great possibility that professionals may unconsciously assume responsibility for the choice of criteria and categories for the participatory diagnosis as well as the indicators for the community epidemiology. The question is important because it goes to the heart of the discussion about popular education and health. In the words of Chaui:

> *It is not the case that anyone may say whatever s/he wants to and whenever s/he wants to. So-called 'competent' discourses thus become mistaken for permitted or authorized institutional language, i.e. language where the interlocutors have already been previously divided into those who will speak and those who will listen. In this framework, places and circumstances have already been predetermined, while content and form have also been authorized.[12]*

This type of problem points towards the need to 'revisit' proposals such as those of Paulo Freire, Carlos Brandào and Fals Borda, among others, and a new discussion of 'alternative investigation' (AI) (participatory research, participant observation and action research), in the light of the new national and international scene.[13] To quote Grossi:

> *Participatory research, for example, is a process whereby the community participates in the analysis of its own reality, with the objective of bringing about social transformation to the benefit of the participants ... To a certain degree, the attempt ... has been looked upon as an approach which could resolve the tension between the process of generating knowledge and the use of the knowledge produced ... No matter how poor the communities may be, and even if they never have all of the necessary resources, they are endowed with creativity which makes them capable of visualising the development suitable to their interests. In this way, an attempt is being made to establish the idea that knowledge is not the product of the intellectual capacity of one sector of society, but is socially produced through a process in which all sectors take part.[14]*

There are several motives which may induce professionals to assume hegemony not only with respect to health and education services but also during a joint investigation. Frequently the threat of an epidemic or the rush to obtain data can result in the imposition of what some call the 'urgency dictatorship', thus permitting almost all initiatives to be taken by professionals. If, on the one hand, this line of action may satisfy academic and political interests, on the other hand, important insights that only the popular sectors might offer will most probably be ignored. Haste, in the way described above, or in simply passing 'preventive measures' against dengue fever or cholera, for example, reinforces the hegemony of the professionals, and impedes the dialogue that expresses the living conditions of the popular sectors. Such a dialogue could modify the very manner in which the preventive measures are discussed.

One point that may need further justification is that of the choice of alternative investigation (AI) as a methodology for PD and CE. A hasty analysis might lead one to evaluate that this preoccupation with avoiding the hegemony of the professionals, with the resulting participation of the popular sectors, is better because it is more democratic. Although such a view is basically correct, it may at the same time reveal a paternalistic posture on the part of the professionals in 'allowing' the popular sectors to participate. Marilena Chaui states the question in the following ways: '... people are induced to be submissive to the language of the specialist who retains the secrets about a certain reality, and who indulgently permits the non-specialist the illusion of taking part in his knowledge'.[15]

The significance of the term 'democracy' in this sense is more profound, because it refers to a concept of participation which is essential for knowledge construction. In other words, only with the participation of popular sectors can one construct the knowledge necessary for solving public health problems:

> The participation and intervention of men and women in
> historical events is, from a theoretical and practical point of
> view, a central political requirement. It is this participation
> and intervention which determines what is intrinsic to social
> reality. Social reality is never presented objectively, but always
> constructed socially.[16]

Edson Nunes justifies this position when he demonstrates that those whose suffering is 'necessary' must have an active role in determining it as such, and that '... it is necessary that there be activity on the part of these individuals, in the sense that they elaborate their original feelings about the necessity they are living: otherwise the "needfulness" will never exist'.[17]

Material living conditions, of the professionals or the popular sectors, contribute considerably to the way in which the content of knowledge is assimilated. Although professionals may make efforts to 'deduce' the material conditions of the popular classes, new factors constantly arise, which require consideration in the knowledge construction process. There are many examples that demonstrate the insufficiency of the mere 'passing on' of knowledge content.

Two examples, among others, can be cited. The first refers to the sanitary campaigns against the dengue fever epidemic, carried out in Rio de Janeiro, where the main recommendation of the authorities is that favela residents should keep their water storage cans covered, since it is in clean water that the dengue mosquito breeds. This recommendation is hard to follow when people receive water in their residences only once a week, and only for a period of four hours.[18]

The second example is from a Rio de Janeiro favela during a neighborhood association meeting about the water distribution problem. One of the participants heard a woman whispering to another that after washing the breakfast plates, instead of letting the dirty water go down the drain, she would throw this water in the toilet in order to clean it. This example, besides helping to understand why so many people throw their used toilet paper in a waste basket, also indicates that excrement may remain in the toilet for hours, since flushing the toilet would waste the same water necessary for drinking, taking baths, washing clothes and cleaning the house. Certainly this is an interesting piece of information for professionals who include in their recommendations for the prevention of cholera the flushing of the toilet after defecating, It is not that the popular sectors do not understand the message; but their material living conditions permit them to read the content of the message in another way.[19]

Thus, the haste and 'urgency' with which professionals seek to 'resolve' the threats of cholera and dengue, for example, result in the separation of the content of preventive measures from the origin of the problem they are meant to address. In this way, the question of basic sanitation, frequently looked upon as a costly technical problem to be resolved on a long-term basis, becomes a touchy political problem during epidemics, and is thus postponed to a more suitable time.

Popular participation, therefore, is not only necessary for the resolution of immediate problems, where, for example, a neighborhood association pressures the local government to resolve its water problem, but it is also a continuous process of formation of public opinion about the need for the universal provision of these basic services. Even if local governments are progressive and popular, pressure from grass-roots groups is vital, so that these governments will have political support in investing public money in works that frequently do not interest those citizens who already have their basic necessities satisfied, and seek to pressure the government to invest the money in more glamorous and superficial works.

Alternative Investigation

The theoretical formulation of alternative investigation is frequently more satisfying than its application and praxis. The application of AI raises a number of difficulties that may not be easy to resolve, especially during the current neo-liberal era.

One of the problems arises from the model that is frequently presented in the AI literature: work with small groups of farm workers or small village dwellers. Besides the problem of how a restricted experience can be used as the basis for generalizing the results for wider audiences, there is also the challenge of how to adjust the model to metropolitan areas.

Brasil's minimum salary is probably the lowest in the world, a substantial part of the working class spends from three to four hours a day travelling by bus and train, to work and back to home, and in this way, consumes a large part of leisure and/or domestic hours. Meetings as well as surveys and small research projects undertaken with popular sectors are frequently questioned by armed drug traffic groups who assume wider control each year of the Rio de Janeiro favelas. Although it is not uncommon that once these groups understand the objectives of these projects, they do not offer opposition; nevertheless there is always an environment of distrust that the popular education professional may be a disguised member of the military or federal police.

Initially, it is important to understand the basic reason for the alternative investigation:

> ... it is not just the objective method of scientific work that determines the quality of the relationship between the research participants; on the contrary, it is frequently the premeditated intention, or the evidence of a personal relationship and/or established political involvement (or even a political involvement to be established) that points towards the choice of specific ways of carrying out the task of thinking out the research.[20]

AI requires long hours and for this reason, certain costs cannot be ignored – two demands that are not always accessible in the light of the above-described material living conditions. An ideal AI project presupposes the effective participation of the popular sectors in the elaboration, execution, evaluation and diffusion/devolution of the investigation.

Alternative investigation in Latin American metropolitan areas requires a combination of formal and informal techniques when one is gathering and registering data. What is being proposed is the construction of what could be called a 'mosaic', that is, giving more emphasis, for example, to the field diary rather than to the planned interviews. Thus, information from many sources would make up the research results: information extracted from neighborhood and favela organizations bulletins and newspapers, informal conversations with professionals and neighborhood residents, articles from the large daily newspapers, official data from federal, state and municipal secretaries, and, of course, formal interviews. A hasty examination of this mosaic proposal might lead one to think that there is little difference between this and the traditional field research. On the other hand, it is important to call attention to the emphasis on the informal, the unexpected chat, the spontaneous complaint of the favela resident, the small talk among residents during a neighborhood association meeting, especially at a time when the planned and formal interview (open or semi-open) may not be viable. If there are formal and prepared interviews or meetings with the residents where it is possible to discuss and prepare the research program, so much the better. But in the absence of these possibilities, there are other sources, which in other circumstances might be looked upon as complementary, and today in Latin American metropolitan areas these may be the principal sources of data for a research program.[21] What is important is that the information collected be registered, organized and returned to the people that made it possible.

There are a number of organizations that could undertake a research program such as the one described above. Certainly non-governmental organizations, as well as progressive church groups and political parties, would be in the best position to carry out such a proposal, since they frequently possess the motivation as well as the material resources for such a task.

The devolution of the results can be guaranteed by methods ranging from the very simple to the very sophisticated. Such instruments may include the simple exposition of results at a neighborhood or church meeting, as well as popular theatre presentations or poster displays. Simple mimeographed bulletins, as well as more elaborate popular journals, are also ways of broadcasting the research results. And all of these forms of dissemination may and, in fact, should attempt to incorporate the efforts of all those involved in the research process.

What seems to be essential to the method is the idea that a knowledge production is not only the result of the work of university-trained professionals, but that it is also the result of the endeavors of popular group organizations. In this sense, such proposals should be looked upon by both groups in such a way that they perceive that without their contribution, the knowledge would not have been produced, nor would the information have been made available.

Concluding with Questions

There are questions posed in this proposal that have not been answered. For example, if the very reason for alternative investigation is the possibility of bringing about a transformation on the part of the participants, be they professionals or popular sectors, how is the problem of participation resolved? Do all of the participants that take part in a participatory research or an action research process have to know that they are participating, or is 'conscious participation' more precisely one of the *aims* of the research group's joint effort? Is it possible for a group of professionals and working-class neighborhood residents to undertake such an investigation from the beginning, with everyone treating the 'informal' process as the principal orientation, while guaranteeing the formal interview whenever possible?

Ema Rubin de Celis calls attention to the fact that the participation of the popular sectors in these investigations may mean their involvement from the very beginning of the process, but it may also indicate just data collection by professionals.[22] Michel Thiollent also suggests that action research and certain kinds of participatory research:

> *... would be the best way to adjust the investigation to the questions and problems found in the midst of the working population ... Due to the channels of communication established by the research process itself, it is possible to immediately make public the results considered useful within the social milieu which generated them.[23]*

Finally, although this article primarily intended to question the original models of alternative investigation (derived from rural areas and small villages), it is also possible to question whether the Rio de Janeiro favela or working-class neighborhoods are the only places for undertaking investigations on the living conditions of their inhabitants. Thus, one might pursue some ideas that have resulted from other experiences; for example work with public school children whose parents live in these neighborhoods or the activities of groups that meet regularly within the many different churches that work with these populations.

Whatever the choice may be, Marilena Chaui's observation about the relationships between middle-class professionals and popular sectors is worth observing:

> *We are accustomed ... to supposing that the working population uses a limited perceptual and linguistic code (euphemism to avoid words such as 'inferior', 'poor', 'narrow'), since we use our own codes as paradigms: we are incapable of apprehending the difference of the other code, concise in words and expressive in gestures, marked by fatigue and by a relationship with work characterized by weariness. In other words the very way of designating space and time is determined by exhaustion.[24]*

Notes and References

[1] V. V. Valla (1992) A construção desigual do conhecimento e o controle social dos serviços públicos de educação e saúde, paper presented at the 15th Annual Meeting of Graduate Programs in Education, Caxambú, MG.

[2] The author believes, along with other Brasilians involved in public health work, that health information is useful for a population only if the very basic necessities have been satisfied, such as primary schooling as well as

the universal distribution of water and sewage works, policies that should be undertaken by means of governmental initiatives, be they federal, state or municipal. School and health recommendations are of little help in combatting cholera, for example, if the population has little access to running water and sewage.

[3] V. V. Valla & E. N. Stotz (1991) *Participação Popular e Saúde. Petrópolis. CDDH and CEPEL*. Séries Saúde e Educação, 2nd edn. 'Popular civil society' is a term I am using to refer to sectors of Brasil's civil society such as labour unions, neighborhood associations, progressive political parties and churches. In this way, I am calling attention to the difference between these groups and other civil society organizations, such as entrepreneur associations and conservative political parties and churches.

[4] C. Reyna (1991) A Peruvian sociologist who lectured on the Peruvian cholera epidemic at the National School of Public Health, Rio de Janeiro.

[5] The Brasilian *favela* is a housing solution devised by the poor sectors of the population, principally in the big cities. Somewhat similar to what is known as 'shanty towns', today many Brasilian favelas are composed of self-constructed brick homes, generally on government sites or on ecologically reserved land, such as the hillsides of Rio de Janeiro. Due to the fact that the favela residents frequently do not possess property titles, municipal governments tend to invest much less in urban equipment in these neighborhoods than they do in middle-class ones.

[6] Dá para ser feliz, cidadão?, *Se Liga No Sinal*, Centro de Estudos e Pesquisas da Leopoldina, Rio de Janeiro, No. 2, 1991. See also V. V. Valla & E. Hollanda (1989) Fracasso Escolar, saúde e Ciddania, in N. Costa et al (Eds) *Demandas Populares, Politícas, Públicas e Saúde*, pp. 104-141. Petrópolis: Editora Vozes.

[7] 'Civil Society': all the (private) social institutions of production, trade, culture, education, local pressure groups, etc. as opposed to the formal, public institutions of 'the state', including local government.

[8] Construindo o banco de dados, *Se Liga no Sinal*, No. 4, December-February, 1991-92.

[9] Valla, op. cit.

[10] M. A. P. Carvalho (1991) Vigilância epidemiólogica: a busca do controle das formas de viver, adoecer e morrer. O controle do destino, working paper produced for the Health, Education and Citizenship Nucleus, National School for Public Health. See also G. Tognoni (1991) Epidemiologia *Salud comunitaria, Salud Comunitaria*, Lima, 1(1). The experience of participatory diagnosis has been proposed by the non-governmental organization CEPEL, the Leopoldina Study and Research Center, while the community epidemiology experience has been proposed by another non-governmental organization. MOSIS, Movement for an Integral Health System. Correspondence: CEPEL, Rua Uranos, 1496,

Sala 401, Olaria, Rio de Janeiro, RJ 21.060-070, Brasil; and MOSIS, San Luis, 1327, 5000 Cordoba, Argentina.

[11] 'Hegemony': political and cultural domination by socially powerful interest groups.

[12] M. Chaui (1990) O discurso competente, in *Cultura e Democracia,* 5th edn, p. 7. São Paulo: Editora Cortez (my translation).

[13] See, for example, P. Freire (1983) *Pedagogia do Oprimido*, 12th edn. Rio de Janeiro: Editora Paz e Terra, C. R. Brandão (1986) *Pesquisa Participante*, 7th edn. São Paulo: Editora Brasiliense, and (1987) *Repensando a Pesquisa Participante*, 3rd edn., Sào Paulo; D. F. Borda & C. R. Brandão (1986) *Investigacion Particpativa*. Montevideo: Instituo del Hombre, Ediciones de la Banda Oriental.

[14] P. V. Gross (1981) Socio-political implications of participatory research, *Convergence*, 14(3), p. 43; N. J. Coletta, Participatory research or participatory putdown?, *Convergence*, 9(3), p. 43; also P. Demo (1988) Elementos metodólogicos da pesquisa participante, in C. R. Brandão (Ed.) *Repensando a Pesquisa Participante*, op. cit., p. 126 (my translation).

[15] Chaui, op. cit., p. 13.

[16] Demo, op. cit., p. 115 (my translation).

[17] E. Nunes (1989) Carências urbanas, reivindicações sociais e valores democráticos, *Lua Nova*, 17, p. 77, June.

[18] Dà para ser feliz, cidadà?, op. cit.

[19] An investigation undertaken by the Leopoldina Center for Studies and Research, Rio de Janeiro, revealed that more than half of the residents in the Penha Favela Complex received water in their homes only once a week, for a period of four hours, and frequently only once a month during the summer period.

[20] C. R. Brandão (1988) Participar-pesquisar, in C. R. Brandão (Ed.) *Repensando a Pesquisa Participante*, op. cit., p. 8 (my translation).

[21] 'For many years I have worked as a researcher on social problems in rural areas, and particularly, on social conflicts, land struggles and social movements ... I have witnessed innumerable times the experience of not being able to undertake an interview with certain persons nor to obtain information from them privately ...[since] there was always also a group of people, sometimes a large group, listening and giving opinions. Which certainly makes sense. Thus, it was not rare that the interview resembled an assembly, with comments being made by others present, some of whom would be leaving and others arriving, offering suggestions and corrections'. José de Souza Martins (1991) Regimar and her friends – children and their struggles for land and life, in José de Souza Martins (Ed.) *The Massacre of the Innocents. Children Without Infancy in Brasil*, Ch. 3, pp. 55-56. Sao Paulo: Editor HUCITEC.

[22] M. Gajardo (1988) Pesquisa participante: propostas e projetos, in C. R. Brandão, op. cit., p. 44.

[23] M. Thiollen (1988) Notas para o debate sobre pesquis-ação, in
   C. R. Brandão: ibid., p. 87 (my translation).

[24] Chaui: op. cit., p. 47 (my translation).

First published in *Educational Action Research*, Volume 2, Number 3, 1994

Changes in the Culture of Teaching and Learning and Implications for Action Research

PETER POSCH

Two Developments in Industrial Societies

The Complexity of Conditions of Life

One could say that the increasing complexity of brain functions allowed human beings to step out of animal life by becoming conscious of their ability to influence action and to gradually increase control over instincts. J.G. Herder, a German philosopher, created the metaphor of the 'the first freedman of creation' (der erste Freigelassene der Schöpfung).

In our millennium, in fact in the last three hundred years, the human capacity to access, store, process, use and communicate information has surrounded human kind with a rapidly increasing array of artificial 'cognitive limbs' and has created a new type of complexity; a complexity not only within each person (in terms of brain potentials), but also and perhaps primarily between people and their human-made environment, i.e. their artificial extensions of their anatomical outfit. The huge variety of artificial limbs and their manifold interactions with natural systems have created the complexity which we experience today. The effects and side-effects of this development become less and less foreseeable and controllable and have created a situation in which the enormous 'life potential' of economic and technological development is confronted with a growing 'death potential' (i.e. through global threats created by this development).

But this is not the only effect. Another significant effect of growing complexity is the decrease of problem-solving capacity of large socio-economic systems and centralised power structures. This is illustrated in tendencies to 'privatise' public services, to devolve responsibility for environmental quality, for social security, and even for safety to the

179

individual citizens. In the past, the ability and willingness to shape professional and public life has been limited to the élites in society, to politicians, entrepreneurs, academics, artists. Now, it seems that these competences and the values associated with them are demanded from more and more citizens.

Let me give you three simple illustrations from the emerging patterns of work:

> The proportion of human routine activities, i.e. of those activities for which the correct algorithm can be predetermined, is decreasing. They are being taken over by technical systems. As a result, the demands on professional qualification increase.
> The mutual dependence between hierarchical levels increases. As a result, cooperation in teams gains in importance.
> The heterogeneity of demands on the individual employee increases; more and more they comprise organisational, executive and supervisory tasks.

The Individualisation Process

Complexity and growing risks have been enforcing a decentralisation of initiative, responsibility and competences. One can assume that elements of power are only given up if through a given distribution of power it is no longer possible to keep the diversity of influences in society under control. So power is devolved inasmuch as this appears to be necessary in order to sustain power. The paradoxical character of this relationship indicates that this is not a linear process.

However, this process has enormously increased the interdependence of people. Paradoxically again, this interdependence can be seen as a primary force towards individualisation. The increasing diversity of demands provides more and more individuals with influence over others and through this process their potential 'value' increases.

There are phases in the devolution of power; at first, power is devolved to subcultures or lobbies if the centre is no longer able to control the emerging diversity. As more and more subcultures develop and/or the diversity within subcultures increases, the ability of the central power structure to provide safety and legitimation within this system again decreases. The social units that have to develop their own coping and adaptation strategies become smaller and smaller moving towards the smallest possible social unit, the individual.

There is little dispute about the global process of individualisation. For Sloterdijk (1993, p. 48) this is a late stage of human development, when 'cosmic singles' are populating bigger and bigger cities. According to Fend (1990, p. 50), 200 years after the Age of Enlightenment 'the right, duty and possibility to use one's mind without being led by somebody else, and to shape one's life at one's own terms is only now becoming a widely held claim and an emerging reality' (or in Frank Sinatra's words: 'to do it my way').

This individualisation process highlights a serious problem that has been described by game theory. Let me illustrate it with an example. Two players are involved in the same game. Let's assume that they are playing against a bank. Both have two strategies at their disposal: to defect and to cooperate. If both of them cooperate, they gain three points each for cooperation. If both defect, their gain is one point each. If one deserts and the other cooperates, the defector gets five points and the other nothing. What would be a rational behaviour in such a situation? The rational player would clearly choose to defect. This is the best choice if the partner cooperates. The gain is five points. But it is also the best choice if the partner defects. The gain is still one point and cooperation would bring nothing. Therefore both players will defect and receive one point. If both had cooperated each would have gained three points (Sigmund, 1992, p. 46).

This rather formal model is a variation of the prisoner's dilemma. It is not too difficult to illustrate by examples from everyday life. It may explain a widespread and puzzling attitude towards the environment. One's own environmentally sensitive ('cooperative') behaviour brings less comfort and has in many cases no advantage if all others do not care (i.e. if they 'defect'). On the other hand, one's own carelessness is very advantageous if the others behave in an environmentally sound way. As a result it is 'economical' to do both: to plead for an environmentally responsible behaviour of others and not to care about it in one's own behaviour. There is an interesting message in this example. If we start from the assumption that, in general, people do what they consider useful to them, one would expect defective rather than cooperative (i.e. morally defensible) behaviour. And this is actually what we get.

Challenges Schools will Face in the Future

Using these two sketches of ecological and social developments: what are some of the challenges schools will face in the future and which will demand answers in terms of changes in the culture of teaching and learning?

Challenge No. 1: negotiation of rules

No society can survive without rules and conventions. If established social structures lose some of their stability and legitimation, the rules have to be developed by negotiation. This process has started in many areas of life. An important example is provided by the socialisation of the young in their families. The authority relationships in families have dramatically changed during the past thirty or so years: what is allowed and not allowed is no longer a lone parental decision but is negotiated. With these experiences pupils come to school and are confronted with a culture of predefined demands and without space for negotiation. This clash of two 'cultures' appears to be the reason for many conflicts. Schools in general have not yet found ways to cope with a social development in which negotiation of rules and norms is gaining importance. How can they contribute to this process?

Challenge No. 2: social continuity

If traditional social networks lose stability and legitimation, the social continuity and social control are reduced. However, continuity of social relationships appears to be an indispensable condition for cooperative behaviour and social responsibility. This has also been illustrated by experiments in game theory. If a relationship is kept up for a longer time, the tendency to defect decreases and the mutual trust that is necessary for cooperation can develop (Sigmund, 1993). It is perceivable that one of the reasons for the apparently increasing violence in big cities has to do with the decline of continuity in society, which has accompanied the individualisation process. It has promoted the tendency to instrumentalise social relations in terms of short-term gains: to defect and not to cooperate. Can schools create situations in which the young experience continuity in social relationships and are shown that to cooperate is better than to defect?

Challenge No. 3: dynamic qualities

The growing complexity of public economic and private situations enforces a decentralisation of decision-making structures. This means that more and more individuals will have to be able to cope with unstructured situations, define problems, take positions and accept responsibility for them. As an example, the power of political authorities to change basic conditions of life such as the production and consumption of energy is increasingly dependent on individual initiatives in the population. Presently there is an incongruity between the diversity of influences young people feel subjected to and their own opportunity to exert influence. There appears to be a growing quest among the young to be taken seriously, to be able to influence their conditions of life and to leave traces in their environment. A quotation from a seemingly well educated skinhead in a radio report gives a vivid illustration of this hypothesis: 'I throw stones, ergo sum' in an interesting rephrasing of Descartes' statement on the nature of human existence, 'I think therefore I am'. There is a need for frameworks in which the young can contribute to shaping their environment in a responsible and constructive way and experience that they 'matter' in society.

These arguments provide a strong case for the promotion of dynamic qualities in the wider population. Can schools provide opportunities to the young to experience that they can make a difference?

Challenge No. 4: reflection and a critical approach to knowledge

Beck (1986, p. 35) has argued that the understanding of most risks in industrialised societies is transmitted by arguments. Consciousness of risks is theoretical or 'scientific' consciousness, because causal interpretations cannot be observed and are theories. As a result, the dependence on scientific knowledge has enormously increased; on the other hand, however, science is regarded also as a producer of risks and therefore tends to be met with increasing doubt and scepticism. This creates a paradoxical situation in which substantive knowledge becomes as important as a fundamental scepticism against whatever is offered as knowledge. It may imply that the definition of 'important knowledge' can no longer be left to traditional authorities only but must be established also by negotiation involving more and more peripheral and smaller social units. As a result, communication between these social units becomes important as different perspectives have to be dealt with and become a basis for establishing 'local truth'. 'Confidence shifts from confidence in contents – established rules, data, methods – to confidence in processes that allow us not to eliminate but to keep error under control' (Losito & Mayer, 1993, p. 72). Can schools provide opportunities to combine advocacy of knowledge with inquiry and to promote both an appreciative and critical stance towards knowledge?

Elements of a Culture of Teaching and Learning for the Future

The prevalent cultures of teaching and learning are still attuned to a relatively static society, in which the necessary knowledge, competences and values are predefined and stored in curricula, tests and accredited textbooks. Schools are expected to prepare the majority of children and young people to meet satisfactorily the demands others have defined for them. The main characteristics of this culture are as follows:

> *A predominance of systematic knowledge.* Priority is given to well-established facts, allowing schools to maintain a close relationship with the results of academic knowledge production. Low priority is given to open and controversial areas of knowledge and to personal experience and involvement.
>
> *Specialisation.* Knowledge is compartmentalised in subject matter fields which more or less correspond to the academic disciplines. This again facilitates an orientation towards established standards of quality and gives teaching and learning a clear and predictable

structure. On the other hand, complex, real-life situations tend to be disregarded because they cross the disciplinary boundaries.

A transmission-mode of teaching. This mode facilitates the retention of the systematic character of knowledge and its reconstruction by the student. It tends to discourage the generation and reflective handling of knowledge.

A prevalence of top-down communication. This facilitates the external control of pre-defined knowledge structures, provides stable frame conditions, and facilitates the maintenance of control in the classroom. However, it discourages self-control and cooperation among students (or teachers) and networking within and across school boundaries.

These few arguments indicate an important and difficult feature of the culture of teaching and learning in the future. This culture will have to comprise contraries. It will have to retain the strengths of static elements and will have to complement them with dynamic ones. The balance of the two will have to shift if schools attempt to find answers to the social changes presently occurring. What are some of the dimensions of a learning culture of the future? Let me give you a few examples which are still compatible with present infrastructural possibilities.

In a school in Austria, one day a week in a class of 11th grade students was declared as project day. Three subjects provided the necessary curricular time: chemistry (one hour), social science and religious education (2 hours each). The issues and patterns of work for each of these days were decided upon by a steering group of students of this class together with the teachers of the three subjects. Some of the issues identified were: communication, a child is born, the environment, science and research, being handicapped, etc.

The procedures consisted of visits, e.g. to the university or to a home for the handicapped, of invited lectures, readings, workshops prepared by students of the steering group for their colleagues, etc. For each two or three issues a newspaper was produced in which major findings, experiences and reflections were documented. Through the year each student of the class participated at least once in the planning activities of the steering group. The basic idea of the whole exercise was to gain understanding and substantial knowledge on salient themes as perceived by the students (Rauscher, 1986).

In this example students are confronted with situations which are not entirely prestructured but have open spaces. They get the opportunity to decide certain things on their own. Work on this project day is not assessed by the teachers for grades. Quality control is provided by the students themselves in their reflections on the process.

In a school in Scotland a student group carried out an environmental audit in their own school to find out about strengths and weaknesses and provide a basis for action. In another Scottish school students were involved in several investigations on 'Travel, Tourism, Transportation and Tipping' and results were made public through exhibitions and weekly articles in a local newspaper (McAndrew & Pascoe, 1993, pp. 23, 33).

In both examples 'local knowledge' was produced which had not been available so far and which was considered useful for a specific audience. A final example shows still another dimension (Axelsson, 1993, p. 42): all teachers and students of Pårydskolan in Sweden have taken up challenges in their own vicinity and reserved two hours per week for environmental projects. They started from their own interests and from requests from outside. A parent, e.g., had ponds that were now overgrown with trees and plants – could the school help them with these? The school now has fish breeding in the ponds. Similar initiatives resulted in a shop in which the school sells environmentally friendly detergents, in a green house, and in the restoration of a water mill. Some of these initiatives involved hard work. If it turned out too hard for students to do themselves, parents came to the school on Saturdays to help:

> *This school has managed what so many schools envy them for:*
> *it has become the centre in a small village ... People also come*
> *to school asking for help about ponds, about acid water in*
> *their wells and about different environmental issues. The*
> *school is a place where knowledge is to be found. (Axelsson,*
> *p. 43)*

In this example an additional dimension is illustrated. Students are able to leave traces in their environment. They can participate in shaping some of the conditions in which they live and experience that what they do is not only aimed at competences to be utilised in the future but is making a difference here and now.

In these examples the concept of learning is extended: the dominant paradigm of learning is based on the classical separation of knowledge and action and on the hope that transmission of knowledge will enable students to act responsibly in the future. An extended concept of learning views learning also as a process of joint seeking, joint experimenting and joint construction of reality. On a more fundamental level, it affects the structure of exchange processes at the heart of education (cf. Elliott & Rice, 1990). As a 15-year-old student put it: 'To prepare for life means to do something now' (Mair, 1990, p. 9).

What Does this Mean for Action Research?

Teachers and students who leave the 'stable state' (Donald Schön) of systematic knowledge transmission and involve themselves in school initiatives of this kind have to cope with open-ended, uncertain, unpredictable, sometimes contradictory situations entailing risks. In situations of this kind, teachers are often unable to control the teaching and learning process alone but have to rely on their students' capacity for self-organisation. As a consequence, an interest in negotiating work with students develops. Often, competences in other subject matter fields are needed. As a result an interest in communication and interdisciplinary cooperation develops. If teachers involve themselves in initiatives of this kind, they become highly dependent on the flexibility of infrastructural conditions for their work, such as curriculum, time budget, use of space and school facilities, materials, etc. So an interest emerges in influencing the regulations determining the structures of work in school. Finally, in many cases, these teachers need the cooperation of persons and institutions outside school. As a result, an interest develops in building networks of communication with other parties and to cross the boundaries between school and environment (Posch, 1994).

These types of interests arising from characteristics of the teachers' work are likely to be a breeding ground for action research. In these contexts, systematic individual and collaborative reflection on action and communication about the knowledge that has been generated appears to be a 'natural' means to realise the values of teachers and students (Altrichter et al, 1993). At present, action research is in most cases an element of externally-led courses promoting teachers' career interests or an ingredient of externally stimulated research projects. If schools move towards a more dynamic culture of teaching and learning action research will become less dependent on these external structures but will more and more become a necessary correlate of what teachers and students want to do.

It is, I believe, not a coincidence that Stenhouse's idea of the 'teacher as researcher' developed in the framework of the Humanities Curriculum Project (Stenhouse, 1975, p. 49). In a curriculum based on the discussion of controversial issues with the teacher as neutral chair-person, open spaces are created and teacher control is reduced. In such a context 'reflective conversations' (D. Schön) with lowly structured situations become imperative not only to keep risks under control but also continually to create understanding as a basis for action.

In the meantime the social pressures on schools to allow students to experience and to create meaning have increased – even if they are not in line with present governmental policy as it appears to be the case in England. As a result, Stenhouse's view of 'extended professionalism' becomes even more relevant than it was in his time: 'The concern to question and to test theory in practice as a basis for development' (Stenhouse, 1975, p. 144). These challenges are probably the main reasons why action research is becoming an international movement.

Traditionally, schools are the recipients of demands from power structures in society. In the future it will be necessary for students and teachers also to express and realise their views of the society they want to live in. Action research is in a sense only another word for this.

References

Altrichter, Herbert, Posch, Peter & Somekh, Bridget (1993) *Teachers Investigate their Work: an introduction to the methods of action research*. London: Routledge.

Axelsson, Harriet (1993) *Environment and School Initiatives – ENSI*. Göteborg: University of Göteborg Department of Education and Educational Research, Report No. 1993-01.

Beck, Ulrich (1986) *Risikogesellschaft – Auf dem Weg in eine andere Moderne*. Frankfurt: Suhrkamp.

Elliott, John (1991) Environmental Education in Europe: innovation, marginalisation or assimilation, in OECD/CERI: *Environment, Schools and Active Learning*, pp. 19-39. Paris: OECD/CERI.

Elliott, J. & Rice, J. (1990) The Relationship Between Disciplinary Knowledge and Situational Understanding in the Development of Environmental Awareness, in Maarten Peters (Ed.) *Teaching for Sustainable Development: report on a workshop at Veldhoven-Netherlands, 23rd-25th April 1990*, pp. 66-72. Enschede: Institute for Curriculum Development.

Fend, Helmut (1990) Bildungskonzepte und Lebensfelder Jugendlicher im sozialhistorischen Wandel, in Leo Leitner (Ed.) *Wie öffnet sich die Schule neuen Entwicklungen und Aufgaben?*, pp. 42-66. Wien: Bundesverlag.

Losito, Bruno & Mayer, Michela (1993) *Environmental Education and Educational Innovation: Italian national report on ENSI research*. Frascati: Centro Europeo del Educazione.

Mair, G. (1990) Lernen durch Handeln in Projekten: Schülerinnen beeinflussen die kommunale Umweltpolitik. Bundesarbeitsgemeinschaft Bildung & Die Grünen (Ed.) *Forum zur ökologischen Bildung vom 14-15 September 1990 in Mimberg*, pp. 8-10. Berlin: BAG Bildung/Die Grünen.

McAndrew, Colin & Pascoe, Ian P. (1993) *Environment and School Initiatives (ENSI) Project in Scotland. The National Report: case studies in environmental education*. Dundee: Scottish Consultative Council on the Curriculum.

Posch, Peter (1994) Networking in Environmental Education, in M. Pettigrew & B. Somekh (Eds) *Evaluation and Innovation in Environmental Education*. Paris: OECD/CERI.

Rauscher, Erwin (1986) PRODO – Ein projektorientierter Unterricht stellt sich vor, *Erziehung und Unterricht*, 4, pp. 242-249.

Sigmund, Karl (1993) Spiel und Biologie: Vom Mitspielen zur Zusammenarbeit, in Hans-Christian Reichel & Enrique Prat de la Riba (Eds) *Naturwissenschaft und Weltbild: Mathematik und Quantenphysik in unserem Denk- und Wertesystem*, pp. 45-58. Wien: Hölder-Pichler-Tempsky.

Sloterdijk, Peter (1993) *Im selben Boot*. Frankfurt: Suhrkamp.

Peter Posch

Stenhouse, Lawrence (1975) *An Introduction to Curriculum Research and Development*. London: Heinemann.

Thonhauser, Josef, Moosbrugger, Marina & Rauch, Franz (1994) *Evaluation of the Austrian Environment and School Initiatives Project*. Research Report commissioned by the Institute for Interdisciplinary Research and Continuing Education, Salzburg.

First published in *Educational Action Research*, Volume 2, Number 2, 1994

Thai Buddhist Philosophy and the Action Research Process

ARPHORN CHUAPRAPAISILP

While some aspects of Thai culture may be seen to inhibit the action research process, other aspects have the potential to assist it. Traditional aspects of culture can be particularly important when emancipatory modes of research are contemplated. When the participants in an action research study not only have their Thai culture to draw upon, but also have a strong background in Buddhism, there are possibilities for heightening the reflective stages of the action cycle through meditation, developing a 'mindfulness' which is akin to the western notion of 'consciousness raising' and using the Mandala Wheel to add a Buddhist dimension to studies of cause and effect. This leads to an examination of 'dependent origination', the Buddhist Law of Conditionality.

There have been criticisms of the effectiveness of action research in that it depends more on personal and interpersonal factors than methodological factors (Reason & Rowen, 1981). The model (see Figure 1) outlined here helps individuals to overcome personal limitations by developing mindfulness (Satipatthana). Since mindfulness helps to free the mind from self-confusion and bias, the individual is able to focus more on the method than on personal factors. In this way, the introduction of a specific Buddhist method would enhance the actual process of action research.

This model, which arose from an original study in a nursing context (Chuaprapaisilp, 1991), is a spiral of action research based on Buddhist culture. It is a modification of the action research spiral developed by Kemmis & McTaggart (1988) highlighting the importance of Buddhist culture to participants in the study. The central theme of this model is 'Satipatthana'. 'Satipatthana' (Sati = mindfulness, Panthana = cultivating, developing) is a Buddhist technical term which means the 'foundation of mindfulness' (Khantipalo, 1981). The foundation of mindfulness is to be actively aware of the present moment. Mindfulness is also the state of mind which represents full awareness of present actions, feelings, state of the mind, and truth. *Satipatthana* is similar to what Fay (1987) called 'consciousness raising') in developing critical thinkers. *Satipatthana* can be developed through meditation and is a cause for the arising of self-awareness and wisdom.

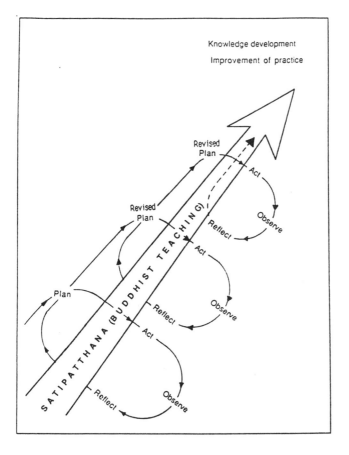

Figure 1. Action research spiral based on Buddhist culture.

This can be explained through the process of *Samatha* and *Vipassana* meditations. *Samatha* meditation leads to a state of relaxation and concentration where you focus on only one thing and are able to block out distractions. *Vipassana* meditation follows *Samatha* meditation and includes the process of contemplation of four foundations of mindfulness: contemplating the body/daily activities, *Kayanupassana*), the feelings (*Vadananupassana*), the state of the mind consciousness (*Cittanupassana*) and the mental objects (*Dhammanupassana*) which are in turn divided into five categories: hindrances, bases, aggregates, factors of enlightenment and truths (Sujiva, 1991). Contemplation of the four foundations of mindfulness leads to the emancipation of the mind and understanding of truth. In this state, the mind becomes calm, clear and unbiased, you can see things 'as they really are'. Then reflective skills are heightened further, leading to insight and wisdom. This Buddhist teaching complements the action research process (plan, act and observe, reflect and revise plan), and thereby enhances knowledge development and improvement of practice.

At this level connections can be made between Buddhist teaching, the reflection stage of the action research cycle and concepts such as emancipation. According to Samyutta Nikava (Ajahn Brahmavamso, 1991; cited in *Forest Sangha Newsletter* by the kind permission of the Pali Text Society):

> *Concentration is the supporting condition for the knowledge and vision of things as they really are,*
> *The knowledge and vision of things as they really are is the supporting condition for disenchantment,*
> *Disenchantment is the supporting condition for dispassion,*
> *Dispassion is the supporting condition for emancipation,*
> *Emancipation is the supporting condition for knowledge of the destruction of the most deeply rooted obstructive habits (asavas).*
> *(Samyutta Nikaya 2, 29)*

The above formulation of linking factors shows the link by which one can develop (or purify) the mind to gain freedom from confusion and bias, to attain wisdom and enlightenment. This state of the mind (i.e. mindfulness) helps us to overcome what Marxist philosophy calls 'false consciousness' and to see things as they really are. thus, mindfulness is the way in which we gain insight and enlightenment since it enhances understanding and eliminates confusion through the attainment of a penetrating wisdom. It is the personal knowledge that one must practise (through meditation) to gain the results (i.e. understanding).

Through *Vipassana* meditation, individuals are able to achieve emancipation at a personal level. A distinction should be made here between the forms of group emancipation which are mentioned in the literature on action research and individual forms. However, forms of collaborative consciousness associated with emancipatory action research are more likely to occur when participants have refined their individual skills are then able to apply them in a group situation.

The benefits of meditation are not only recognised by those following an Eastern philosophy, but also by researchers in the west. In recent times, significant research has been carried out by Wallace (1991) on the 'neurophysiology of enlightenment', showing how Transcendental Meditation transforms the human body. For health care workers using action research there are double benefits. Not only can meditation help them in their research, but it can also be used by patients and researchers alike to improve their own health. Worth mentioning here are the works of Simonton (1994) and Gowler (1992).

The Buddhist Mandala Wheel and Action Research

One aim of action research is to learn from experience. Action research is already familiar, but to non-Buddhist readers and researchers it may now be helpful to provide details on the philosophy's underlying beliefs. What do we mean by Dependent Origination and what is the link with the Mandala Wheel? How can Dependent Origination be interpreted? What are the implications for practising Buddhists involved in action research?

The notion of Dependent Origination, or the Buddhist Law of Conditionality, is well described by Payutto (1994). Payutto's translator, Bruce Evans, argues that the principle of Dependent Origination is one of the most profound and intellectually intriguing of all the Buddha's teachings. Payutto argues that the teaching of causal interdependence is the most important of the Buddhist principles, describing the law of nature. the progression of causes and conditions is the reality which applies to all things. It includes the natural environment which is an external physical condition, and also the events of human society, ethical principles, life events, happiness and suffering, which are all manifest in our minds. As all things are seen to be interconnected, and all tend to affect one another, success in dealing with the world depends on creating harmony with it. The Mandala Wheel is a symbol showing how, as in action research, all things are connected.

There are two significant interpretations of the Buddhist Law of Conditionality. One involves a process of moving from lifetime to lifetime. The other is a more immediate process, occurring in the space of moments of consciousness (from moment to moment). The former may be of more significance when we consider action research as a vehicle for long-term personal and professional development, while the latter may be of more significance when we are working within one phase of an action cycle. Whether we interpret 'Dependent Origination' as covering many lifetimes or occurring in one mind moment, we are dealing with matters beyond normal perception.

The main implication for practising Buddhists is that they can bring techniques from meditation to be applied in the reflection process of action research. In addition, the main purpose of the Buddha's teaching is to overcome suffering, and similarly the purpose of action research is to overcome the contradictions and suffering of participants' practice. Furthermore, when Buddhism and action research are operating in harmony or unison, happiness and 'loving-kindness' ('*Metta*') are consistently in evidence, which results in the spontaneous conducting of action research to achieve the desired outcome. In this process every factor of the situation is integrated harmoniously, like the Mandala Wheel that moves forward together with reflection from the past to improve the present practice and plan for the future, so that the results will be successful and appropriate.

Conclusions

Buddhism thus provides a world view and a set of insights which may help participants to view events in a highly perceptive manner. This world view is likely to produce results which are very different to those experienced in a western non-Buddhist setting. Those Thai practitioners who are experienced in *Vipassana* meditation may be well placed to apply their reflective skills to an enhancement of the action research process and work is currently in progress to explore the practical implications of the ideas presented in this outline.

References

Ajahn Brahmavamso (1991) Samatha Meditation, *Forest Sangha Newsletter*, Amaravati Buddhist Centre, England, October 4-6.

Chuaprapaisilp, A. (1991) Improving Learning from Experience: action research in nursing education in Thailand, in C. Colins & P. Chippendale (Eds) *Proceedings of the First World congress on Action Research and Process Management*, Vol. 2, pp. 43-56. Brisbane: Association for Action Learning, Action Research and Process Management.

Fay, B. (1987) *Critical Social Science: liberation and its limits*. Cambridge: Polity Press.

Gowler, I. (1992) *You Can Conquer Cancer*. Melbourne: Hill of Content.

Kemmis, S. & McTaggart, R. (1988) *The Action Research Planner*, 3rd Edn. Geelong: Deakin University Press.

Khantipalo, Bhikku (1981) *Calm and Insight: a Buddhist manual for meditations*. London: Curzon Press.

Payutto, P.A. (1994) *Dependent Origination: the Buddhist Law of Conditionality*. Bangkok: Buddhadhamma Foundation.

Reason, P. & Rowan, J. (1981) *Human Inquiry: a source of a new paradigm research*. London: Wiley.

Simnton, O.C., Henson, R.M. & Hamton, B. (1994) *The Healing Journey*. New York: Bantam Books.

Sujiva, Venerable (1991) *A Pragmatic Approach to the Practice of Vipassana Meditation*. Petaling Jaya: Buddhist Centre.

Wallace, R.K. (1991) *The Neurophysiology of Enlightenment*. Fairfield: Maharishi International University.

First published in *Educational Action Research*, Volume 5, Number 2, 1997

PART 4

Action Research
in Practice Settings

Three of the articles in this final part describe action research in contrasting professional settings, social work, teaching and nursing. The fourth discusses the particular value for action research that is created when people from different professional settings share their understandings, their conceptual frameworks and their experiences.

The article by Angie Titchen & Alison Binnie is a methodological paper from a long-term and highly influential study illustrating the methods and principles of action research in the context of hospital nursing. The project was concerned with developing 'patient-centred' nursing, i.e. a move from a conception of nursing dictated by centralised routines (for which the ward sister retained responsibility) to a model in which responsibility for nursing care was devolved to staff nurses, and where the emphasis would be on preserving continuity in the caring relationship. The principles for 'patient-centred care' are described by Titchen & Binnie as 'individualistic, holistic and humanistic'. One of the most interesting aspects of the work is that it focuses very centrally on the facilitative and mutually educative relationship between the two authors. And yet its overall emphasis is on the nature of all the relationships within an action research process, not only between the collaborating initiators but also the relationships between nurses, and between nurses and patients. This emphasis on the general form of action research relationships as one which was equally applicable to the research process and to the practice relationship between professional and client (or 'patient' or 'student') was later summed up in Angie Titchen's eloquent phrase 'critical companionship' (see Higgs & Titchen, 2001), which has a powerful and general resonance for action research in general, as a mode of intervention in social affairs.

A similar theme is found in Carol Munn-Giddings's complex and wide-ranging article, which argues explicitly that the collaborative and reflexive relationships required by action research are also those required by social work practice committed to the empowerment of clients. The first stage of her argument is unusual in the action research literature in that it starts from the author's experience of undertaking qualitative observational and analytical work in the role of 'expert researcher'. Her conclusion is that such work is much better undertaken by practitioners themselves, if there is to be much chance of acting on any of the findings. She goes on to argue that the skills required by social research are those which are both required and fostered by the experience of social care:

> *Many of the skills involved in semi-structured interviewing,*
> *group discussions and, in particular, participant observation,*
> *are those which in many cases would be developed and*
> *expressed by a committed and sensitive practitioner ... A good*
> *social practitioner should always be both participator and*
> *observer, continually checking out their clients' understanding*
> *of events and their actions, and the practitioner's own*
> *understanding of the situation and their actions, and it is that*
> *reflection on their practice which enables its development.*
> *Research then becomes a highly relevant possibility even for*
> *busy social care practitioners.*

Her conclusion is twofold. First, action research could and should aspire to develop 'a methodology as akin to practice as possible'. Second, 'the research process itself can be seen as a positive, empowering way in which to work with and for clients'. Social work staff will find this article to be a helpful articulation of action research as a key strategy for bridging the gap between official policies and the individual relationships of social care.

Pete Strauss's article 'No Easy Answers: the dilemmas and challenges of teacher research' is an eloquent account of a teacher's journey of personal learning and insight through action research. He begins by explaining how listening to tape-recordings of his own work with children helped him to recognise the gap between his own espoused ideals of open interaction and the residual prescriptiveness of his actual practice. He goes on to describe the feelings of pain and even despair that this engendered, and then provides us with several moving extracts from his personal reflective diary that he used as a method of moving his thinking forward in response to the difficulties that his action research had begun to make explicit. This powerful article focuses on action research as an individual practitioner's self-questioning, but at its heart is an ideal of re-creating professional workers' relationship with those for whose wellbeing they are responsible, in terms of a mutually empowering and educative process. In this sense it has much in common with the two previous articles in this section.

These three articles all describe action research undertaken in professionally specific areas. However, important initiatives are under way which emphasise the need for collaborative working between staff of different professions, if the needs of clients (children, students with difficulties, families with problems, etc.) are to be addressed more effectively. It is this aspect of the current professional scene that is specifically discussed in the important article by Belinda Watts & Shirley Jones with which this section concludes. Their basic argument is that action research processes may be essential if the barriers created by different professional ideologies are to be transcended. Conversely, action research methodology in general may be able to learn from the processes developed through attempts at inter-professional collaboration. Thus, in an ingenious tabular presentation they present a variety of different intellectual and interpersonal processes that are equally applicable in considering what is needed for success when one is aiming to *explore* and *develop* practice and when one is negotiating the sharing of roles with staff from 'adjacent' professions in reinforcing a focus on client need. Their list is challenging and suggestive, including, for example: recognition and acceptance of multiple realities, working through conflict, re-framing problems, pluralism and reflexivity, risk-taking, deriving power from knowledge rather than status, value clarification. A testament both to the scope and the optimism of action research's general philosophy.

Reference

Higgs, J. & Titchen, A. (Eds) (2001) *Practice, Knowledge and Expertise in the Health Professions*. Oxford: Butterworth Heinemann.

A Unified Action Research Strategy in Nursing

ANGIE TITCHEN & ALISON BINNIE

Background

We are engaged in a four-year action research study of the development of patient-centred nursing in the medical unit of an acute hospital. Early in 1989, one of us (Alison Binnie, a senior sister at the John Radcliffe Hospital) successfully approached the National Institute for Nursing, Oxford, to propose setting up a collaborative study. Angie Titchen was appointed by the Institute in May 1989 as the project researcher. We developed the complementary roles of 'actor', in the form of a change agent/facilitator role, and 'researcher', both within a collaborative partnership. Alison was mainly an 'actor', whilst Angie was mainly a 'researcher'. Over time, we have developed and refined our complementary way of working, fine-tuning our relationship within our practice and our research, becoming what we now see as an effective 'double-act' (Titchen & Binnie, 1992).

The project, entitled 'Patient-centred Nursing in Practice', was designed to help the nurses on two study wards to move gradually from traditional nursing to patient-centred nursing, using the work organisation method of primary nursing. The major focus of the study is the unravelling of the complex organisational, personal and professional changes required for such a practice shift. The aim is to provide UK nurses with a 'map' of the processes involved and to point to the kinds of strategy that are likely to be effective in achieving the change.

Primary nursing is a system that devolves to a staff nurse the authority to manage the nursing care of a small group of patients from admission to discharge. Continuity of care allows nurses to practise in patient- and family-centred ways, through the development of close therapeutic relationships. Humanistic values underpin these relationships and care is given in an individualised and holistic way. This style of nursing is a major departure from traditional practice which is governed by standardised routines and procedures and where authority for key decisions about patient care rests with the sister.

Our Action Research Strategy

The eclectic nature of our approach arose because we were trying to achieve a variety of goals. We therefore developed several different, but interconnected strategies (which were used in parallel) for:

> introducing innovation and facilitating change;
> helping practitioners research their own practice;
> facilitating professional learning and reflective practice;
> democratising health care through the emancipation of nurses from the nursing hierarchy and the traditional role of doctor's handmaiden;
> generating and testing theory.

Although these strategies are generally seen as quite separate, we saw them as connected or unified in various ways. For example, we felt that if we could help the nurses and sisters to research their own practice and innovations, and thereby generate and test theory, they would inevitably develop personally and professionally, as they learned to think critically, analytically and reflectively. We anticipated that a bottom-up change strategy would help nurses to empower themselves and raise their self-esteem. The creation of new roles and a new work organisation design would also mean that nurses would have to learn to think and act in new ways – thus organisational change could lead to personal and professional learning. Moreover, researching or reflecting upon their own practice would help nurses to articulate their unique contribution to health care and might, therefore, help nurses to enter into more collegiate relationships with doctors because their own roles were clearer. We found support for the notion that action research unifies quite distinct activities in the educational field (Elliott, 1991).

Introducing Innovation and Facilitating Change

Our investigation centred around practitioners' perceived needs to change the cultural norms and values in their ward settings. Our strategy involved not only addressing problems and issues identified by ourselves as the change proceeded, but also the problems identified by the nurses. We studied our effectiveness as change agents and facilitators in:

> establishing a felt need for change;
> devising and facilitating a bottom-up change strategy;
> developing appropriate structures for patient-centred nursing;
> providing support;
> creating a non-judgemental climate where creativity is fostered;

feeding back data;

helping people to look critically at what was happening to them/what they were doing;

disseminating information/sharing ideas about the change;

facilitating communication and clearing up misunderstandings/ misinformation.

In addition, we helped some of the sisters to become change agents, facilitating innovations on their wards. The staff nurses in Alison's wards found that the project helped them to innovate and improve practice because it enabled them to reflect upon and evaluate their work. They found the experience of being asked open questions about their practice and being fed back data on their actions particularly helpful. Several staff nurses also became key change agents in the ward.

At the outset of the work, we recognised the potential value of some kind of theoretical framework to help us in three areas. First, we needed a framework to guide us through the complexities of facilitating organisational changes; second, to help us to understand the actors' experiences of the change; and third to help us recognise when the nurses were practising in the new patient-centred way.

Taking the first area, there is a huge literature, both theoretical and empirical, on the management and facilitation of organisational and professional change with which we are familiar and which we used in the project, as actors or change agents. Our actions, therefore, could be considered to be 'ideas-in-action', with ideas drawn from the literature, our own data and our personal knowledge and experience. In other words, our actions in managing and facilitating the change were theoretically informed; we were using a theoretical framework. However, very little is known about the other two areas – the experiences of the actors in this particular change and the nature and characteristics of patient-centred nursing. In relation to patient-centred nursing, we initially developed a theoretical framework derived from the literature on primary nursing and from our personal experiences, but we rejected this framework, eventually, on the grounds that much of the empirical work is methodologically flawed. We decided, therefore, not to develop, at the outset, theoretical frameworks for our study in these two areas, but to suspend our personal theoretical understandings until later in the field work. We doubt whether it is possible to achieve an entirely 'atheoretical' position, but we attempted to suspend or 'bracket' (Schutz, 1962) our personal theoretical understandings by making them explicit and by Angie adopting the role of 'stranger' who goes into the situation, naively, and without preconceptions of what will be found. Success, or otherwise, at 'bracketing' was monitored and recorded (Titchen & McIntyre, 1993).

Practitioner-as-Researcher

The notion of the practitioner-as-researcher is well described in the educational literature. It has also been described as an ideological movement aimed to bring about a democratisation of educational research, with a move away from the assumption that only academics are legitimate generators of knowledge, towards a situation where it is acceptable for practitioners to research their own practice. Carr & Kemmis (1986) suggest that the notion of the practitioner-as-researcher became popular at a time when teachers were developing professionalised roles and seeking opportunities to establish a research role in which they investigate their own practice. This kind of research was seen as more useful and relevant to practice than that carried out by outside researchers and academics. Teachers had also adopted the 'accountability movement' which required a self-monitoring to justify practice and to critique the contexts in which practice is conducted.

The current nursing climate is very similar to the one described by Carr & Kemmis. Nurses are seeking professionalised roles (for example, the primary nurse role) in which individuals are accountable for, and have to justify, their own practice. Research carried out by academic nurse researchers has sometimes been seen as irrelevant for practitioners, although MacGuire (1990) states that there is little research evidence to support this claim. We considered that the adoption of the practitioner-as-researcher strategy would provide a means of personal and professional development, through the process of self-monitoring, and would generate knowledge that would be relevant to practice.

Facilitating Professional Learning

From the literature and from our different experiences of promoting innovations in health care, we knew that the change we were anticipating would require considerable personal and professional development of the nurses. They would need to develop new roles and relationships and, to be able to fulfil their new obligations and responsibilities, deepen or refine existing skills and develop new ones. We saw the action research process as a way to help people to learn – either as researchers or as reflective practitioners.

We helped the nurses to learn by creating opportunities or seizing unexpected ones and by creating a conducive climate. Specific behaviours we adopted were being sensitive to nurses' readiness to learn, making our own values explicit and valuing the nurses' contributions to the development. We used a variety of learning processes, including working with individuals and groups, role-modelling and acknowledging effort and progress. In addition, we built time into the working day for reflection and theorisation of practice and we made a conscious effort to articulate our own theorisations of practice experiences.

The idea that action research must be educational, in itself, has emerged recently in the literature. It is argued that it must help people to make sense of their everyday practice (McNiff, 1988). Action research improves practice by 'developing a practitioner's capacity for discrimination and judgement in particular, complex, human situations' (Elliott, 1991) and helps practitioners to make sense of the social, historical and political content of their work situations. We attempted to create opportunities where the nurses could examine their personal and social assumptions and values. We helped them to look for contradictions and inconsistencies between their espoused values and the values that had shaped the context in which they worked. We hoped that their enhanced understanding of the situation, through seeking explanations for any contradictions and inconsistencies, would enable them to formulate strategies for improvement (O'Hanlon, 1988).

Empowerment and Democratisation

Traditionally, nurses at the bedside were oppressed by a rigid, bureaucratic nursing hierarchy, which meant that they had very little control over their working lives. The traditional, oppressive 'hand-maiden' role of nurses had also trapped them in an unequal power relationship with doctors. We considered that an environment where nurses could empower themselves might be best achieved by helping the sisters in the medical unit and the staff nurses in Alison's wards to work with us in the kind of way described by Kemmis and his colleagues (Carr & Kemmis, 1986; Kemmis & McTaggart, 1988), that is, as a group of practitioners who question the relationship between the actual and the possible in nursing and embark on a 'critical project' or 'struggle for reform'.

Early in the work, we invited the sisters to join us as co-action researchers (as described by Kemmis & McTaggart, 1988). However, although the sisters were supportive, interested and collaborated with the work (by acting as informants when we were collecting data on the effects of our actions and by carrying out action they had planned with our facilitation), it was always seen as 'Alison and Angie's project'. They did not see it as their own. We now realise that this outcome was probably inevitable, because the project was not set up with this strategy in mind and so the sisters were not involved in the project proposal. Our advice to others who wish to develop a Kemmis & McTaggart co-action researcher model is that the group needs to be involved from the very beginning.

We were, however, very successful in facilitating a different kind of collaborative group model of action research, where sisters and staff nurses became reflective practitioners and change agents (Titchen & Binnie, 1993). In addition, two staff nurses became researchers in an observational study of their colleagues' views and experiences of a new assessment and care planning strategy, developed by Alison during the project (we call them researchers rather than action researchers because they were not exploring the effects of their own actions). These various experiences, not available in everyday nursing life, provided insights and skills which contributed to the growth of confidence and maturity, already beginning to transform the nurses' working relationships with health professional and medical colleagues and their control over their work.

Theory Generation and Testing

We used action research as a strategy for generating and testing theory and, in retrospect, we were able to see that we operated within the following research criteria:

1. Theoretical understandings of the substantive area are initially suspended.

2. Observational studies are used for the generation of theory.

3. In the observational studies, general, open questions are asked to get at the actors' perspectives (to begin to generate theory about appropriate actions to achieve certain goals).

4. Action hypotheses are generated from the data collected in the observational study for testing in the field (i.e. in situations of type X, strategies of type Y will achieve goals of type Z).

5. Theoretical understandings guide one's action planning and carrying out of the action.

6. Questions are generated to determine the effectiveness of achieving the goals.

7. Data are collected on the actions and their effects.

8. Theoretical sampling of people and situations is carried out.

9. An attempt is made to theorise and generalise findings – we used three methods:

(i) providing readers with a rich description, interpretation and explanation of the situation, they are able to make judgements about whether the findings of our specific case are relevant to their particular situations because our rich description invites them to say, 'This is like my situation' or not;
(ii) drawing on substantive social science theory and existing empirical data where relevant;
(iii) establishing abstractions and generalisations across individual cases. Brown & McIntyre (1988) assert that such 'generalisations are better

described as naturalistic and as forming hypotheses to be carried from one case to the next rather than as general laws applying across a population'. These generalisations together create a provisional theoretical framework to make explicit the participants' experiences of the processes, strategies and outcomes of change.

10. Findings and theorisation are laid open to public scrutiny.

We found the formal action research schemes in the literature (Ebbutt, 1985; Kemmis & McTaggart, 1988; Elliott, 1991) to be lacking, in that they tend to under-emphasise the observational studies which are essential for theory generation. Both Elliott and Ebbutt recognise that the Kemmis & McTaggart scheme does not allow for observational studies to take place after the initial reconnaisance, and they have built, at intervals, such studies into their schemes. On the other hand, Brown & McIntyre (1981) suggest that theory generation, through action research, should be based not only on prior observational research in which a theoretical analysis of the situation is carried out, but should also be combined with an explicit ignorance of some of the problems that might arise during the action. This position implies a continuing development of the exploratory observational research, running in parallel with the action and its outcomes.

We built on Brown & McIntyre's (1981) ideas and asked open questions when trying to understand the situation we were aiming to change, the changed situation itself, and the actors' experience of change. Our questions were more focussed when we were trying to establish whether our actions had been effective. We were, therefore, generating and testing theory simultaneously. The following is one of our action hypotheses:

> When Alison works as a full-time team member, if she makes explicit why she is there, i.e. not to check up on the nurses, but to facilitate their learning and act as a resource for them, then the nurses will see her presence as useful, rather than showing them up by unfavourable comparisons.

While gathering evidence to test this hypothesis, we were also asking open questions about the staff nurses' experiences of Alison working on the ward. Data generated from the open questions enabled us to gain a better understanding of the ways of achieving certain goals (theory generation), it also helped us to develop a better hypothesis next time round for theory testing.

In a discussion of how we developed this strategy, we had the following conversation:

> *AT: At first, we didn't see ourselves as generating action hypotheses, we simply identified the practical goals we wished to achieve and then investigated the means by which the goals*

*could be attained, that is, the change strategies and processes.
Thinking in retrospect now, we were aware that there may be a
number of means of achieving the goal and that we had
hypothesised, in a crude way, that one particular way would
work. If it didn't work, we moved on to the next hypothesis,
until we were in a position to refine a hypothesis which was
grounded in the data. I only made our research criteria
explicit half way through the fieldwork, after discussions with
Donald McIntyre. Alison, what was your reaction when I first
put them to you?*

*AB: My initial reaction was, 'I'm not doing that. It just feels
like a lot of long words'. However, when we started to use the
criteria, I felt that they made sense and that it would have
been helpful to have had them earlier to guide our action and
research.*

*AT: As mainly responsible for data collection, I felt guilty that
I had not made the criteria explicit at an earlier stage. The
only reasons that I can offer are that we took our research
knowledge for granted and that explicit articulations of theory
generation and testing in action research have not been well-
documented – the notable exception being the paper by Brown
& McIntyre (1981). At that time, what we were doing just felt
like common sense – we were using tacit knowledge gained
from our previous research.*

*AB: Yes. I think what has happened since is a process of
making our tacit knowledge of research explicit.*

Conclusion

In this article, we have outlined our collaborative action research
strategy, with its five distinct activities. First, we conclude that the
activities, although distinct, are unified. Our strategy helped
practitioners to empower themselves and this empowerment brought
about a democratisation of professional practice. A major philosophical,
organisational and cultural shift was achieved, nurses developed
personally and professionally and theory was generated and tested. We
went up a blind alley, methodologically, by trying to set up the Kemmis
& McTaggart (1988) model of co-action research after the project had
been set up. But as we were successful in achieving our goals, as action
researchers, we question whether it is necessary for other participants, in
a collaborative project, to be co-action researchers to innovate or
empower themselves. We found that by helping the sisters and staff

nurses to become reflective practitioners and change agents, these goals were achieved. Our experience of action research in nursing, therefore, supports Elliott's (1991) claim that action research unifies quite different activities.

Secondly, we suggest that the research criteria we present here may help action researchers to generate and test theory more effectively, than when operating on tacit knowledge. Meeting these criteria can be demanding; however, working in an action research partnership enabled us to meet the challenges of both the action and the research.

Acknowledgements

We would like to thank warmly all the participants in this study who worked so hard with us to achieve patient-centred nursing. Our thanks also to Donald McIntyre for his skill in helping us to understand complex methodological issues.

References

Brown, S. & McIntyre, D. (1981) An Action Research Approach to Innovation in Centralized Educational Systems, *European Journal of Science Education*, 3, pp. 243-258.

Brown, S. & McIntyre, D. (1988) The Professional Craft Knowledge of Teachers, *Scottish Educational Review*: Special Issue on the Quality of Teaching, pp. 39-47.

Carr, W. & Kemmis, S. (1986) *Becoming Critical: education, knowledge and action research*. Lewes: Falmer Press.

Ebbutt, D. (1985) Educational Action Research: some general concerns and specific quibbles, in R. Burgess (Ed.) *Issues in Educational Research*. Lewes: Falmer Press.

Elliott, J. (1991) *Action Research for Educational Change*. Milton Keynes: Open University Press.

Kemmis, S. & McTaggart, R. (Eds) (1988) *The Action Research Planner*, 3rd edn. Geelong: Deakin University Press.

MacGuire, J.M. (1990) Putting Nursing Research Findings into Practice: research utilisation as an aspect of the management of change, *Journal of Advanced Nursing*, 15, pp. 614-620.

McNiff, J. (1988) *Action Research Principles and Practice*. London: Macmillan Education.

O'Hanlon, C. (1988) Alienation within the Profession: special needs or watered down teachers? Insights into the tension between the ideal and the real through action research, *Cambridge Journal of Education*, 18, pp. 297-311.

Schutz, A. (1962) *Collected Papers*, Volumes 1-3. Dordrecht: Kluwer.

Titchen, A.C. & Binnie, A.J. (1992) A Double Act: co-action researcher roles in an acute hospital setting, unpublished paper, National Institute for Nursing, Oxford.

Titchen, A.C. & Binnie, A.J. (1993) Research Partnerships: collaborative action research in nursing, *Journal of Advanced Nursing*.

Titchen, A.C. & McIntyre, D. (1993) A Phenomenological Approach to Qualitative Data Analysis in Nursing Research, in A. Titchen (Ed.) *Changing Nursing Practice through Action Research*, pp. 29-48, 83-86. Oxford: National Institute for Nursing,.

First published in *Educational Action Research*, Volume 1, Number 1, 1993

'A Different Way of Knowing': social care values, practitioner research and action research

CAROL MUNN-GIDDINGS

Introduction

This article has as its central theme the relationship between social care values (of empathy and empowerment), qualitative research and action research. This may seem like a rather ambitious task, but rather than making a conclusive statement I hope this article will provide one possible framework which can be developed through future submissions to the journal *Educational Action Research*.

Action research only rarely takes place in social care practice; it is certainly not written about or debated in any sustained or thoughtful way. This article therefore focusses on the importance of action research as a means of improving practice through reflecting on the problems arising from a piece of traditional research.

I have used as an example an ethnographic research project that I carried out in 1988 with a community unit of a health authority service for people with learning disabilities. My perspective and reflection on this experience is as a 'traditional' researcher but I discuss in the latter section why I think this approach and undertaking would be particularly important and relevant for social care practitioners, and thus begin to indicate the value of action research in the social work profession. It is contended that both the epistemology of qualitative research and its associated technique of participant observation *potentially* mirror the philosophy of undertaking critical reflection on practice. This article therefore starts out at a distance from action research but through its process will argue that because of the values that purport to underlie social care practice, practitioner research and action research should be very closely aligned.

The Project

In Britain, the development of a policy known as 'community care' has led to the run-down of institutional long-stay hospital care for people with learning disabilities. This policy has promoted for them, as alternative options, support either in their parental home, staffed community homes (run by either statutory, voluntary or private sector) or unstaffed community homes. However, physically moving people from hospital settings into the community has not necessarily led to their participation in a community life which is similar to that experienced by most other people. A health authority in the south east of England which was in the process of moving people from hospitals into staffed community homes, and which was keen to encourage its clients to form relationships with people outside of the service, commissioned myself and a consultant researcher (Adrian Adams) to:

> *initiate and investigate a programme of participation in*
> *community based activities for people with learning*
> *disabilities through the use of volunteers.*

Six volunteers were recruited from the local neighbourhood and matched by age and gender with clients in both community homes and the hospital. The volunteers' only brief was to share their time doing what they or the client would normally be doing for an agreed period of time each week (Giddings & Adams, 1989). The project was intended to inform and promote strategies that would enable clients to participate in the local community and to obtain information relevant to staff training.

The Research Methodology

The research methodology was qualitative and multi-method and included semi-structured interviews with volunteers, staff and those clients who were able to speak, group discussions with volunteers throughout the duration of the study and participant observation with the matched couples. All of the methods were designed to gain the views and perceptions of the volunteers, clients and staff.

This commitment to the view of those being studied means that the researcher is involved not only in expressing that view but deciding on how that view is to be gained. This commitment is expressed in ethnography (Hammersley, 1983), humanist research (Plummer, 1983) and particularly feminist research (Oakley, 1981; Finch, 1986; Harding, 1982; Stanley & Wise, 1983) all of which, although coming from different theoretical traditions, have common concerns – since all three use peoples' lived experience as their central concern.

The specific focus of this article is the participant observation work that I carried out, which was intended to elicit the key characteristics of the relationships that developed between the volunteers and the clients (their partners) and to identify barriers and opportunities in the formation of these relationships. The fieldwork involved me in accompanying the volunteers and clients for six months during their meetings together and making comprehensive notes (onto a tape which was later transcribed) after the meetings, detailing events, interactions and contexts. The examples from the findings that follow result from the analysis of the field-notes which were taken over 56 outings (72 hours). The data were analysed both by myself and by the collaborating researcher (independently of each other) to identify recurrent themes and concepts which were agreed, then used to code and sort the data.

The research technique was particularly important in elucidating how the volunteers and clients formed their relationships since the process of the relationship over time could be followed. Although it must be acknowledged that the presence of a third member must affect the dynamics of the relationship developing, I would argue that the flexibility and informality such a research method allowed (especially over time, as staff, volunteers and clients became used to my presence) was crucial in gaining an understanding of the non-measurable influences in relationship formation. In terms of working with people with learning disabilities it was also crucial in (a) getting close to the subjective experience of people who cannot communicate verbally, and (b) gaining an understanding of the difference between staff and volunteers' stated beliefs and their actions.

Examples from the research will help to illustrate and clarify these points. In presenting the information, I have chosen two themes crucial in the understanding of the formation of the relationships and indicated how the method was able to elucidate the issues.

Examples of the Uses of the Approach

A crucial factor in the development of the relationships was the way in which authority and control was negotiated between clients, care staff, volunteers and the public. Being able to observe the initial reaction and contact of the pairs elucidated how lay beliefs affect the interaction of people with and without learning disabilities and how service staff's handling of the situation influences the beginning of their relationships. For example:

> *Sally [the lay volunteer] was introduced to Tessa [a client] at Tessa's house. Sally was feeling very apprehensive about meeting Tessa and confided that 'I don't quite know what to expect'. Tessa and a staff member greeted Sally at the door. Sally was shown into the dining room and spent some time alone with Tessa and the researcher whilst the staff member made some tea. Sally commented several times on her own*

feelings of awkwardness saying to the researcher: 'I don't know
what to say to her' and 'I feel stupid'.

It was important to Sally to make some sort of sense of Tessa's behaviour,
for example:

Tessa went over to the music centre and rocked by it, pointing.
'What does she mean?' Sally said to the fieldworker. Similarly,
Tessa finished her tea and stood by the record player and
began to dance about. 'What do you want me to do?' asked
Sally.

In trying to make sense of Tessa's behaviour, Sally deferred to the
researcher and the staff member to ratify or correct her explanations. The
staff member involved told Sally the things that Tessa particularly
enjoyed, and explained that all the people in the house like different
things, stressing their individuality.

During Sally and Tessa's first meeting the staff intervention was
minimal and the only clue Sally got to Tessa's identity through the staff
were in terms of what Tessa enjoyed. This contrasts with some of the
other meetings where staff's emphasis on giving the volunteers warnings
or non-personal information about the client served to increase their own
concern and led them to attribute negative aspects to the client's identity.
For example:

She's no problem, quite sociable, loves to go out, never
aggressive ... will do anything for biscuits.
She's also incontinent, but easy to change; do you want to see?

The information was no doubt presented by staff out of concern for the
volunteer and as a way of asserting their control, but staff's presentation
of clients was particularly important in these initial meetings because of
the importance that the volunteers attributed to making sense of the
clients and their behaviour in the absence of verbal clues. One such
negative presentation led a volunteer to comment in the workshop:

Well they sort of brought her into the room, didn't they,
wheeled her in and put her there ... as if she was on show or
something. I didn't like that. The staff member stood there, I
tried to speak to her, but I must admit I did give up after a bit
because I didn't know what to do ... but the staff member was
just saying, this is how you feed her, how she eats this ... she
said they take them out for walks occasionally but she didn't
say she likes this or this.

Staff views were also influential in shaping volunteers' interactions with
other clients living in the same house as the client with whom they had a
relationship:

> *Ethel was sitting in a chair in the lounge, she was dribbling,
> her head was down. Sally kept looking across to her and
> frowning as if she didn't know what to make of Ethel. She
> asked 'Is she asleep?' . A member of staff replied 'No, she
> pretends to be'. After that, Sally made no attempt to talk to
> her.*

Sally's awkwardness in the introductory meetings was a common experience in all of the relationships; for example, another volunteer commented to the researcher directly after the introductory meeting:

> *I felt quite out of place, not really knowing what to expect, not
> knowing what to do … because she couldn't speak and her
> physical handicaps as well. I just couldn't speak to her, I
> didn't know what to do.*

The awkwardness suffered by the volunteers seemed to stem in part from the social awkwardness/ambivalence involved when meeting someone who cannot express themselves verbally. The volunteer matched with someone who could speak did not experience such a degree of awkwardness but did so with other people she met in the house. Being unsure about the way the client felt and was thinking confused the volunteers who expected to establish a form of communication between themselves and the client, despite having been told that they might have profound speech/ communication impairments. This presented the volunteers with an uncertainty about their role and confusion about the identity of the client. These feelings were compounded/relieved by a number of factors.

The allocation of authority and control, and blame for unwanted outcomes, which was negotiated between clients, care staff, volunteers and the public was a crucial factor in the formation and maintenance of relationships. Underlying or even unconscious attitudes were illuminated by the fieldwork. In interviews with the researchers, staff consistently answered in a positive way about their desire and actions to facilitate the relationships. However, observational work helped to establish that staff reactions and actions often militated against the relationships:

> *Tessa and Sally's first outing was arranged in a foursome with
> volunteer Pauline and a client Jackie. Tessa and Jackie had
> been told in advance by the staff that they were going out with
> Sally and Pauline, and were ready to leave as soon as the
> volunteers arrived. Tessa was asked to hold Sally's arm by the
> staff. As soon as they left the house, instead of turning right
> towards the town (where the volunteers had decided to go)
> Tessa turned left, shook herself free from Sally's arm and ran
> down the road. Sally pursued her, calling out to the researcher*

> *that she didn't know what to do. Tessa became anxious and stood rocking on the spot, indicating that she wanted to go back inside the house. Tessa, Sally and the researcher eventually returned to the house. By this point, Jackie had also become very anxious and was suggesting taking another of the clients to town instead; she refused to go back inside. A staff member appeared and firmly ordered her inside. Tessa calmed down very quickly. A member of the staff explained that 'she probably doesn't know you well enough, she was like that with [a staff member] when she first took her out'. She suggested that Tessa and Sally should go out separately for a while with a member of staff as well. Another member of staff confirmed that 'She has phases like that but she's harmless ... not like [another client, who was in the room] she's broken people's bones before now'. Both volunteers looked shocked. The same staff member suggested that Tessa could show Sally her room, which she did.*

The way staff perceive their role and the responsibilities they felt they had towards the clients often clashed abruptly with the attempts of the volunteer and the client to establish or retrieve their relationships. The staff member who suggested that Tessa show Sally her room, although intervening and directing the interaction did suggest something that enabled Sally and Tessa to be together again. In contrast, after the described incident:

> *Jackie [who, it could be reasonably argued had done nothing untoward outside, but had had her outing curtailed] said to Pauline 'Let's go into the dining room'. 'No Jackie, you're not going in there' said a staff member, 'she just wants her music on'. The staff member walked out. The researcher suggested to Jackie that she show Pauline her room. On the way to it the same member of staff told Jackie to go back to the lounge. The researcher apologised to Jackie and told the staff member that she had suggested it. She shrugged 'I think they need to stay down there for a while'. Jackie sat down and brushed her hands agitatedly through her hair. She repeated 'Music, music'. The staff member said she'd had enough and told her to go to her room. Jackie went. 'What will she do up there?' Pauline asked the staff member. 'Sit. I won't leave her there for long'. [staff] 'Just sit?' [Pauline] 'Yes' [staff].*

The example starkly points out the tension between the staff's perception of their responsibility and control for their client and the negative aspects this can have both on the development of relationships outside of service delivery and on the volunteer's perceived identity of the client, i.e. as dependent and subject to control by the staff, and undoubtedly on the client's own self-identity.

As the relationships developed and the volunteers and clients became more confident about their role and relationship with the client they were much more ready to question some of the staff's behaviour towards the client, although feeling unable to confront it, for example:

> *The volunteer was standing by the client's door looking*
> *uncomfortable. A staff member opened the door and called*
> *out hello. The client was standing with her trousers down,*
> *having a pad put in her pants. The volunteer was looking in*
> *her wardrobe for a coat. 'Is this hers?' she pulled out a drab,*
> *worn grey coat. 'Oh that's awful, I'll get her X's coat, it's more*
> *trendy' [staff member]. Later on the way to the pub the*
> *volunteer commented 'I was really shocked back there in her*
> *bedroom, just taking her pants down like that ... I mean*
> *privacy is really important, that's why I was trying to keep her*
> *door closed ... that's happened before, she has been taken to*
> *the toilet, the door's left open, anyone could see'.*

This sense of staff's role *vis-à-vis* their client and *vis-à-vis* the volunteer in relation to them was still apparent at the termination of the fieldwork and put some tacit constraint on the relationships. Again this information was only made apparent because of the research method being used – spontaneous comments made to the researcher clarified the role relationships between volunteers and staff.

The participant observation work that formed the basis of the case study analysis provided a way of understanding relationships between those socially identified as 'people with learning disabilities' and those who are not. The analysis of lay-attitudes as opposed to professional views and assumptions that tend to dominate health and social care programmes can add a new dimension and direction to the planning of services. The method also provides a chance to use the experiences of clients to shape the policies and practices that affect them.

Discussion

In this section of the article I discuss why I now believe that this type of research would be more usefully undertaken by practitioners who have both a continuing relationship with the client and whose job it is to develop the service *with* their clients. I then move on to look at how this method of research links with good, reflective practice in social care work and thus establishes the link between social work practice and action research.

Research and Action

My experience was essentially as an 'arms-length' researcher in the sense that I was specifically contracted to undertake the research and would have no ongoing contact with either staff or clients individually or service development more generally. My colleague's position was different since being a social worker himself and involved throughout the duration of the project in joint health/social services training he was utilising the material from the process of the research to inform his practice. He was not, however, directly involved on a longer term basis with either the staff or clients who took part in the study.

Many pertinent issues arose from the study which were none too easy to relay back to the staff who at the time I felt were defensive and unwilling to concede the 'blatant truths' with which they were presented. On reflection I have considerably more understanding of their reaction. At the same time that they were being 'retrained' to move from hospital to community settings, having to follow new local and national policies in which they had no part in framing, they were also being subject to 'observation' by a researcher who had no clinical experience, informing them that they were basically working to the detriment of their clients!

I would still stand by the results of the study and would still argue that professions should not be entirely self-regulating, *but* there is a fundamental problem in research becoming an 'expert service' disconnected from the issues and services it wishes to explore and improve. Not least is the danger that if the data are not owned by those who can ultimately act upon it, it is unlikely to be directly utilised. An important dynamic therefore exists between those who purport to explain and illuminate issues and those who are charged with the task of acting upon them. In the context of social work and other social care work there has been a lot written about the relationship of research to policy but there has not been a corresponding interest in the crucial relationship of research to practice.

The model of the 'expert researcher' is one against which educational action researchers have reacted, but this reaction and tradition is nowhere near so developed in social care practice, where the division of labour and professionalisation of different aspects of service delivery has effectively mitigated against the philosophy of action research. However, with the increasing interest in developing services through individual and collective critical reflection on practice (i.e. the reflective practitioner), research, and action research in particular, has the opportunity to be seen as integral to practice rather than separate from it.

Qualitative Research and Practitioner Research

Alternative philosophical traditions are used for qualitative research, 'a different way of knowing' as Rist (1984) puts it and one based on involvement, empathy and experience. In looking for 'meanings' rather than 'causes' and in rejecting the positivist view from which quantitative methodology is derived, the task of social research is seen as resting on the meaning of social events and processes derived from an understanding of the point of view of the person or group being studied.

This endeavour is very similar to the 'empathy' practitioners commonly strive for with their clients. For example Rogers's (1980) definition (which is extensive) of empathy in relation to a counselling relationship includes:

> *... entering the private perceptual world of the other and becoming thoroughly at home with it ... it means temporarily living in his/her life, moving about in it without making judgements, sensing meanings of which he/she is scarcely aware ... by pointing to the possible meanings in the flow of his/her experiencing you help the person to focus on this useful type of referent, to experience the meanings more fully and to move forward in the experiencing.*

This understanding of both experience and feelings is important in many practitioner–client relationships. The parallels with the type of research described above seem to me to be quite striking and offer a way in which a practitioner or practitioners could use the material gained from such a study to work with both individuals and groups. It also *potentially* offers practitioners the chance to recognise how their own values and understandings of situations can impact on their work with clients. Plummer (1983) has described how in his life-history work (now a part of many programmes for people with learning disabilities) the interviewees' cultural system (i.e. way of organising the world) may differ greatly from that of the researcher, so it has to be intimately entered if sense is to be made of the social world. The social researcher is not a mere medium through which knowledge is discovered, s/he can also be seen as constructors of knowledge; it is therefore important for the researcher to be aware of and reflect on how their own values, race, gender, class, etc. and the procedures they use can affect their research. This acknowledgement of the human dynamic in research known as reflexivity (rather than the vision of the researcher as a neutral vessel through which information passes) is hotly contested in research (Hammersley, 1983) but it is most persuasively and strongly argued by feminists (see Harding, 1982; Finch, 1986) whose work facilitates a model of understanding based on empathy between persons. Using a 'reflexive' framework to reflect on practice seems to me to be the most constructive way forward for practitioner researchers. Starting from the viewpoint of those being studied, knowledge is not conceived abstractly but is viewed as a dynamic process in which theory develops from practice. It is a perspective that facilitates the understanding, undertaking and use of research by practitioners.

Many of the skills involved in semi-structured interviewing, group discussions and in particular participant observation, are those which in many cases would be developed and expressed by a committed and sensitive practitioner. In justifying participant observation as a useful research tool the justification and necessitation of the practitioner as a researcher becomes obvious. A good social practitioner should always be both participator and observer, continually checking out their clients" understanding of events and their actions, and the practitioner's own understanding of the situation and their actions, and it is that reflection on their practice which enables its development. Research then becomes a highly relevant possibility even for busy social care practitioners if data can be gathered with little additional effort through the course of their work – this endeavour has been seen as important for educationalists (see Winter, 1982 who also discusses alternative ways in which to analyse data) and I would argue is even more so for social workers and nurses who have both a severe shortage of time and little institutional support for their own research. The development and use of a methodology as akin to practice as possible is an important task that would be usefully explored through this journal.

I would further argue that this method and framework of enquiry links to the *potential* empowerment of clients, because (1) it offers a way in which power relationships can be examined and acknowledged; and (2) 'empathic understanding' can lead to clients feeling that their experience is both valued and being used to help to develop services. In this way the research process itself can be seen as a positive, empowering way in which to work with and for clients.

Practitioner Research Practice and Action Research

Even without an action research framework then, practitioner research can be seen as an empowering process. However, the philosophy of empowerment also clearly links to the conceptual framework of action research. Action research can be conceived of as a continuous spiral of:

planning of action,
action,
observation on action,
reflection on action (Kemmis et al, 1982).

This also describes the critical reflection on practice promoted in social care work today, especially that of social work. In these terms critical reflection describes both good social care practice and research. Action research is also centrally concerned both with reflexivity and with collaboration (Winter, 1989). Collaboration with 'clients' (be they students or users of social services) is only possible if a critical stance is adopted towards the power relationships in which the service is delivered. If action research is about change, then change requires a critique of existing power relationships. Any research undertaken to do so should be sure that power relationships are challenged in both its design and in the process of undertaking it; this involves looking critically at who is doing the research and what their role is in the proposed change. An empowered client is not someone who has things done to *them* but someone who is worked *with*. If research is to be part of that process and to reflect those values, then the obvious researcher is the practitioner.

I have used the world 'potentially' at several points in this article. This is because I believe research is a process and at each stage of that process there exists the possibility to use it in either an oppressive or constructive way. The methodology of social research is a political framework which defines the relationship of the researcher to the researched. I have argued in this article that a qualitative methodology used by practitioner researchers is a potential way to examine and begin to address the researcher/researched relationship and also to define some of the central values of social work practice itself. This argument suggests the important contribution that can be made if researchers are practitioners researching with their clients as part of their practice. In this way we can begin to conceive of a constructive relationship between practice and theory.

I am aware that the ideas contained here need further development and refinement and would welcome practitioners' views and comments.

Acknowledgement

I would like to acknowledge Jane Nichols for discussion and contribution to these ideas.

Bibliography

Finch, J. (1986) *Research and Policy: the uses of qualitative methods in social and educational research*. Lewes: Falmer Press.

Giddings, C. (1987) Ways of Knowing: an exploration of the issues concerning the use of a qualitative framework. Dissertation (unpublished).

Giddings, C. (1990) Qualitative Research and Social Policy. MA dissertation (unpublished).

Giddings, C. & Adams, A. (1989) Image and Identity: report on the Timeshare project (unpublished).

Hammersley, M. (1983) *Ethnography: principles into practice*. London: Tavistock.

Harding, S. (Ed.) (1982) *Feminism and Methodology*. Milton Keynes: Open University Press.

Kemmis, S. et al (1982) *The Action Research Planner*, 2nd edn. Geelong: Deakin University Press.

Oakley, A. (1981) in H. Roberts (Ed.) *Doing Feminist Research*. London: Routledge & Kegan Paul.

Plummer, K. (1983) *Documents of Life*. London: Allen & Unwin.

Rist, R. (1984) On the Application of Qualitative Research to the Policy Process: an emergent link, in L. Barton (Ed.) *Social Crisis and Educational Research*. London: Croom Helm.

Rogers, C. (1980) *Empathic: an unappreciated way of being, in* A Way of Being. Boston: Houghton Mifflin.

Stanley, L. & Wise, S. (1983) *Breaking Out: feminist consciousness and feminist practice*. London: Routledge & Kegan Paul.

Ward & Mullender (1991) Empowerment and Oppression: an indissoluble pairing for contemporary social work, *Critical Social Policy*, 32, Autumn, pp. 21-31.

Winter, R. (1982) 'Dilemma Analysis': a contribution to methodology for action research, *Cambridge Journal of Education*, 12, pp. 161-174.

Winter, R. (1989) *Learning from Experience*. Lewes: Falmer Press.

First published in *Educational Action Research*, Volume 1, Number 2, 1993

No Easy Answers: the dilemmas and challenges of teacher research

PETE STRAUSS

Feeling Disturbed and Unsettled

About a year ago, as part of my part-time Masters course at Nottingham Trent University.[1] I decided to try and find out more clearly what it was that the children in my Year 4 class of 8-9-year-old children were learning. I tried lots of different approaches, all of them with an emphasis on the qualitative rather than the quantitive. I wanted to explore some approaches to assessment that moved away from the current orthodoxy of National Curriculum levels [2], and concentrate instead on the learning that couldn't necessarily be ticked off in a box because it was either too complex or too subtle. It's been a fascinating year. Some of my methods worked better than others, but on the whole, I have found out a huge amount of interesting and useful information about what the children in my class are learning.

I ought to be really pleased that my time as a teacher-researcher has been so fruitful (and of course I am pleased with the insights I have gained), but the trouble is, I don't just feel pleased. I also feel something else entirely: I feel disturbed and unsettled. The truth of the matter is, that although I set out with the intention of exploring the children's learning, I (inevitably of course) ended up, examining my own teaching too. Now, as I look back over the inquiry, I feel drawn towards considering these more disturbing ideas related to teaching, rather than the really quite positive and encouraging things I have discovered about learning.[3]

Becoming a teacher-researcher has, I think, raised some important and challenging issues for me, and I hope that by drawing the issues together and discussing them, I may raise some questions that are of interest to others too. I want to focus on five distinct areas:

(1) Am I the teacher I think I am? Is there a gap between my espoused principles and my actual practice?

(2) How can I as a researcher come to terms with the feelings of despair that an inquiry into my own practice is likely to generate?

(3) How can I as a teacher and a teacher-researcher come to terms with being pulled in different and sometimes opposite directions by the established educational systems and orthodoxies on the one hand, and my own ideals and visions on the other. I have called this 'professional schizophrenia'.

(4) What role does the writing down of personal reflections have in illuminating my own practice, and resolving such dilemmas?

(5) How can I go forward after my time as a researcher has ended, working within the system, but maintaining my critical/self-critical approach?

My Shifting Sense of Self

One of the most troubling things I have discovered is that I am not the teacher I thought I was. When I set out on the inquiry, I actually set down my personal and professional commitments, and very grand they sounded too. I cited Paulo Friere's *Pedagogy of the Oppressed* (1972) and wrote in my Personal Reflections (see later in this article):

> *I see education as being about helping people to take control over their lives, and to feel at home in the world in which they live. Furthermore, I see education as a two-way process between teacher and learner; as a dialogue during which both teacher and learner are learning as well as teaching and teaching as well as learning.*

As the inquiry progressed though, I began to find evidence that there was something of a gap between my proclaimed ideals and my actual classroom practice. It was made particularly obvious to me in listening to tape recordings of myself in conversation with the children in my class.[4] I made a note of the following exchange:

> *I had a brief conversation with Charles about his coke can dragster. I asked him where the energy came from to move it and he said the rubber band. I then asked where the rubber band got the energy from and he said muscles. I then asked where the muscles got their energy and he said food. I asked where the food got its energy to grow and he said the sun.*

As soon as I listened to the tape, I was struck by the fact that this wasn't a conversation at all, but rather a catechism, in which Charles responds almost ritually to my leading questions, with established and predictable answers that provide me with nothing more than reassurance. I was also struck by how I was never quiet. There were no silences during which Charles might have had the opportunity to say something unexpected, or even ask a question himself!

On another occasion, I taped myself working with Aaron who was engaged in a maths investigation. He was trying to find out how many different triangles he could construct using a 16-pin geoboard.

> *PS: What do you mean you don't know how you're getting along?*
> *AL (laughs): I've thought of all the ones going that way and I've thought of of all the ones going that way.*
> *PS: Have you got them all?*
> *AL : No.*
> *PS : These three are like a group aren't they? What about going to this pin or this pin or this pin? Aren't there six other possible triangles there?*
> *AL : I don't know. (pause). What do you mean 'go to this pin'?*
> *PS : Well, on the first one you've gone to this pin (I try to explain).*
> *AL : So instead of going to the bottom, go to the next row along?*
> *PS : Yeah. You could do. Does that help?*
> *AL : Yeah.*

This showed me to be very much in the business of steering and directing Aaron's learning along my own predetermined lines. There was not a lot of room here for Aaron to devise his own solutions to the problem. I didn't give him the space.

More generally, I came to find that rather than my educational practice being 'liberating' I had in some ways been seduced by the power of being a teacher:

> *One of the aspects of this inquiry that has startled me most, has been my discovery that in many ways I have unconsciously and involuntarily embraced a dangerously powerful and dominant role in the teaching and learning processes that go on in our class. I don't mean that in a naive sense ... of course I have more power than the children I teach, and I spend a good deal of my time ordering them to do things they don't really want to do (working through playtime if I judge that they have been messing about instead of getting on with the task at hand). I mean the less obvious power that I wield through the way I talk, the way I question, the way I direct thinking and so on. I suppose I knew that I was doing it, but I had never really stopped to consider how much. In many ways, I think I am the kind of teacher that does encourage independence, responsibility and criticism, but, nevertheless,*

*there are aspects of my practice that probably undermine
those ideals and which, if I am not very careful, I can remain
quite ignorant of.*

The troubling aspect of all this however, is not about whether my
teaching style is right or wrong. The point is that my ideas about what
kind of a teacher I was, were mistaken. Crucially, I would perhaps never
have realised that I was mistaken, unless I had first of all articulated
what my guiding principles were, and then, subsequently, taken a closer
look at what was really happening in my class.

Dealing with Despair

Perhaps it was inevitable that I would go through a period of self-doubt
and even despair during my inquiry. Perhaps anyone who stops and
takes a closer look at what they are doing in life is first startled and then
depressed by the shortcomings they find. Certainly, I went through such
a period.

On one occasion I wrote:

*Mary Jane Drummond says that 'words such as love, beauty
and truth ... do not often appear in educational texts of the
90's' and yet they are words which should be central to the
kind of education I believe in. As I begin to consider the
learning in my class, I can't help but dwell on the teaching. It
isn't dreadful, by any means, but I do think there is something
missing. And as I examine and reflect on the learning in my
class, the more I feel ... here is something missing.*

And later on:

*I have begun to ask myself questions like – 'what is the point
of bringing children in at the end of an activity or topic to ask
them what they have learned?' Surely I should be bringing
them in at the outset, to ask them what they would like to
learn? 'This was brought home to me when Colin and I were
discussing his Topic Web and in answer to my question, 'What
did you find most interesting in the Victorian Topic?' he
started at me blankly, and replied 'nothing really'.[5]*

Sometimes I felt almost overwhelmed by these darker feelings of self-
doubt.

*Maybe I'm just not a very good teacher. Maybe teaching is,
knowing what the children are learning and responding to that
knowledge. Maybe there's nothing else to it, and I'm not very
good at it.*

My areas of concern for the inquiry consequently shifted dramatically. One – no doubt inevitable – result of looking more closely at learning in my class, was that I found myself also looking closely at teaching in my class. Whereas I started off asking What are the children in my class learning? I gradually came up with these much wider and more unsettling questions:

How can I have more quality time in conversation with the children?
What am I teaching?
How am I teaching?
What meaning and relevance do the children attach to my teaching?
Could the children be more involved in deciding what they learn?

I don't really think there are any easy answers to this, and yet the risk of personal discomfort is absolutely central to both reflective practise in general and formalised action inquiry in particular. Marion Dadds (1993, pp. 287-303) has argued that it is possible to intervene in order to prepare for and then manage the possible trauma of self-study. I'm sure she's right, but as she herself points out 'putting oneself at risk is not a monolithic or standardised phenomenon'. In any case, I suspect that taking moral responsibility for one another's emotional support, as advocated by Dadds, in a sense misses the point. I increasingly feel that some prior conditions need to exist for people to be able to take part in a potentially wounding self-study.

In the case of formal action inquiry through award bearing courses, there has to be established right at the outset, a culture of advancing theory and insight through discourse and debate. Critical friendship cannot be imposed or legislated for but it does have to be nurtured. Students embarking on action inquiry courses ought to perhaps spend a lengthy period engaged in intensive debate about questions like: What is the point of education? We need to bring our personal and political baggage out into the open. Only then, it seems to me, will we be in a position to trust one another sufficiently to provide the support that Marion Dadds is asking for, which might help us get through the pain of self-scrutiny.

Similarly, reflective practitioners who are not involved in formal award-bearing courses as such, but are interested in asking themselves awkward and challenging questions about their practice, cannot really be expected to sustain their project in isolation. It could be argued that there can be no such thing as reflectiveness in one person. Reflectiveness depends on colleagues talking to one another and trusting one another. A staffroom culture of 'fear and loathing' is unlikely to generate discussions about the purpose of education, and yet those discussions are a prerequisite of reflective practise.

Creating such a prior-culture is obviously problematic. Maybe the bottom line is to at least try and understand, from the start, that self-study – if rigorous – is almost bound to be a painful business. (If it ain't hurtin', it ain't workin' as they say). It seems to me that any serious scrutiny of one's professional practice is likely, at one point or another, to lead to questions like: *Why am I doing this job? What is the point of it all?*

For myself, I am able to identify one particular area of my inquiry that has been helpful to me in bringing to the surface and working through the more troubling aspects of my study, and that was the writing down of my Personal Reflections (see below). Paradoxically, it was writing that brought feelings of despair up to the surface in the first place, but it was also writing that allowed me to face these feelings and work them through.

Hypocrisy and Schizophrenia

There have been occasions over the past year when I have felt distinctly schizophrenic. I have been engaged in a search for more qualitative approaches to assessing children's learning, whilst at the same time continuing to work with the English National Curriculum's levelled assessment procedures. For example, I took part in a number of agreement trialling activities over the year, including a science investigation into dissolving and a maths activity concentrating on investigative skills. I have experimented with opening up decisions about the content of the curriculum to the children themselves, but at the same time, have continued to plough on with organising a very prescriptive and top-down National Curriculum for most of the time. I have encouraged the children to ask questions and set targets for themselves, and take a measure of control over their learning during the inquiry, but at the end of the day, the context in which we work doesn't allow an awful lot of pupil autonomy.

I felt almost as if I was inhabiting two different worlds, doing the formal assessment because I had to, and pursuing my own methods because I wanted to. Presumably I am not the first teacher to struggle with these feelings of professional schizophrenia. It is something that we all feel at different times. Indeed, I have since been introduced to Jack Whitehead's (1989, pp. 67-77) concept of the teacher as a 'living contradiction' ... 'the experience of holding educational values and the experience of their negation'. The question is, how do I cope?

The educational and political culture within which we operate is fairly inflexible. As a teacher who has spent a good deal of time, worrying about and questioning some of the aspects of teaching and learning in my class, I find myself continually knocking into that reified culture.

Paradoxically, by taking a closer look at my class, and the teaching and learning that goes on inside it, I have opened up a view of schooling as a whole. Again, maybe this is an inevitable result of examining one's professional practice, that you 'see the wood for the trees' and start asking awkward questions about it. This approach to the problem of 'professional schizophrenia' seems to echo Whitehead's call for educational theory 'in the living form of dialogues'. I may be inhabiting two worlds, but at least by acknowledging that fact, I am in a better position to understand the world I'm in, and create my vision of a better one.

Personal Reflections

One of the most illuminating and fruitful methods of research that I adopted over the year, didn't in fact take place in the classroom at all, but happened later on, back home, in the evenings. I got into the habit of writing down personal reflections about the previous day or two, and over the course of my inquiry I wrote altogether about thirty-six thousand words, usually over about three evenings a week. Mary Louise Holly (1989) has argued that it is through journal-writing that teachers can give full expression to their creativity and do justice to the massive complexity of their situation. For myself, I can endorse Holly's belief that it is through writing that teachers can come to know themselves properly. Writing has certainly helped me.

I used the reflections to bounce ideas around, to throw them out and see how they came back to me.

They were also therapeutic, helping me to feel better about aspects of classroom life that were worrying me, just by writing them down.

Current Concerns

1. The class are too noisy when I want them to be quiet (i.e. when I want their attention).
2. The children I'm not working with directly seem to spend too long off task, chatting.
3. I'm not getting anywhere with Colin. I seem to be telling him off all the time. If he wasn't leaving in a fortnight, I'd be more worried.
4. Gavin and Robert Br. really upset a little Reception boy today, by pushing open the door of the toilet while he was in there. I was very depressed when I heard, though I didn't show it. I've had to send a letter home to Gavin's mum and dad. I hope he doesn't get walloped.
5. I don't seem to spend much quality time with the children. I am always running around 'spinning plates' as the well worn cliche has it. Maybe that's what this inquiry is all about really. Maybe the biggest problem in my class isn't that I don't know what the children are learning, but that I don't spend enough quality time with them. Too much moaning about the noise. Too much organising of activities and providing of experiences. Not enough conversation.

I sometimes used them to record any observations I had made about significant learning that had taken place in class [6]:

> *Robert B. impressed me in the Maths group. He showed a real*
> *flexibility of approach in dividing a shape in half. Robert C.*
> *was very good with the computer too. Very independent, even*
> *managing to print his work by himself. Aaron laughed at all*
> *the subtle funny bits in Sheep-Pig. Bill spotted that after 1/2,*
> *1/4/, 1/8, would be 1/16 and noticed that the number was*
> *doubling. I missed a lot though. Charles seemed to be working*
> *really hard with the shapes, but I never talked to him about it.*
> *I'll try to tomorrow.*

I also made notes about individual children:

> *I noticed on two occasions how Julie got discouraged when*
> *faced with a task that she didn't think she could manage.*
> *Once with the Coke Can dragster, when it didn't work properly*
> *and she went off in tears, and later doing the census data base*
> *at the Comprehensive School, when she kept telling me that*
> *she wouldn't be able to do it by herself. As it happened, and*
> *quite by chance, she was one of the two children who ended*
> *up working all by herself and she did really well. I'm sure that*
> *her skill and confidence with the computer will have grown*
> *tremendously, but it was only by sheer fluke that she didn't*
> *end up sitting with someone else, in which case I'm pretty sure*
> *she would have hung back and got her partner to do it all.*
> *Where would we be in education without fluke!*

I found myself reflecting on events in the class that seemed at first sight to have no bearing on the inquiry:

> *Colin and Mark both went home in tears today, both claiming*
> *that the other had thumped the other with no provocation. I*
> *spoke to both mums, who both seemed to think that the other*
> *boy was to blame, and promised to try and get to the bottom of*
> *it tomorrow. Colin had come to me earlier in the day*
> *complaining that Mark was hitting him, but I didn't take any*
> *notice, because I thought Colin was probably winding me up.*
> *Perhaps I should have intervened earlier.*
>
> *We had an interesting discussion about the new School*
> *Council. To begin with nearly all the children in the class*
> *wanted to put their names forward as candidates to be class*
> *councillors, but when I said that they would have to talk for 30*
> *seconds to the rest of the class about why they thought they*
> *should be elected, one or two of the boys and practically every*
> *single girl dropped out. I asked why that had happened and*
> *Mark A. said girls were more shy; Robert Pe. said they had*

smaller brains than boys (which caused gasps of amazement from the girls and a pitying look from Wendy). Julie said that the boys could just stand up and say any old rubbish, which I thought was very astute and probably had a lot of truth in it. This wasn't resolved and we will go back to it. It was striking how girls who were mostly very bright and apparently very confident did not apparently feel confident enough at talking about themselves in front of the class. I took this to be a lack of self-esteem on the girl's part, and possible worry about some of the boys' possible responses. It doesn't reflect too well on the class as a whole, on me as a teacher and the boys in particular, if we have a class in which girls don't feel happy about putting themselves forward in a public way. I shall try and tackle this further in class.

Sometimes I used the Reflections to review the day and to pick out features of the teaching that had apparently gone well. I could also try to hammer out any worries I had, about teaching that was not working out as I wanted, and to suggest to myself possible strategies for improving the situation.

Writing these reflections down took an enormous amount of time, often after I'd come home from work feeling pretty tired after my day's teaching. I think it unlikely that I could sustain such a project over a long period of time, and when I stop being a teacher–researcher and go back to being just a teacher, I will almost certainly stop writing them. The thing is though, that writing those reflections down was immensely useful. It was through that process of dialogue with myself, that I began to make sense of what was happening in my classroom, and of the discrepancies that existed between my ideals and my practice. The key question is then – if these reflections are so important, what can I realistically do instead to ensure that I continue to reflect on what I'm doing as a teacher day to day?

Where Do I Go From Here?

One of the fascinating aspects of the last year has been how my attempts to get closer to the children's learning have given me a greater understanding of myself, not just as a teacher, but as a learner. My tutor has pointed out to me the interesting parallels that exist between the children as learners during their time in my class, and myself as a learner during the course of this inquiry. The children and I have, in a sense, been travelling the same road. They and I have both been engaged in the same process of taking time to stop ... to stop and talk about, to stop and look at, and to stop and reflect on the work we are involved in. That taking time to stop and look has, I think, given me insights into the children's learning; given the children insights into and consciousness of their own learning; and given me insights into my own practice as a teacher.

I have learned a lot during this inquiry, and much of it has been unanticipated and unplanned for. I set out originally to find out more about the children, and find myself having discovered a good deal – but not just about the children. I have discovered a good deal about myself. The fact that we have all been engaged in this project together (albeit a project initiated by me) has in a way made tangible and real the ideal I originally espoused in my earliest work – about the children and I all being learner-teachers and teacher-learners.

The trouble is that I now face the future with a good deal of unanswered and difficult questions hanging over me. I have made an attempt to resolve what I can ...

> *The important thing, it seems to me now, is not to lose the will to question and reflect, but also, not to wear myself down by futile collisions with the established structures and systems of schooling today. It is going to be a matter of compromise. The dangers lie on both sides ... the danger of being absorbed into an unquestioning acceptance of reified forms of educational culture; and the danger of being worn down by unrealistic and impossible gestures of dissent.*
>
> *I increasingly find myself seeing the way forward as being built on a search for flashes or sparks of liberating insight in what can otherwise be a rather restrictive and ever oppressive environment. The important thing, it seems to me, is to be ready for those flashes of insight when they come; to know them and to recognise them for the inspiration and the liberation that they can represent. I have a crucial role in trying to enable those flashes of insight to happen.*

My own professional practice as an educator may have turned out to be less liberating than I had liked to believe, but my short time as a teacher researcher has most definitely been a liberating experience. I have been particularly interested in and inspired by the ideas of Joe Kincheloe (1991) who sees Qualitative Inquiry as an emancipatory activity, liberating both teachers and learners from a dominant Taylorist production-line ideology and approach to education. In my case, the emancipation has been in asking questions that had previously not occurred to me. One of the themes that emerged in my study was how little questioning children actually do in school. Well, the fact is that until this inquiry, I wasn't asking many questions either.

The question is, now that the inquiry is over, how can I keep up the momentum? They say that a journey of a thousand miles begins with a single step, and possibly asking the questions that I have raised here is sufficient to begin the long journey of continuing to be a reflective practitioner. I have to say, though, that I think there is a danger of losing the impetus. I can imagine myself becoming gradually less thoughtful, asking fewer and fewer questions, and becoming ever more complacent.

Perhaps the answer is to adopt Noam Chomsky's idea (1992) of 'courses in intellectual self-defence.' I may not be able to sustain the effort of writing up thousands of words of personal reflections for the rest of my time as a teacher, but I could perhaps meet together with a small group of fellow teachers, simply to ask one another awkward, difficult and unsettling questions every now and then.

Laurence Stenhouse (1975) wrote that good classrooms are those in which questions are asked to which people don't know the answer. Perhaps the same goes for good teachers too ... that they are teachers who band together in 'self-defence' to ask themselves questions that – at very least – don't have easy answers.

Acknowledgement

I would like to gratefully acknowledge the support, advice and encouragement I received from Kath Green, my tutor at Nottingham Trent University.

Notes

[1] This article was written as part of the requirements of an MEd through Action Inquiry course at Nottingham Trent University in July 1994.

[2] At the time of writing, the English National Curriculum sets out the content to be taught to school children across nine separate subjects. It divides each subject into 'attainment targets' or themes (for example 'Life and Living Processes' in Science or 'Shape and Space' in Mathematics.) Each National Curriculum attainment target is in turn divided into ten levels, representing levels of difficulty, and each of these levels is descibed by one or more 'statements of attainment'. These statements are supposed to be used in the classroom as the criteria for assessing children's achievments. As we go to press some aspects of the National Curriculum are undergoing review. The ten levels will remain in the revised curriculum, though they have been renamed as 'level descriptors'.

[3] For an example of the *content* of my research, see Pete Strauss (1995) Julie's story, *Forum*, 37, pp. 23-25.

[4] The names of all the children have been changed.

[5] A 'topic web' traditionally refers to a model of planning used by many primary teachers in England, but in this case refers to my attempt to encourage the children to map out what they have learnt, and how it connects together, in the form of a flow chart.

[6] Readers may notice an apparent imbalance in the number of references to boys and girls in the class. I ought to point out that there was an

imbalance in the composition of the class and that boys outnumbered girls by more than 2:1.

References

Chomsky, Noam (1992) *Manufacturing Consent* (Mark Achbar & Peter Wintonick, Necessary Illusions/National Film Board of Canada).

Dadds, Marion (1993) The Feeling of Thinking in Professional Self-study, *Educational Action Research*, 1, pp. 287-303.

Drummond, Mary Jane (1993) *Assessing Children's Learning*. London: David Fulton.

Friere, Paulo (1972) *Pedagogy of the Oppressed*. Harmondsworth: Penguin.

Holly, Mary Louise (1989) Reflective Writing and the Spirit of Inquiry, *Cambridge Journal of Education*, 19, pp. 71-79.

Kincheloe, Joe (1991) *Teachers as Researchers: qualitative inquiry as a path to empowerment*. London: Falmer Press.

Stenhouse, L. (1975) *An Introduction to Curriculum Research and Development*. London: Heinemann.

Whitehead, Jack (1989) Creating a Living Educational Theory from Questions of the Kind, 'How Do I Improve My Practice?', *Cambridge Journal of Education*, 19, pp. 67-77.

First published in *Educational Action Research*, Volume 3, Number 1, 1995

Inter-professional Practice and Action Research: commonalties and parallels

BELINDA WATTS & SHIRLEY JONES

Introduction

Action Research has a number of conceptual approaches, but it would usually claim to have at least four common characteristics:

focuses on problem solving;
promotes partnership and collaboration;
creates a change in practice;
redefines or develops theory.

Action research has a number of common traits with inter-professional practice in that both are mutually collaborative, value good inter-personal relationships as nexus to problem solving and the adoption of change, strive to make the best possible use of resources in the work place, challenge the epistemological basis of practice, and seek to address power and boundary relationships. It would seem logical to suggest, therefore, both that action research could be a vehicle to promote and enhance inter-professional practice, and that the procedures emerging from inter-professional practice can illuminate certain aspects of action research.

Inter-professional Practice

The delivery of effective health and social care is currently a major political issue. Burdening costs, technological advances promising greater longevity and raised expectations, together with the increasing complexity of the problems faced in clinical practice, have seen the demand to a change in working practices escalate. The increasing public outcry for improved standards of care and access to seamless service provision have significantly impacted on current thinking about health and social care delivery. The rigidity that has characterised the NHS and the demarcation of the professions and services available, is no longer seen as the way to meet modern health and social care needs. Greater efficiency in the use of resources is essential. The need to streamline services and prevent unnecessary duplication together with the need for evidenced-based practice is now a key requirement for service delivery.

A key solution to addressing some of these problems is the promotion and development of inter-professional practice, whereby professionals who contribute to patient/clients care, collaborate to provide integrated health and social care provision across a range of services. Much of the work and challenges facing inter-professional teams will be directed to solving problems in practice, generating evidence to support practice and promoting change. However, promoting and implementing inter-professional practice is inherently challenging and problematic, since it seeks to draw together professionals from different backgrounds with unique identities, ideologies, values, knowledge, culture and power base. Gillett characterises human relationships as encompassing the whole range of 'human intractability, incompetence, power politics, greed and negativity, together with, of course, sweet reasonableness, great imagination, creativity, generosity and altruism' (Gillett, 1995, cited in Hudson, 2000).

Since inter-professional practice is inherently based on complex human processes, successful teams will require good inter-personal relationships if compatibility, rather than competition is to flourish. We acknowledge that inter-professional practice is a difficult, contentious and complex endeavour, but would argue that it is ultimately essential to the attainment of greater flexibility and choice in meeting the diverse needs of clients.

Several terms are used to denote inter-professional practice, e.g. 'multi-professional', 'multi-disciplinary' and 'inter-disciplinary'. The terms are often used inter-changeably, but may be ascribed different definitions (Leathard, 1994). A comparison can be made between 'multi' as being made up of many, who may not interact, and 'inter', which implies interaction between members (Petrie, 1976).

From our perspective, we see inter-professional practice as essentially relating to collaborative inter-disciplinary team working, rather than the multi-disciplinary situation in which team members may operate sequentially, but independently.

Team and team working has been well scrutinised, particularly in the management literature. Often the emphasis is on how teams tackle particular problems or tasks. A great deal has been written about teamwork in Primary Care (Ovretveit, 1993, 1995; West & Slater, 1996) providing insight into the characteristics of successful and less successful teams. However, less has been written about the ongoing and more nebulous nature of teamwork and inter-professional practice in the wider health and social care arena, and in particular how successful inter-professional team working can be attained (Miller et al, 1999).

Many writers allude to the barriers, which prevent effective teamwork and collaboration, but it is clear that effective collaboration is pivotal to successful inter-professional practice. Attempts at inter-professional collaboration are inherently likely to create conflict because there are deep-rooted social differences in the ways individual professions work. This arises from their different knowledge base, their rituals of socialisation and enculturation via education and training 'tribalism', (Atkins, 1998; Dombeck, 1997; Beattie, 1995) and their differing priorities of working heightened by the direct competition, amongst professions, for power and resources. Ross & Tissier (1997) highlight that even when different professional groups value inter-professional working, incompatible organisational structures can fetter effective integration, especially at the multi-agency interface e.g. the involvement of educational welfare staff, probation workers and teachers concerning cases of school truancy. It is therefore essential at an operational level that individual practitioners are committed to service co-operation and collaboration.

In order to overcome these barriers, certain requisites are fundamental:

the development of mutual trust and respect between individuals, leading to the fostering of a safe environment for learning and practice (Mackay et al, 1995; Miller et al, 1999).

the need for negotiation and role clarification which may impact on and challenge traditional role boundaries (Ovretveit, 1993; Beattie, 1995; Rees & Jolly, 1998; Miller et al, 1999);

shared planning and decision making (West & Poulton, 1997; Miller et al, 1999);

shared responsibility and accountability (Henneman, 1995);

the adoption of reflective processes both individually and collectively (Tsang, 1998);

the development of a common value base (Dombeck, 1997; Wilmot, 1995);

non-hierarchical relationships based on knowledge and expertise, rather than status or title, in which issues of power can be addressed (Henneman, 1995);

open and responsive communication (Miller et al, 1999);

commitment to new ways of working and consequently to professional change (Miller et al, 1999);

the development of new, shared and common knowledge, generated from reflection on practice between colleagues utilising contrasting professional perspectives (Checkland, 1981; Miller et al, 1999).

Also, we would wish to add:

willing participation and engagement in continual professional development.

Given this perspective one can see how inter-professional practice may illuminate concepts that are the foundation of action research. In common with inter-professional practice, successful action research is dependant upon collaboration, negotiation and group decision-making, requiring individuals to constantly challenge power relationships amongst its members. Action research therefore offers practitioners working inter-professionally a strategy for change and development, and in this sense, it can become part of a process of practice that is integral to the every day work of practitioners (Hudson & Bennett, 1997).

Pivotal to the action research process is the desire to bring about change and improve practice. Research issues/questions that are initiated by practitioners, are grounded in practice, contextually defined and future orientated. Thus, the development of knowledge is practice driven, enabling practitioners to bridge the theory/practice gap and to adopt, rather than merely adapt to change (Hart & Bond, 1995).

Inter-professional practice values:	Action research promotes:
Collaboration	Mutual collaboration
Problem-solving in practice	Interactive processes and contextual working: reflection in action and the reframing of problems in situations
Innovation – resulting from the sharing of knowledge and values	Engagement in continuous feedback and dialogue to effect change and improve practice
Recognition and acceptance of multiple realities	Pluralism and reflexivity
Value sharing and clarification, breakdown of tribalisim, role identification and clarification	Democracy, power based on knowledge and expertise, not status
Shared knowledge base grounded in practice experience so that practice is subjected to theoretical redefinition	Bridging the gap between theory and practice: little or no separation of knowing and doing: defining and redefining theory
Teams or individuals working through conflict	Risk taking, inter-personal relationships
Ownership of change – improve morale and team identity	Empowerment/emancipation
Personal growth and development	Educative processes through reflection and practice development

Table I. Supportive links between inter-professional practice and action research.

As previously highlighted, tensions and contradictions are prevalent in inter-professional practice. Central to action research is the notion of reflexivity, whereby practitioners engage in critical reflections on the nature of the collaborative process, examining, for instance, the role and influence of power, dilemmas resulting from differing professional perspectives and value bases, and the impact of different types of knowledge, on the research process (Winter, 1989). The recognition of a pluralistic perspective is highlighted by Hudson & Bennett (1997), who illuminate the importance of identifying the different players in a given setting, who will all perceive the situation differently. This enables practitioners to enter into an open, honest and meaningful dialogue essential to illuminative evaluation, and the generation and reconfiguration of new, shared and common knowledge.

To summarise, there are a number of overlaps and mutually supportive links between inter-professional practice and action research, which Table I attempts to illustrate.

Conclusions

The links between inter-professional practice and action research can provide reciprocal opportunities. For newly formed inter-professional teams seeking to form a cohesive group, action research offers a vehicle by which they can develop a common approach and philosophy, which transcends individual professional perspectives and cultures, to find new ways of working. For action research, effective inter-professional practice can generate creative research opportunities, which enrich action research by challenging the potential impoverishment that may arise when research is undertaken from a uni-professional base.

References

Atkins, J. (1998) Tribalism, Loss and Grief: issues for multiprofessional education, *Journal of Interprofessional Care*, 12, pp. 303-307.

Beattie, A. (1995) War and Peace Among the Health Tribes, in K. Soothill, L. Mackay & C. Webb (Eds) *Interprofessional Relations in Health Care*. London: Edward Arnold.

Checkland, P. (1981) *Systems Thinking, Systems Practice*. Chichester: John Wiley

Dombeck, M. T. (1997) Professional Personhood: training, territoriality and tolerance, *Journal of Interprofessional Care*, 11, pp. 9-21.

Hart, E. & Bond, M. (1995) *Research for Health and Social Care*. Buckingham: Open University Press.

Henneman, E. (1995) Collaboration: a concept analysis, *Journal of Advanced Nursing*, 21, pp. 103-109.

Hudson, B. (2000) Inter-agency Collaboration: a sceptical view, in A. Brechin, H. Brown & M. A. Eby (Eds) *Critical Practice in Health & Social Care*. London: Sage Publications & Open University Press.

Hudson, H. & Bennett, G. (1997) Action Research: a vehicle for change in general practice? in P. Pearson & J. Spencer (Eds) *Promoting Teamwork in Primary Care: a research based approach*. London: Arnold.

Leathard, A. (1994) *Going Inter-professional. Working Together for Health and Welfare*. London: Routledge.

Mackay, L., Soothill, K. & Webb, C. (1995) Troubled Times, the Context for Interprofessional Collaboration, in K. Soothill, L. Mackay & C. Webb (Eds) *Interprofessional Relations in Health Care*. London: Edward Arnold.

Miller, C., Ross, N. & Freeman, M. (1999) *Researching Professional Education. Shared Learning and Clinical Teamwork: new directions in education for multiprofessional practice*. Research Report series No 14 ENB.

Ovretveit, J. (1993) *Co-ordinating Community Care: multi-disciplinary teams and care management in health and social services*. Buckingham: Open University Press.

Ovretveit, J. (1995) Team Decision Making, *Journal of InterProfessional Care*, 9, pp. 41-45.

Petrie, H. G. (1976) Do You See What I See? The Epistemology of Interdisciplinary Inquiry, *Journal of Aesthetic Education*, 10, pp. 29-43.

Rees, L. & Jolly, B. (1998) Medical Education in the Next Century, in B. Jolly & L. Rees (Eds) *Medical Education in the Millennium*. Buckingham: Open University Press.

Ross, F. & Tissier, J. (1997) The Care Management Interface with General Practice: a case study, *Health and Social Care in the Community*, 5(3), pp. 153-161.

Tsang, N. M. (1998) Re-examining Reflection – a common issue of professional concern in social work, teacher and nursing education, *Journal of Interprofessional Care*, 12, pp. 21-31.

West, M. A. & Slater, J. (1996) *Teamworking in Primary Health Care: a review of its effectiveness*. London: HEA.

West, M. & Poulton, B. (1997) Primary Health Care Teams: in a league of their own, in P. Pearson & J. Spencer (Eds) *Promoting Team Work in Primary Care*. London: Arnold.

Wilmot, S. (1995) Professional Values and Interprofessional Dialogue, *Journal of Interprofessional Care,* 9, pp. 257-266.

Winter, R. (1989) *Learning from Experience: principles and practices in action research*. London: Falmer Press.

First published in *Educational Action Research,* Volume 8, Number 2, 2000

239

Notes on Contributors

Alison Binnie held senior clinical posts at the John Radcliffe Hospital, in Oxford, for 16 years. During that time, she led major practice development initiatives, aimed at developing a genuinely patient-centred nursing service. Her own work with patients was always a central part of her professional life. She found it to be her main source of inspiration and energy, as well as a powerful medium for influencing the practice of others. Alison now works independently as a practice development consultant in hospitals in the United Kingdom and Ireland.

Colin Biott is Professor of Professional Education and Development at the University of Northumbria. He is engaged currently in a number of evaluations and action research projects related to government policies in the field of social inclusion, studies of life histories of school leaders, and induction for newly qualified teachers. Recent work has included national evaluations of the training needs of community children's nurses, and of career entry profiles for new teachers. Books include: *Working and Learning Together for Change* (with J. Nias) and *Collaborative Learning in Classrooms and Staffrooms* (with P. Easen).

Arphorn Chuaprapaisilp is currently an Associate Professor and Associate Dean at the Faculty of Nursing, Prince of Songkla University Thailand. She graduated with a BSc in Nursing and Midwifery, and received MSc in Nursing from Thailand. Her PhD in Health Personnel Education was undertaken at the University of New South Wales, Australia. She finished her PhD thesis entitled 'Improving Learning from Experience: action research in nursing education in Thailand' in 1989. It was the first action research project in nursing profession in Thailand. Her post- doctoral special studies in Philosophy of Nursing Science & Interpretive Research Methods took place at the University of California, San Francisco School of Nursing. Her research projects involve HIV/AIDS prevention and care, quality of life of cancer and AIDS patients, end of life care, application of Buddha Dharma and Eastern wisdom in holistic nursing. Her special skills are action research and qualitative research methods, self-healing, interpersonal healing and Vipassana meditation.

Jean-Claude Couture works with the professional development staff of the Alberta Teachers' Association in Edmonton, Canada. His current research utilizes a psychoanalytic cultural critique of the intensification of teachers' work. He has worked extensively with school communities using action research as a way to interrogate the contemporary difficulties of teaching. He has written in media studies and on the impact of technology in education. His publications include 'The Tie that Bonds' in *Multi/Intercultural Conversations: a reader* (Ed. S. Steinberg) and 'Teachers' Work: Living in the Culture of Insufficiency' in *Tech High* (Ed. Marita Moll). He has co-authored social studies textbooks and has been involved in numerous curriculum development initiatives in western Canada.

Christopher Day is Professor of Education and Co-director of the Centre for Research on Teacher and School Development at the School of Education, University of Nottingham. He has worked as a schoolteacher, teacher, educator and local authority adviser. He has extensive research and consultancy experience in England, Europe, Australia, South East Asia, and North America in the fields of teachers' continuing professional development, action research, leadership and change. He is editor of *Teachers and Teaching: Theory and Practice*, co-editor of *Educational Action Research* and *Journal of In-Service Education*. He is a Board Member of the International Council for Teacher Education (ICET). In addition to *Leading Schools in Times of Change* (Open University Press, 2000), recent publications include *The Life and Work of Teachers: international perspectives in changing times,* (co-editor and contributor; Falmer Press, 2000); *Educational Research in Europe: Yearbook 2000* (co-editor; Leuven-Apeldoorn, Garant, 2000); *Developing Teachers: challenges of lifelong learning* (Falmer Press, 1999).

John Elliott is Professor of Education within the Centre for Applied Research in Education, which he directed from 1996-99. He is well-known internationally for his role in developing the theory and practice of action research in the contexts of curriculum and teacher development, and has directed a number of funded collaborative classroom research projects with teachers and schools. He is currently an Advisory Professor to the Hong Kong Institute of Education and a consultant to the Hong Kong Government on the strategic development of its curriculum reform proposals.

Kath Green began her teaching career in the 1960s in inner city primary schools before moving into higher education. Her present post, as an Education Adviser for postgraduate medical and dental education, involves her in working with hospital consultants and dental regional advisers to support the development of teaching in a variety of workplace settings such as ward rounds, theatres, clinics etc. Kath has two children, Rachel and Thomas, who have both 'caught the bug' and embarked on careers in teaching and she remains in regular contact with James, her 35-year-old foster son. She is proud to be classified as 'resistant to change' whenever that means refusing to give up on cherished educational principles and finds cooking meals for a kitchen full of friends to be the best antidote to some of education's current orthodoxies.

Shirley Jones qualified as a physiotherapist in 1976 and worked as a clinician until 1980 in a variety of nhs hospitals. In 1980 she moved into teaching, and taught on undergraduate physiotherapy courses, initially as a lecturer and then as a senior lecturer until 1992. In this period she completed her masters degree in education at Liverpool university . In 1992 she joined Anglia Polytechnic University as a senior lecturer to support the teaching on a multi-professional top up degree in Health Studies. In 1998 she co-wrote an undergraduate and post-graduate mutli-professional programme in response to the Government initiatives for Health & Social Care and collaborative working. She currently leads the BSc Hons Health & Social Studies.

Maggie MacLure is Professor of Education at the University of East Anglia. She has an unhealthy interest in research methodology – particularly those mutations that go by the name of poststructuralism and deconstruction. She is co-author with Ian Stronach of *Educational Research Undone: the postmodern embrace* (Open University Press).

Carol Munn-Giddings worked for many years as a social researcher in various health and social services settings, undertaking, managing and facilitating projects related to service users perspectives. In her current post at Anglia Polytechnic University, School of Community Health and Social Studies she is Reader in Participative Inquiry and Director of Research. Her work includes research with self-help groups, teaching research to practitioners and supporting staff in developing their research. She recently co-wrote with Richard Winter *A Handbook for Action Research in Health and Social Care* (Routledge, 2001).

Susan E. Noffke taught elementary and middle school children for 10 years before pursuing a doctorate in Curriculum and Instruction at the University of Wisconsin. She is now Associate Professor at the University of Illinois-Urbana/Champaign, where she teaches courses in Elementary Education, Curriculum Studies, and Action Research. Her publications have included *Educational Action Research* (with Robert Stevenson) and articles in *Review of Research in Education*, *Theory into Practice*, and *Teaching and Teacher Education*. She is coauthor (with

Kenneth Zeichner) of the chapter on 'Practitioner Research' in the newest edition of the *Handbook of Research on Teaching*. She is currently working on a long term field project involving facilitating action research with classroom teachers who are exploring issues of social justice in their educational practice.

Christine O'Hanlon is an Honorary Research Fellow in Education at the University of East Anglia. She has researched and published widely on the topic of action research as a means of professional and personal development in teacher education. She has worked at the University of Ulster and the University of Birmingham developing teacher education courses through action research. She currently organises and teaches courses for teachers and other professionals in support of 'inclusive' education to reduce the marginalisation of specific individuals and groups in mainstream schools. Her latest book to be published shortly is entitled *Teacher Action Research for Inclusion*.

Peter Posch has teaching degrees in English and Geography, and a PhD in Education and Psychology. He has conducted studies and research activities at the Universities of Innsbruck and Constance and the Vienna School of Economics. Now retired, he was Professor of Education at the Institute of Education at the University of Klagenfurt in Austria since 1976, and was Visiting Professor at the School of Education of Stanford University in 1992.

Bridget Somekh was a secondary English teacher before becoming a full time researcher at CARE, University of East Anglia, in 1987. She was Co-ordinator of the Collaborative Action Research Network between 1987 and 1995 and is a founder Editor of the journal *Educational Action Research*. Bridget is currently Professor of Educational Research at Manchester Metropolitan University. Her main research interests are educational change for individuals and organisations, information and communication technologies, curriculum, pedagogy and learning. She is also an experienced evaluator of innovatory educational programmes.

Pete Strauss is 43 years old and has been a primary school teacher in Nottingham for ten years. After working as a carpenter for several years, he began his teaching career at Greythorn Primary School in 1991 and then became Deputy Head of Forest Fields Primary School in 1996. He has been the Head Teacher of Arkwright Primary and Nursery School since 1998. Since completing his action-research-based MEd at Nottingham Trent University, he feels guilty that he has not done as much reading, writing or research as he would have liked.

Angie Titchen is a Senior Research and Practice Development Fellow based at the Royal College of Nursing Institute, Oxford. Her work is rooted in clinical experience as a physiotherapist and now in her high challenge/high support facilitation of nurses and health care professionals who are developing effective, patient-centred care. Her research interests focus around the facilitation of transformational, learning cultures, experiential learning and the use of creative arts in research, practice development and education. She has published widely in these areas. She loves to walk, dance, practise Tai Chi and paint by a beautiful lake near her home.

Victor Vincent Valla was born in Los Angeles, but has resided and worked in Brasil for more than 35 years and is today a Brasilian citizen. Valla is professor and researcher at the National School for Public Health, Oswaldo Cruz Foundation and the School of Education, Fluminense Federal University in Rio de Janeiro where he carries on research projects and lectures on the living and health conditions of the poor and their relationships with popular education and collective organization. Within this line of research, he is currently studying religious practices of the poor and the effects on their health conditions.

Melanie Walker currently teaches in the School of Education at the University of Sheffield. She began her career in education by teaching history and english in a number of different South African schools. She subsequently became involved in curriculum materials development, and in pre and in-service teacher education. Her enduring concerns with social justice, and a concern with the gap between practice and theory in educational research in South Africa generated her first action research project with African primary school teachers. More recently she has pursued action research in higher education with lecturers at the University of the Western Cape and the University of Glasgow.

Belinda Watts qualified as a nurse in 1977 and worked in the National Health Service and the private sector in a variety of roles until 1984. In 1984 she moved into nurse education where she was involved with leading and teaching to a number of pre-registration and post-registration programmes. In 1992 she completed a degree in law from Liverpool University and in 1996 a Masters in Educational Research from the University of East Anglia. She joined Anglia Polytechnic University in 1995 to lead the BSc (Hons) in Health Studies. In 1998 she co-wrote an undergraduate and postgraduate multi-professional programme in response to the Government initiatives for Health and Social Care and collaborative working. She currently leads the MSc Interprofessional Practice in Health and Social Care and Primary Care.

Richard Winter is Professor of Education at Anglia Polytechnic University. After many years in the School of Education, where his work focused on action research as a mode of inservice professional development for teachers, he transferred to the Faculty of Health & Social Work in order to develop a practice-based degree in social work. He has published a number of articles and books on action research, including *Learning from Experience*, Falmer Press, 1989 (on action research methods), *The Investigative Imagination*, Routledge, 1999 (on the role of writing and sharing creative fiction in professional development) and *A Handbook for Action Research for Health and Social Care*, Routledge 2001.